THE JEZEBEL SYNDROME

A Restoration To Godly Womanhood

Daniel Klender

ISBN 978-1-63630-241-6 (Paperback)
ISBN 978-1-63630-242-3 (Hardcover)
ISBN 978-1-63630-243-0 (Digital)

Covenant Books, Inc.
11661 Hwy 707
Murrells Inlet, SC 29576
www.covenantbooks.com

To my beloved daughters Tiffany and Abigail, whom I love with tender affection. May God grant both of you the grace to embrace Lady Wisdom to the end of your lives.

ACKNOWLEDGMENTS

If I believed in luck, I, like baseball great Lou Gehrig, would consider myself the "luckiest man alive." For God has mercifully supplied me with grace beyond measure. A part of that fortune comes from the gracious people the Lord Jesus has placed in my path to prepare me for my life's work. Among them are Rev. James Andrews and Dr. J. Carl Laney, mentors beyond measure who have shaped my thinking in more ways than I can count. I am also deeply indebted to many ministry colleagues. Colonel Andy Meverden (retired), who has served as an outsized advisor and friend. Dr. Jim Baugh is a friend who has been a model of steadfastness and encouragement. RADM Darold F. Bigger (retired), Chaplain Larry Zirschky (US Navy CDR, retired), LTCOL Tam Cookson, and the late Dr. Glen Riddle, have been faithful friends who have all contributed immeasurably to my life. Meriting special mention is Chaplain Chris Sutton and Commander Curtis Culwell, who have made invaluable contributions to the author's thinking on this topic. The author would also like to thank Chaplain Mark DiConti (CDR retired), for his exquisite modeling of servant-leadership. The author is also immensely grateful for the faithful prayers for my friend and battle buddy, Navy pilot, Capt. Steve Drake (retired), whose faithful prayers were palpably felt throughout the writing of this project. Immense gratitude is in order for Dr. Gordon Ainsworth whose passion for God's Word and love for remains an anchor in my life.

Thanks also is due to my college buddy Rev. Brian Chandler, who shares my passion for advancing the kingdom of Christ, and longtime friend, author, and cartoonist, Jonny Hawkins, who many years ago encouraged me to write. The author would also like to thank his parents Curt and Carol Klender, his brother Rich, and sister Wendy Wilson. Thanks also is in order for Lori Klender, Thad Wilson, Bill and Sandy Klender, Debbie and Trent Poling, Brenda Tanner, Rick and Emelyne Sablan, Terry Fifer, and Scott Whipple.

The author would also like to thank the inspiring Sarahs in his life. Among them are Susan Nash, June Curd, Phyliss Hull, Patty Payne, Ann Wykoff, Betty Allmand, Mary Conlin, Hannah Joya, and my dear friend Marta Plopper whose encouragement and servant's heart have a manna from heaven. Last but not least, to my beautiful daughters Tiffany and Abigail. May you forever embrace Lady Wisdom!

CONTENTS

THE JEZEBEL SYNDROME

Few gifts are more beautiful than a godly woman. Godly women are invaluable assets to the world, who are praised by God and loved by multitudes. Writing under the inspiration of God three thousand years ago Solomon asserted, "Charm is deceitful, beauty is vain, but a woman who fears the LORD shall be praised" (Prov. 31:30). The praise of godly women comes from one's Creator, husband, father, daughters, sons, even enemies. Godly women contribute immeasurably to world civilization as beautiful expressions of feminine wisdom.

If the maxim "the hand that rocks the cradle shapes the world" is bottom-line true, it is imperative that the world thoroughly examine that hand. Is it a hand that places the world on a positive or negative trajectory? Is it a hand that fears the Lord, or fears a negative image in the world? Today, there is a breed of woman masquerading as virtuous, trafficking in the public square. She is a woman outfitted with the wardrobe of false piety that militates against God's design for marriage, the church, and the world. Following the perverse dictum of socialist pioneer, Saul Alinsky, these women, "do the best they can with what they have, and then clothe it with moral arguments."

One place where this woman surfaced was in the cultural tsunami known as the "Me Too" movement. This socialistic wave crested during the Brent Kavanaugh Senate confirmation hearings. During the hearings it was asserted by some that all women had a right to be believed. Such an assertion is not only unconstitutional, but unbiblical. Constitutionally it fails to meet the legal standard of "innocent until proven guilty." Additionally, and more importantly, it fails the smell test of biblical integrity. Though the allegations made against Justice Kavanaugh were proven to be spurious, considerable violence was perpetrated on this good man and his family. While the devious political agenda of Me Too was exposed when Vice President Joe Biden was accused of sexual malfeasance by former staffer Tara Reade, this miscarriage of justice will continue to inflict its torture on good men and their families.

What Jesus and Solomon Would Have Said About "Me Too"

Claims made by the Me Too movement frequently fail the acid test of biblical womanhood. Solomon asserted, "If a man answers a matter before he hears it, it is a folly and a shame to him" (Prov. 18:13). Whether a man or a woman rushes to judgment in a charge as serious as sexual harassment, they are wrong. In this regard, Christ-followers are compelled to heed the words of Jesus, "Judge not according to appearance but judge righteous judgment" (John 7:24). Solomon similarly rhapsodizes in Proverbs 25:2, "It is the glory of God to conceal a matter, but the glory of kings to search out a matter."

Pursuant to Me Too, the author has witnessed the abuse of this movement firsthand. In nearly forty years of ministry, I have ministered to a plethora of men who were falsely accused. Some of these men have unjustly served time as a consequence of these false allegations. Consequently, they will bear the scars of such reproach the rest of their lives. Such injustices alone signal an urgent need to return to biblical womanhood. False accusations leveled by women against men have done untold damage. Such as that inveighed against Richard Jewell, the hero of the 1996 Atlanta Summer Olympics bombing who died prematurely after being falsely accused by a female reporter then summarily indicted in the court of public opinion. While eventually exonerated, slander had perpetrated its deviltry on his soul. He died at age forty-four.

Misogyny Versus Misandry

It is cruelly ironic that the charge of misogyny (the hatred of women) is carelessly leveled against men today in America, while misandry (the hatred of men) is increasingly palpable and equally destructive. Moreover, if you accuse someone of being a misogynist today, you have a better than average chance of being understood. However, labeling them a misandryist (man hater) is likely to elicit blank stares and confused looks. This cultural disparity exists for several reasons. One is the widespread social acceptance of male bashing. Today it is politically correct for women to bash men incessantly on television, social media, in movies, sitcoms, and public discourse without fear of reprisal, while a mere scintilla of like criticism of women sparks international outrage. Meanwhile this cultural embrace of the denigration of males has taken an unconscionable toll on the family, society, and the church. Freely issuing hall passes to women for such aberrant behavior leads to the devastation of legions of marriages while conditioning women to embrace a cultural rather than biblical model of womanhood.

MGTOW

This boomerang effect of feminine disdain for men is witnessed by the groundswell of disillusioned men described by the acronym MGTOW (Men Going Their Own Way). This grassroots movement of men resolving to decouple themselves from women, refusing to marry, cohabitate, or court the fairer gender. This vow of celibacy is an acidic reaction to the cultural pendulum swing toward feminism in America. While most men have not resorted to such draconian measures, the silent streams of resentment coursing through the veins of many American men is highly toxic.

A Case of Contempt

The American landscape is littered with the lives of disillusioned men testifying that women have butchered their mother tongue of respect. The devastation wrought by feminine contempt is no longer a theory, but a fact. Scientific proof is supplied by celebrated marriage and family therapist, Dr. John Gottman. Gottman has ascertained through conducting clinical studies that the rancorous contempt wives harbor for their husbands currently ranks either first or second as a catalyst for divorce. While examining over two thousand marriages in his "love laboratory," Gottman has predicted with 91 percent accuracy whether couples would stay together or divorce. Gottman concluded that the two determining variables predicting marital success or failure were love and respect.

Pursuant to respect, the venomous rhetoric women routinely spew toward men in society is akin to that of a spitting cobra, and every bit as lethal. To paraphrase T. S. Eliot, "Men cannot bear much contempt." Such an assessment should not surprise Christ-followers since God's design for marriage calls for the husband to love his wife and the wife to "see that she respects her husband" (Eph. 5:31). Unconditional respect is the high-performance motor oil lubricating the engine of a man's soul.

Conversely, the flood of contempt has levied an unconscionable toll on the spirits of men to the point of disillusionment, depression, even death. In the last few decades, this author has known men who cited the mistreatment of their wives as a major trigger for disillusionment and chronic depression. Sadly, some of these men whom I served as a chaplain or friend, terminated their own lives as a result.

Jezebel's Pedigree

Since the feminist movement was birthed, the pendulum swing of identity socialism has not championed gender equality, but female superiority. Yet none of this should surprise the perceptive Christ-follower as the historical taproots of false accusations and blame-shifting, and female domination of men, have longer tentacles extending far beyond the past fifty years. For such distortions of godly feminism have been with us since the dawn of time. Eve blamed the serpent for deceiving her. Eve's role was reprised when a domineering queen confiscated the property of a godly Jew after falsely accusing him of treason. The queen named Jezebel leveraged her authority deviously, while filing trumped up charges against this godly man. After convicting him in a kangaroo court, the unruly queen presided over his execution.

While the Bible is chocked full of examples of godly woman-hood, it is also replete with examples of women afflicted with a malaise this author terms the Jezebel Syndrome. This too should not be surprising to the Christ-follower, for the cesspool of human wickedness is emblazoned upon the pages of Scripture. God has given us such examples as proofs, "to the intent that we should not lust after evil things as they also lusted" (1 Cor. 10:6). Paul further underscores the major purpose of these negative examples in 10:11, "Now all these things happened to them as our examples, and they are written for our admonition, upon whom the ends of the ages are come" (see also, Rom. 15:4).

Sadly, in recent years, both the church and the culture have issued hall passes to the Jezebels of our day. The last several decades have witnessed a disturbingly indifferent approach to the woman's role in marriage and in the church. Regarding the former, Christian marriage expert, Emerson Eggerichs has correctly asserted that we are not telling the whole truth about marriage. Eggerichs further contends that similar to the oath taken in a court of law, "Do you pledge, to tell the truth, the whole truth, and nothing but the truth, so help you God?" it is incumbent upon Christ-followers scrupulously pursue the truth of how the image of God has been distorted in women.

The Urgency of Truth-Telling

In the military subculture, it is imperative that warriors continuously traffic in brutal honesty. The motivation for such earnest candor is the devastating nature of falsehood. Simply put, lies kill. In a similar vein, failure to engage in meticulous truth-telling concerning God's design for godly womanhood produces mounting casualties in marriages, society, and the church of Jesus Christ. The truth however, will set us free (John 8:31–32). The Word of God is the GPS navigating us through "the whole counsel of God, regarding men and women" (Acts 20:27).

This counsel comes to us through the Chief Engineer and Architect of the universe who understands with pinpoint precision where the image of God in women and men has misfired and is due for an overhaul. The objective of this book is to champion godly womanhood while identifying where womanhood has been derailed. While men are in no way inherently better than women, it is this writers' belief that the church has done a commendable job assisting men in ascending to their high calling. Conversely, sparse literature is available to assist the fairer sex in fulfilling their calling. Tragically, this vacuum of teaching continues to exact a costly toll on marriages, society, and the reputation of Jesus Christ in the world.

The Daughters of Sarah

Among the many saintly women praised by God in the Bible is the matriarch of the Jewish nation, Sarah. Sarah is set forth as a positive template of biblical womanhood by one of Jesus's closest disciples. While advising Christian wives suffering the plight of a disobedient husband, Peter cites Sarah's godly example, "For in this manner in former times, the holy women who trusted in God also adorned themselves, being submissive to their own husbands, as Sarah obeyed Abraham, calling him lord, whose daughters you are if you do good and are not afraid with any terror" (1 Pet. 3:5–6).

Sarah's unconditional respect for her husband Abraham received high praise among the matriarchs who feared God. It is this writer's conviction that there is an urgent need today for the daughters of Eve, to be reborn as the daughters Sarah. Today's Christian woman does well to mimic the holy women of God named Sarah, Ruth, Abigail, Esther, Anna, Eunice, Lois, Rehab, and Mary, among others who implicitly trusted and obeyed their God.

Jesus's Disdain of Jezebel

While critiquing the behavior of the compromising church of Thyatira, the Lord Jesus cited a woman who wedded immorality to heretical teachings, while teaching others to follow her example. He denounced the teaching and conduct of this woman while calling her by a pseudonym, namely, Jezebel. Jezebel, the wicked queen of Ahab, sought to wed the worship of Baal to the worship of Israel. This hybrid brand of "COEXIST" religion was detestable to the risen Christ. Jezebel's role was reprised in the ancient church of Thyatira as she became a metaphor for fallen behavior and beliefs. She is the anti-heroine of the Bible whose teaching and conduct, Jesus commands His church to join Him in disavowing. The Savior inveighed against the church of Thyatira, "Nevertheless, I have a few things against you because you allow that woman Jezebel, who calls herself a prophetess, to teach and seduce My servants to commit sexual immorality and eat things sacrificed to idols" (Rev. 2:20–21).

The Jezebel of which the Savior spoke was a real woman who perpetrated idolater and seduction. This crafty idolatress who seduced God's people into believing a lie. John Walvoord wrote of her, "She is…the epitome of subtle corruption and a symbol of immorality and idolatry."[i]

Jesus rebuked His servants for failing to renounce the wicked ways of a first-century Jezebel while expelling her from their fellowship. The daughters of Jezebel surround us. Their ungodly manner must be exposed and discredited as displeasing to the God of glory. Following the example of his Savior, the author has employed Jezebel as a metaphor designating dysfunctional womanhood in the body of Christ and society.

The Jezebel Syndrome

By the Jezebel Syndrome, the author is referencing a spiritual disease that has infected women today.

The Jezebel Syndrome is not a book that diagnoses problems without prescribing cures. Contrarily, its primary objective is to clearly answer the question, what does God intend for women? What is the measure of a godly woman and wife?

The purpose of examining this pandemic is to identify where biblical womanhood has veered off course. The author's objective is to empower the daughters of Eve to spiritually morph into the daughters of Sarah. The goal is not to level undue criticism against women, but rather of identify where mid-course corrections are in order. Since the best defense against the Jezebel Syndrome is a good offense, a large portion of this book is committed to positively examining the daughters of Sarah. There is much at stake. The consequences for failing to biblically define the role of women in the church and family, are enormous. It is the author's sincere prayer that this book will benefit men, women, wives, and husbands in their quest to mirror God's image to a lost world.

Daniel Klender
San Diego, California
July 2020

IT ALL BEGAN IN
THE GARDEN

"Have you not read, He who made them at the
beginning made them male and female."
—Matthew 19:4

It all seemed so harmless. A casual conversation between the First Lady of the human race and a disgraced elite angel expelled from heaven's shores. What could go wrong? Certainly, to Eve, Lucifer, displayed no ruthless appearance, but a beautiful array of color, she judged too good to be bad. Certainly, an offline conversation with this eye candy creature equipped with a melodic voice could do no harm. Surely Eve was far too sophisticated to engage in chitchat with one resolved to hasten her death.

The conversation was anything but benign. It reflected the adage, "Satan appears a comfortable friend until he has his hands around your neck and is choking you." Per the devil's standard operating procedure, he fed Adam's bride, a whopper of a lie. The lie was that if she imbibed in the fruit of the tree of the knowledge of good and evil, she would be like god discerning both good and evil. Unlike a baby rattlesnake, unable to control its venom, Satan resembles a spitting cobra who paralyzes his victims with pinpoint accuracy. The slanderous lie He told was scripted to torment the human race until God once again made all things new. Adam and Eve's eyes would most certainly be opened, yet not in a way that they envisioned. The Adversary's deceitful strategy was to ambush the first couple, causing them to spiritually implode. Jesus comments on this first lie of the father of lies in John 8:44.

He rebuked, "You are of your father the devil and the desires of your father you will do. He was a murderer from the beginning and abode not in the truth for there is no truth in him. He is a liar and the father of lies" (John 8:44). Jesus later labels Lucifer as the thief whose endgame is "to steal, kill and destroy" (John 10:10).

Eve bought the lie. She ate the fruit. She gave this delectable fruit to her husband who also partook. Immediately the shiny veneer of Lucifer's lie began to peel away like cheap paint. The unvarnished truth is that Adam and Eve would immediately be subjected to the self-consciousness of sin (Gen. 3:7). Henceforth, debilitating fear, despair, loneliness, alienation, shame, and guilt, would be baked into the human condition. Toxic masculinity and femininity were born on that fateful day.

Though grace and forgiveness was theirs for the asking, their sin catalyzed a chain reaction of consequences spiraling out of control. Such far reaching consequences would saddle all of their posterity with a sin nature begging for redemption. Since God is of "purer eyes to behold evil, and cannot stand to look on iniquity" (Habbakuk 1:13), it was imperative that He judge their sin. Adam, the head of the human race was judged first. The LORD cursed the first man in the field. He would toil and harvest crops by the sweat of his brow. The soil from which Adam originated would perennially bear thorns and thistles. Eve was cursed in the home. Child-bearing was made excruciatingly painful due to the first couple's rebellion.

Though God cursed the woman with sorrow and pain in child-bearing, ultimately there would be a silver lining to the maternal pain she was called to suffer. Eventually, the seed of her pain would blossom into a glorious flower of redemptive hope. This hope was embodied in a Son who would ultimately crush the head of the serpent with a fatal blow (Gen. 3:16). This was the first gospel, the good news foretelling of God's plan to redeem fallen humanity. The bad news was that until Paradise Lost became Paradise Regained, there would be a titanic struggle unfolded in Eve's curse. Moreover, though her deception cursed all of her posterity, she and all of her daughters would retain her dignity through child-bearing, should "they continue in faith, love, and holiness, with self-control" (1 Tim. 1:15).

The Curse of Eve

Adam and Eve were both guilty of sinning against love by dis-obeying God's mandate to not eat of the fruit of the tree of knowl-edge of good and evil (Gen. 2:17). As such, Adam as the head of the human race bore the brunt of the blame. Paul writes, "Therefore, just as through one man sin entered the world, and death through sin, and thus death spread to all men, for all have sinned" (Rom. 5:12). Adam is identified as that "one man." For the epic status of men and women was captured in the early colonial creed, "In Adam's fall, we sinned all." Though sin entered the world through Adam, God was not exonerating Eve of sin. Rather he was assigning final culpabil-ity for plunging the human race into sin to the first man. Since sin always has consequences, Eve, like Adam was subject to a curse. In Genesis 3:16, God said, "To the woman He said: I will greatly mul-tiply your sorrow and your conception; In pain you shall bring forth children; Your desire shall be to your husband, And he shall rule over you."

The Backdrop of Eve's Curse

In an effort to understand this curse, it is best to examine the nature of Eve's sin. In a general sense, Eve's sin was the same as Adam's. Though she was deceived, unlike her husband Adam, she too joined her husband in sinning against God (1 Tim. 2:14; 2 Cor. 11:3). She disobeyed God by eating the fruit of the tree of knowledge of good and evil. However, there is another nuance to Eve's sin that differs from the sin of Adam. An added dimension to Eve's sin is that she sought to usurp Adam's role of headship by giving him the forbidden fruit to eat (Gen. 3:6). In doing so, she both failed to submit to her husband's leadership which prohibited her from eating the fruit of the tree of knowledge of good and evil. This usurpation of the God-given role assigned to her husband, constituted the sin of Eve. Submitting herself to the Lord's prohi-bition conveyed by her husband Adam would have been the godly course of action.

A Curse Equaling the Choice

As was common in God's history book, the curse corresponded with the nature of one's sin. This is taught most explicitly in Galatians 6:7–8: "Do not deceived, God is not mocked; for whatever a man sows, that he will also reap. For he who sows to the flesh, will of the flesh reap corruption. But he who sows to the Spirit will of the Spirit reap life everlasting."

Since her misdeed was usurping her husband's authority, her posterity would reap a harvest of perpetual rebellion and discontentment. Eve's sin, not unlike Adam's, would be talionic ("an eye for an eye, a tooth for a tooth, a hand for a hand, a foot for a foot, a burn for a burn, a life for a life"; see Ex. 21:4, Deut. 19:21; Gen. 9:6). With this historical backdrop, we are better equipped to interpret Eve's curse in a way that makes sense contextually and historically.

The Burden of Eve and Her Daughters

While there is a general consensus on the meaning of the first half of the curse, there is widespread disagreement on the second half. A traditional interpretation of the phrase, "Your desire shall be to your husband and he shall rule over you" is that Eve's sexual desire will be channeled in the direction of her husband. This view implies that the curse consists of a wife's intensified sexual desire toward her husband. Yet the view that the curse every woman bears is a heightened sex drive, fails the logical litmus test. One must ask, "How was this a curse since Adam and Eve, enjoyed sexual relationships prior to the Fall?" Before their plummet into sin, the LORD commanded them to be "fruitful and multiply" (Gen. 1:26–28).

Such a mandate obviously favored sexual relations for reasons of procreation and recreation. The recreative component of wedded love is embedded in Genesis 2:25 in which the first couple was "naked and not ashamed." This implies that they were not ashamed of their God-given anatomy. Sexual intercourse for the first couple was not a shameful excursion into godless passion, but a pure, unadulterated, celebration of one of God's best gifts! Adam and Eve were hands down the most sexually satisfied couple in history as they did not tote into the bedroom the cumbersome baggage of a sin nature. Elsewhere wedded love is a pristine gift from God (Song of Solomon; Prov. 5:18; Eccl. 9:9), that is both God-honoring and moral. The Bible instructs, "Marriage is honorable in all and the bed undefiled" (Heb. 13:4).

In view of God's original design for sex, the notion that Eve's sexual desire for her husband was the curse is rendered implausible. For rather than the curse elevating sexual desire in marriage, it escalated sexual tensions and domestic conflict both in and out of the bedroom. Paul warned singles of the ensuing struggle they would face should they marry, divulging "such will have trouble in the flesh" (1 Cor. 7:28). So pronounced are these tensions that Paul is compelled to remind married couples of their sexual responsibilities to each other (1 Cor. 7:2–6).

The Crouching Tiger, Hidden Dragon of Sin

If the "desire" of which God spoke was not at its root sexual in nature, then what does it portend? The Hebrew grammar of 3:15, speaks of Eve's sinful rather than sexual desire to dominate her husband. Just as she exerted sinful influence over her husband in in the Garden, so would she struggle to honor him throughout the course of their marriage. Her desire to dominate her husband would in turn reap the bitter fruit of domestic conflict. The LORD informs the future matriarch of the human race that this inordinate desire to dominate Adam will be met with futility. Again, the LORD divines, "Your desire shall be for your husband, And he shall rule over you" (Gen. 3:16). The verb translated "desire," speaks of a "desire to dominate." It was used of a wild animal poised to pounce and devour its prey. God is saying to Eve that try as she will to dominate her husband—he will dominate her. One must not assume that such domination is always physical, though wife battering is a tragic by-product of the fall. The domination could be positionally, financially, psychologically, emotional, et al. While such domination has popularly made perennial victims out of women in the western world, the victimization of the husband must not be ignored. For the curse is a like a double-edged sword that cuts in both directions. One clear outcome of the fall is that Eve "will seek to dominate her husband."

Cain and Abel

The curse of Eve seeking to dominate Adam is illustrated in the sequel to Genesis 3. Eve, meaning, "the mother of all living," gave birth to two sons. The eldest son, Cain became a farmer, demonstrating the curse of his father. The first couple's youngest son, Abel, became a shepherd (Gen. 4:2). In due time, both brought offerings from the fruit of their respective occupations. Cain brought garden variety vegetables to the LORD. Abel brought the firstborn and primo animals of his flock along with their fat. The qualitative difference between the two offerings was stark. Cain's casual sacrifice of the "dregs" of the harvest to the LORD was on a par with Esau's despising his birthright many generations later (Gen. 25:34). Contrarily, Abel brought the first-fruits of the flock and the well pleasing fat desired by the LORD. Cain's primo offering was honored by the LORD. The narrative reports in Genesis 4:4–5, "And the LORD respected Abel and his offering, but He did not respect Cain and his offering. And Cain was very angry and his countenance fell."

According to divine pattern established early in the Book of Genesis, the LORD sought out Cain. He always does. Whether asking Cain's fallen father, "Adam where are you?" Or as the compassionate Father who runs to meet his wayfaring sons and daughters, God diligently seeks that which is lost (Luke 15).

God met Cain in the field seeking reconciliation. He offers an olive branch and a warning in Genesis 4:6–7, "If you do well, will you not be accepted? And if you do not do well, sin lies at the door. And it's desire is for you, but you should rule over it."

God uses the same Hebrew phrase to communicate with Cain as he did with his mother in Genesis 3:16. He informs him, that sinful anger in Cain's case, resembled a hidden wild animal crouching, "lying" (i.e., "crouching"), "at the door," to pounce upon its prey. Sin was like a crouching tiger ready to pounce upon Cain if he failed to take decisive action to slay it with the sword of obedience. If Cain were "to do well," by following God's instructions to offer an excellent sacrifice to the LORD, he would slay the crouching tiger and hidden dragon of sin. If not, his sin would rise up like a wild animal conquering his will while fueling his sinful desire so as to make sin even more enticing. In this vein, Cain's sinful desire would be aided and abetted by the hidden dragon of demonic influence (Eph. 4:26–27). This demonic influence in Cain's case would fuel anger, and eventually first-degree murder (Gen. 4:8).

The Domino Effect of Eve's Sin

Against this chilling backdrop of first degree murder, Eve's curse is best understood. For just as her attempt to rule Adam was met with futility so would her daughters' as their husbands would dominate them. The fingerprints of Eve's curse are evidenced throughout the biblical narrative. Below is the sinful debris churned up in the wake of Eve's attempted domination of Adam in the Garden.

Sarah seeks to dominate Abraham by urging her husband to sleep with her handmaiden Hagar so she might become impregnated with an heir.

- Rebekah seeks to dominate her husband Isaac by urging their son Jacob to prepare a goat and thus deceive her husband Isaac into giving their youngest son the blessing of the firstborn.
- Leah seeks to dominate her husband Jacob by brokering a deal with Rachel, Jacob's favorite wife, to procure an aphrodisiac so she might sleep with Jacob and become pregnant.
- Rachel seeks to dominate Jacob, by secretly confiscating pagan idols after her husband flees from her father Laban.
- Samson's wife seeks to dominate him by improperly disclosing the secret of his riddle to the Philistines.
- Delilah seeks to dominate Samson through incessantly nagging him to reveal the secret of his strength and in turn disclosing that secret to the Philistines.

- Jezebel dominates Ahab by devising a plot to falsely accuse Naboth, execute him, then confiscate his vineyard.
- Solomon's thousand wives dominated him by turning away his heart from the true God to false gods.

The Domination of Eve

Since Eve succumbed to the serpent's craftiness, her daughters have sought to dominate men in every arena of society. History and contemporary culture solemnly testifies to this perennial pandemic. If art imitates life, then women seek to dominate men physically (World Wrestling Federation, *Charlies Angels,* Quentin Tarantino movies), in politics (*Madame Secretary, Veep*), in business and government (*On The Basis of Sex*), and in the church (Ellen G. White, Aimee Semple McPherson), and in society (Modern Feminism, Me Too, Identity Socialism). From the bedroom to the boardroom, women seek to dominate men in society. The smudge-marks of this attempted coup of God's order of creation are everywhere. However, the unintended consequence of this attempted female domination is the male domination of women. For the cruel irony of this age-old sexual revolution is that by channeling the Greek god Sisyphus, women are forever rolling the stone of female domination uphill, only to witness it tumble into the valley of feminine despair. For try as they will, God has not decreed that women commandeer the ship of male leadership on the ocean of history.

Eve's Redemption

Realistically, the curse is a death sentence for Adam and Eve's posterity-yet God extended an olive branch of redemptive hope available to all. The redemption first came through Eve's seed, the God-Man, Jesus Christ. After God's Son, pitched His tent on earth, millions receiving Him were promised distinguished children of God status (John 1:12–13). This speaks of justification, of which the Apostle Paul writes eloquently in Romans 3–5 and Galatians 3–4. Pursuant to sanctification-salvation, the results of the curse are reversed through the renewing of one's mind. Pursuant to this renewal, Paul writes in Colossians 3:9–10, "Do not lie to one another, since you have put off the old man with his deeds, and have put on the new man who is renewed in knowledge according to the image of him who created him."

This book marks a clarion call for a radical return to God's original design for women. The tarnished image of God in women must be restored by a careful examination and diligent application of God's original template for womanhood. While the course leading to spiritual restoration for both male and female image bearers is clearly outlined in the Bible, this book focalizes Christian women. The goal of *The Jezebel Syndrome* is to stimulate careful consideration of what the image of God in woman looks like. It is the author's prayer that reading this book will motivate Christ-followers to champion the quality that most pleases God in women-the praiseworthy quality of a "woman who fears the LORD" (Prov. 31:30).

Questions for Reflection

1) Adam and Eve's fall in the Garden of Eden is the seminal event propelling the devastating force of sin in the world. On a scale of 1–7 (1 being rarely, and 7 being often), how often do you reflect on the devastating consequences of sin in the world?

   1 2 3 4 5 6 7

2) What parallels do you see between Eve and Jezebel's sin?
3) Peter admonishes Christians husbands, "Husbands, likewise, dwell with them [your wives], with understanding, giving honor to the husband, as to the weaker vessel" (1 Pet. 3:7). In what ways is a Christian wife able to protect their wives, while shoring up their weaknesses?
4) In reflecting on the narrative of the fall in Genesis 3, Paul writes, "Adam was not deceived, but the woman being deceived was in the transgression" (1 Tim. 2:14). If you

are a Christian husband, list the ways you can protect your wife from doctrinal deception?

5) The author described Eve's curse as the "crouching tiger, hidden dragon of sin." Eve was cursed in that she desired to rule over her husband, yet her husband would dominate her (Gen. 3:16). On a scale of 1–7 (1 being rarely, 7 being often), do you struggle with a desire to rule over your husband?

1 2 3 4 5 6 7

6) There was redemption for Adam and Eve and all their posterity. That redemption included Eve's seed, Jesus Christ descending the stairway of heaven to die for the sins of men and women. The God-Man Jesus Christ offers eternal life to as many as receive Him (John 1:12). Jesus informed, "For God so loved the world that He gave His only begotten Son, that whoever believes in Him should not perish but have eternal life" (John 3:16). Have you taken the step of believing on Jesus Christ as your Savior?

WHO WAS JEZEBEL?

"But there was no one like Ahab who sold himself
to do wickedness in the sight of the LORD,
because Jezebel his wife stirred him up."

—1 Kings 21:25

"Women today have a lot of choices. They can be
married with kids and work. They can be married with
kids and not work. They can be married without kids
and work. They can be married without kids and not
work. Men only have two choices, work or go to jail."

—Tim Allen

In his book, *Hillary's America,* political historian Dinesh Dsouza, traces
the earliest beginnings of Bill and Hillary Clinton. He chronicles the
circumstances of their meeting at Yale Law School, to Bill's election as
Arkansas Governor, followed by their eight years in the White House.
Dsouza contends that Hillary's marriage to Bill was a convenient
arrangement to increase their political capital. Such political ambitions
are well documented in her senior thesis she wrote at Wellesley College
concerning her mentor, celebrated socialist, Saul Alinsky. Those ambitions fermented during her years at Yale Law School. Dsouza writes,

"Bill and Hillary came to Yale Law School
burning with ambition. Bill wanted to be a major
figure in Arkansas politics, setting himself up to
run for president. Hillary may not have known
then she wanted to be president, but she too shared
Bill's volcanic ambition. She too wanted ambition

27

and power. Hillary had a problem that is no one-male or female-liked her… Hillary decided she needed to partner with a man who was ambitious, gregarious, and naturally likeable. Of course, he might have no use for her in the bedroom, but she didn't necessarily need him for that. Rather, she wanted him to be her "pitch man." His job was to make her attractive, not necessarily to him but to the people Hillary needed to gain influence and power. Of course she might initially have to subordinate her ambitions to his. But only initially; later, she could make her move. At this point, she would have to be sure she could rely on him. In other words, his dependence on her would be complete. From the outset, Hillary didn't need a husband; she needed a partner in crime."[ii]

Ambition Run Amok

Romeo and Juliet. Bonnie and Clyde. Ahab and Jezebel. Though the circumstances differ, such couples head the list of famous romances ending badly. In the case of Ahab and Jezebel, the truth was stranger than fiction. In the Old Testament narrative of the kings, Ahab's fate is inextricable bound to Jezebel's story. Their story is not only a story of love gone wrong, but also of a nation adrift. For similar to a local church mirroring the personality of its pastor Israel had adopted the worship habits of her king and queen. While there was fault on both sides of the royal bedroom, Jezebel's influence on the nations descent into idolatry had polluted the atmosphere of Israel's northern kingdom.

Ahab, the king of Israel, was obligated to follow the Mosaic law and abide by the stipulations of the Palestinian covenant. Failure for him to do would result in the LORD visiting the nation with unimaginable curses (see Deut. 28:15–68). Early on, Ahab made a poor choice. Israel's kings were forbidden to marry foreign wives as well as bottom line treaties with pagan nations. Ahab, following the lead of his predecessors, flagrantly violated both commands.

Perhaps Ahab was captivated by Jezebel's stunning beauty or infectious leadership style. He may have been fascinated by her native intelligence, seduced by her unwavering decisiveness, or managerial prowess. As a king, he might have been intoxicated with the political prospects of being wed to a foreign king's daughter. Perhaps unbridled passion had afflicted him with amnesia causing him to forget that marriage is a package deal. To marry Jezebel would be to marry Baal, the "rain god." Since Jezebel was the daughter of Ethbaal, the king of Tyre, whose name means, "with Baal," her god of choice was a no brainer. Jezebel didn't discard her pagan idolatry in Tyre, but exported it to Ephraim, the northern kingdom of Israel. She lobbied Ahab to make "Baal Worship" the established "state" religion in Ephraim. Since she wore the proverbial pantsuit in her marriage, she successfully achieved this objective. The upshot was that Jezebel seduced Israel in not only worshipping Baal, but offering child sacrifices to idols. The Psalmist laments,

> "[Israelites] poured out innocent blood,
> the blood of their sons and daughters,
> whom they sacrificed to the idols of Canaan,
> and the land was polluted with blood." (Psalm
> 106:38)

Her unspeakable atrocities were further detailed in 2 Kings 17:17–18: "And [Israel] burned their sons and their daughters as offerings and used divination and omens and sold themselves to do evil in the sight of the Lord, provoking him to anger. Therefore, the Lord was very angry with Israel and removed them out of His sight."

As a repayment for such unthinkable bloodshed, Isaiah declared an oracle of judgment on those who worshiped Baal both in the northern kingdom of Israel and the southern kingdom of Judah. In Isaiah 57:5–9, he inveighs:

> "You who burn with lust among the oaks,
> under every green tree, who slaughter your children in the valleys, under the clefts of the rocks…

On a high and lofty mountain, [high places of Baal], you have set your bed, and there you went up to offer sacrifice. You journeyed to the king with oil [Molech]and multiplied your perfumes; you sent your envoys far off, and sent down even to Sheol."

A Modern Jezebel

Margaret Sanger was born in 1879 in Corning New York. She became the most famous eugenicist and birth control activist in the twentieth century. She is infamously known as the founder of *Planned Parenthood*. While a heroine among modern feminists, she advocated the genocide of two thirds of the human race. Under the guise of purifying the human race, she championed a cause leading to the extermination of 73 million babies in America-and counting.

In the 1930's, Sanger gave speeches praising the Nazi sterilization laws. She also recommended that America keep pace with Hitler's campaign of Arian purity. Illustrating the far reaching tentacles of Sanger's perverse influence was Adolf Hitler. The Fuhrer wrote a "fan mail" letter praising Sanger with the declaration, "Your writings are my Bible." In the 1920 she published a book entitled, *The Wickedness of Creating Large Families.* In this book she contended, "The most merciful thing that the large family does to one of its infant members is to kill it."[iii] She referenced blacks in America as "human weeds" in need of eradication. In a letter to Clarence Gamble she wrote, "We don't want the word to go out that we want to exterminate the Negro population…"

Jezebel an Ancient "Bloody Mary"

Mary Queen of Scots murdered two hundred and eighty Protestant Christians earning her the infamous moniker, "Bloody Mary." Jezebel, like Sanger, and Mary Queen of Scots was a cold-blooded killer. She murdered three hundred prophets of Yahweh without batting an eyelash. She later threatened to murder Elijah and probably would have, had God permitted. Not a big Bill of Rights gal, Jezebel had no use for those who disagreed with her.

Jezebel's Influence on Ahab

Ahab was more than a mere willing accomplice in Jezebel's barbarity. The narrative discloses that this unruly queen stirred up the most wicked king in Israel's storied history. While there are unanswered questions in Ahab and Jezebel's relationship, it is absolutely certain that Ahab would have done well to heed the wisdom of his predecessor Solomon, "And I find more bitter than death The woman whose heart is snares and nets, Whose hands are fetters, He who pleases God shall escape from her, But the sinner shall be trapped by her" (Eccl. 7:26–27).

Inevitably, Ahab became entangled with the trip wires of Jezebel's god and her perverse ways. Such ways included the false accusation and murder of a righteous Jew by the name of Naboth. Later she ordered the execution of some three hundred of LORD's prophets. After the LORD had demonstrated Himself to be the One and only True God, she threatened to murder Elijah, a faithful prophet of the LORD, and one of two people in the annals of history to never taste the bitter pill of death. True to Solomon's rhetorical flourish, Jezebel's heart was "snares and nets." Ahab, like a caged bird was imprisoned by Jezebel's tenacious grip. As a result, he committed unprecedented evil in Israel, provoking the LORD to holy anger. Second Kings 16:32 records, "And Ahab made a wooden image. Ahab did more to provoke the LORD God of Israel to anger than all the kings of Israel who were before him." Elsewhere we read, Ahab "sold himself to do evil in the sight of the LORD" (1 Kings 21:20).

The Power of a Godly Woman

The anti-type of Jezebel is a holy woman of God. While a single Bible college student in my early twenties, I was privileged to travel with an evangelist and participate in an evangelistic crusade. I taught the youth and also gave sermonettes each evening before the evangelist preached. While shadowing the evangelist and the senior pastor, they suddenly felt compelled to mentor me in the area of marriage. They prefaced their remarks, "Dan, marriage is a wonderful institution. What you need to know is that marriage will either make you or break you."

Tales from the White House

A story involving the late President George H. W. Bush and his wife Barbara echoes this sentiment. The anecdote finds them at a gas station. Barbara recognizes the service station attendant, affectionately greets him before becoming deeply engrossed in conversation with the man. The President is bewildered by the First Lady's absorption with someone he assumes to be a stranger. When Barbara returns to the car he curiously asks, "Do you know that guy?" The First Lady enthusiastically responds, "Oh yes! He is an old boyfriend." A smug smile creeps across the President's face as he responds, "Well, I bet you are sure glad you married me instead of him?" At which the First Lady chides, "Oh George! Don't be silly! You know that if I had married him, he would be President and you would be pumping gas!"

Jezebel and Ahab: A Marriage Destined for Destruction

Ahab's choice of a marriage partner, put him on a downward trajectory every bit as treacherous as descending Niagara Falls in a rowboat. His reign was staged on a spiritual sinkhole supported by blasphemy, intrigue, apostasy, immorality, and murder. Jezebel was the catalyst for Ahab's chicanery leading to his ultimate demise. First Kings 21:25 reads, "But there was no one like Ahab who sold himself to do wickedness in the sight of the LORD, because Jezebel his wife stirred him up" (1 Kings 21:25). In the final analysis, her shameless idolatry led to the decimation of Israel and her own destruction. After the murder of Naboth, the LORD sent Elijah to Ahab. He delivered a horrific oracle of judgment on Ahab, Jezebel, and their posterity in 1 Kings 21:21–24:

> Behold, I will bring calamity on you. I will
> take away your posterity, and will cut off from

Ahab every male in Israel, both bond and free, I will make your house like the house of Jeroboam, the son of Nebat, and like the house of Baasha, the son of Ahijah, because of the provocation from which you provoked Me to anger, and made Israel sin. And concerning Jezebel, the LORD spoke saying, 'The dogs shall eat Jezebel by the wall of Jezreel.' The dogs shall eat who-ever belongs to Ahab and dies in the city, and the birds of the air shall eat whoever dies in the field.

Ahab foolishly imagined he could escape the Lord's judgment. He intimated to Jehoshaphat, "I will disguise myself and go into battle; but you put on your robes. So the king of Israel disguised himself and went into battle" (1 Kings 22:30). This ruse to deceive the enemy failed miserably. The enemy about to kill Jehoshaphat, mistaking him for Ahab, were kept from their purpose when the king of Judah cried out. Ahab was mortally wounded by the arrow of a Syrian sniper.

Jezebel's Final End

Later, after Jehu executed Ahaziah, he made a beeline to Jezreel, the capital of Samaria. Though Jezebel knew her fate was sealed, she made no introspective probe or spiritual U-turn, but continued traveling the road of narcissistic choices. Instead of repentance, she gave herself a makeover, and donned royal finery, serving to further illustrate the vanity of her shallow existence. Defiant to the end, she shouted, "Is it peace Zimri, murderer of your master?" (2 Kings 9:30–31).

Jehu gave the command to the queen's eunuchs to hurl her off the balcony. It is no accident that the name Jezreel means to "fling something aside," or "throw something away." Jezebel was hastily tossed like a ragdoll into the busy concourse where she was immedi-ately trampled by horses. Weary from battle, Jehu entered the palace dining room. Subsequently, he issued another order, "Then he said,

'Go now, see to this accursed woman, and bury her,' for she was a king's daughter" (2 Kings 9:34). Jehu was willing to give Jezebel a customary burial for a king's daughter, though he was fully aware of the deviltry of this wicked woman. God however, had a different plan. The LORD intervened to suspend the burial customs for Jezebel. For just as the LORD had prophesied through Elijah, the evil queen's flesh was consumed by dogs so that only her skull, the bones of her feet and hands remained.

Queen to Quagmire

The ignominious end of this woman was that her remains would be "like refuse on the surface of the field, so that they shall not say, 'Here lies Jezebel'" (2 Kings 9:37). Jezebel decomposed into fertilizer to be consumed by scavenging birds. One if reminded of Moses's warning to Israel should they rebel, "But if you do not do so, then take note you have sinned against the LORD. And be sure your sin will find you out" (Num. 32:23). As poetic justice would have it, this pernicious queen who murdered a man, then confiscated his vineyard, now served as fertilizer for fruits and vegetables. Truly God had invoked the spiritual law of the harvest, "Do not be deceived. God is not mocked; for whatever a man [woman] sows that shall he [she] will also reap" (Gal. 6:7).

Clearly Jezebel "sowed the wind and reaped the whirlwind" of God's judgment (Hosea 8:7), as she rejected the sweetness of a relationship with the living God to savor the sacred raisin cakes offered to Baal (Hosea 3:1). She chose to idolatrously sacrifice to Baal rather than exercising mercy upon His servants (Hosea 6:6). Her shameful end served as a chilling memorial of how utterly detestable idolatry coupled with the shedding of innocent blood are to the LORD. One testament to her judgment was the name of Hosea's son, Jezreel. Whenever the prophet called his son's name in the streets of Ephraim, terror surged up the spines of pious Jews (Hos. 1:3–5), as they were reminded of the horrific end of Israel's most ignominious queen.

The Upside of Negative Examples

Many years ago, a mentor of this writer remarked to him of the invaluable nature of negative examples. His perspective was biblical. The wicked legacy of Ahab and Jezebel issues a solemn warning for all, "But there was no one like Ahab who sold himself to do wickedness in the sight of the LORD, because Jezebel his wife stirred him up" (1 Kings 21:25).

Ahab and Jezebel's wicked and disgraced legacy pulsates with relevance for today's church. Paul serves notice of this in 1 Corinthians 10:11, "Now these things happened to them as examples, and they were written for our admonition, upon whom the ends of the ages have come" (see also 1 Cor. 10:6). Jezebel serves as a negative template for womanhood. Her sad existence demonstrates how God despises all forms of idolatry, injustice, immorality, and rebellion. Her legacy collides broadside with the solemn reality of Proverbs 14:12, "There is a way that seems right to a [woman], but the end thereof are the ways of death."

A Door of Hope

Positively, Jezebel's horrid end played a role in Israel eventually forsaking idols and worshipping the true and living God. There is hope for modern Jezebel's and generations of believers who wish to follow in the train of a modern Jezebels. The hope is expressed in the Lord's prophecy to Gomer, Hosea's wife in Hosea 2:14–16:

> Therefore, behold I will allure her, will bring her into the wilderness, And speak comfort to her. I will give her vineyards from there, And the Valley of Achor as a door of hope; she shall sing there, As in the days of her youth, as in the day when she came up from the land of Egypt.

The "Valley of Achor" was literally, "the Valley of Trouble" where Achan, the infamous thief who plundered the city of Jericho, then promptly executed was buried. By stealing the accursed things, of a beautiful Babylonian garment, two hundred shekels of silver, and a wedge of gold, he tragically forfeited his life and the life of his family (Josh. 7:21–22). The Valley of Trouble was therefore metaphorical for the traumatic plight Israel would face a result of Ahab and Jezebel's sin. Thank God that was not the last chapter to be written in Israel's history. Yahweh promised that after He judged Ephraim for Ahab and Jezebel's sins, He would open a "door of hope." With the Living God, there is always a hope and a future for God's people (Jer. 29:11; Tit. 2:11–13). Acquisition of that hope requires diligence and in some cases repentance (2 Cor. 7:10–11). The Church of Jesus Christ is not immune to spending time in the Valley of Achor. For her plight is similar to that of Israel's before God judged the nation. The prophet solemnly warns, "My people are destroyed for lack of knowledge; Because you have rejected knowledge, I will also reject you, that you should be no priest to Me; Because you have forgotten the law of your God, I will also forget your children" (Hos. 4:6).

Contextually, one major portion of the law of God Hosea has in view is the first commandment. The LORD commands, "You shall have no other gods before Me" (Exodus 20:3). Israel's indulgence in Baal and calf worship was akin to the brand of idolatry championed by Jezebel. Jezebel, her life, and death serve as an everlasting witness to God's hatred of idolatry. This divine loathing is reinforced by Isaiah, "I am the LORD that is My name; And My glory will I not give to another, Nor My praise to graven images" (Isa. 42:8).

The Cultural Image of the Modern Jezebel

Just as Israel, forsook the living God for Baal, so the west has rendered homage to a cultural icon of womanhood carved in the image of Jezebel. By deferring to Madame Folly over Lady Wisdom they have given voice to this bad actress. As a consequence, both the church and society have paid an enormous price. Now is the time to revisit and rediscover the biblical template of a godly woman.

The following chapters will address the false template of what Jesus called the "way of Jezebel" while unpacking the godliness of

Sarah and the holy women of God. Just as Jezebel models the worst of womanhood, Sarah is established by Peter as a godly model for Christian women of every generation. Below is a compendium of symptoms of the Jezebel Syndrome in addition to the moral graces of Sarah. Both will be explored in the rest of the book.

Symptoms of the Jezebel Syndrome

1) Jezebel seeks to dominate her husband by usurping his role of headship.
2) Jezebel traffics in gossip and innuendo.
3) Jezebels are storytellers who traffic in false accusations.
4) Jezebels like Margaret Sanger, advance an agenda to destroy rather than save life.
5) Jezebels commit hypergamy by attaching themselves to powerful men.
6) Jezebels are easily deceived by persuasive men.
7) Jezebels are emotional cul-de-sacs, all roads end with them.
8) Jezebels employ their sexuality to lure men to destruction.
9) Jezebels often resort to sarcasm and belittlement.
10) Jezebels refuse to celebrate their husband's dreams.
11) Jezebels opt for style over substance, virtue signaling over integrity.
12) Jezebels emotions are the voice of God, a voice that they religiously obey.
13) Jezebels, like Lot's wife, traffic in greed and personal comfort.
14) Jezebel are addicted to male bashing.
15) Jezebel induce suicide and depression through flooding.
16) Jezebels are the queens of vindictiveness.
17) Jezebel seeks to usurp the role of men in the local church setting.
18) Jezebels establish no moral boundaries while encouraging others to participate in their debauchery.

19) Jezebels defraud their husband sexual intimacy, by employing sex as a power tool to manipulate and a weapon to punish.

20) Jezebels are false prophetesses who add to and subtract from God's Word, without mental reservation.

21) Jezebels choose vengeance over forgiveness.

22) Jezebels rush to judgment by believing the first report.

23) Jezebels emotions are the voice of God, a voice eclipsing God's Word.

24) Jezebels engage in group-think rather than God-think.

25) Jezebels are the queens of seduction.

26) Jezebels opt for nakedness and fear over being naked and unashamed.

27) Jezebels ignore the biblical principle of marital water being thicker than family blood.

28) Jezebels traffic in nuanced morality.

Sarah's and Her Daughters

1) Sarahs do not rush to judgment, but rather heed the words of Jesus to, "not judge according to appearance, but judge righteous judgment" (John 7:24).

2) Sarahs sport an enlargement mentality rather than a scarcity mentality.

3) Sarahs rejoice with those who rejoice and weep with those who weep.

4) Sarahs are proactive rather than reactive.

5) Sarahs don't let go and let God, but trust God and get going!

6) Sarahs, like Mary, express devotion to Christ, through words and deeds.

7) Sarahs like Mary delight in spending time at the feet of Jesus.

8) Sarahs major on God-think rather than Group-think.

9) Sarahs, like Ruth, are virtuous women who practice pure religion by compassionately meeting the needs of widows.

10) Sarahs, like Ruth, are virtuous women who go the second mile to meet the practical needs of others.
11) Sarahs pour out gracious words of faith, hope, and love.
12) Sarahs, like Ruth walk by faith and not by sight.
13) Sarahs, like Ruth are tirelessly diligent.
14) Sarahs, like Esther, possess an indomitable spirit that moves them to risk their lives for the sake of others.
15) Sarahs, risk their own lives to protect and provide for others.
16) Sarahs, are faithful prayer warriors.
17) Sarahs give others the benefit of the doubt.
18) Sarahs demonstrate love to their children by teaching them God's Word and by instilling within them to love and fear God.
19) Sarah's genuinely forgive others from the heart, knowing they are greatly loved and forgiven.
20) Sarahs diligently attend to the needs of their husband and children.
21) Sarahs demonstrate unconditional respect toward their husbands, even when they are disobedient to God's Word.
22) Sarahs seek to diffuse conflict with tactful respect.
23) Sarahs courageously trust God-even when it is difficult or uncomfortable.
24) Sarahs quietly pray for their husbands rather than drudging up the past.
25) Sarahs train their children in the Holy Scriptures.
26) Sarahs do good to all people-especially those in the household of faith (Gal. 6:10).
27) Sarahs measure every opinion by the straight edge of God's Word.
28) Sarahs do not obsess with their husband's faults, but celebrate his virtues.
29) Sarahs cultivate a fond affection towards their husbands and children.
30) Sarahs are discontent only with their godliness.
31) Sarahs teach and spiritually mentor younger women.

32) Sarahs joyfully share the gospel.
33) Sarahs strengthen their faith by showing hospitality to others.
34) Sarahs resist the impulse to gossip and male bash.
35) Sarahs cultivate speech seasoned with grace and truth.
36) Sarahs display love to God, their families, and their neighbors.
37) Sarahs are praised by all for their outsized virtue.
38) Sarahs take seriously their calling to meet the sexual needs of their husbands-knowing that it is God's will for them to meet those needs.
39) Sarahs submit to their husbands during public worship because of the angels.
40) Sarahs take their one flesh relationship with their husbands seriously.

While the aim of this book is to inspire women, it also written with the men who love them in mind. It is my prayer that both women and men, single and married, will benefit immeasurably from this volume. Women, by personalizing the principles of godly womanhood, and men by lovingly leading them. One prayer of the author is that married couples will read this book together and apply its biblical principles. By doing so they will embark on a journey marked with joy and peace while anticipating a rich welcome into the eternal kingdom of the Lord Jesus Christ.

Questions for Reflection

1) Jezebel is a template for fallen womanhood, illustrating the sand traps into which women frequently fall. Where do you see Ahab erring with Jezebel? Explain.
2) Jezebel was a notorious idolater who introduced Baal into the Northern kingdom of Israel. What other idols do women struggle, who are susceptible to the Jezebel syndrome?
3) If you are a man, a relevant takeaway from Jezebel's life is that a wife possesses the potential of either making or break-

ing the men who love them. Are there any women in your sphere of influence suffering from the Jezebel Syndrome?

4) If there is a woman in your orbit suffering from the Jezebel Syndrome, what strategy might you implement to help them?

5) If you are woman, to what degree does Jezebel's shameful end motivate you to want to be a daughter of Sarah as opposed to a daughter or Jezebel? On a scale of 1–7 (1 being low, 7 being high), rate your motivation level.

1   2   3   4   5   6   7

6) Proverbs 31:30 briefly summarizes a positive and negative template of a woman God considers vain, and one He considers praiseworthy. It states, "Charm is deceitful, and beauty is passing, But a woman who fears the LORD shall be praise." On a scale of 1–7, rate how well you do cultivating the inner beauty of a God-fearing spirit, vice focusing on temporal external beauty.

1   2   3   4   5   6   7

7) In Numbers 32:23 the children of Israel are warned that spurning the law of the LORD will ensure that their "sin will find them out" (be judged). This verse is graphically illustrated through Jezebel's wicked life and ignominious death.

8) 1 Samuel 2:30 informs us, "For those who honor Me, I will honor, and those who despise Me shall be lightly esteemed." What steps are you taking to cultivate God's "honor principle" in your life?

9) The biblical narrative of Ahab's life reports that Jezebel stirred him up to perform evil deeds. If you are a single man dating a woman, does your girlfriend motivate you to do good or evil? Explain.

PROFILING JEZEBEL

"Women have come, women have gone, everyone
trying to cage me. Some were so sweet, I barely
got free, others they only enraged me."
—Bob Seger, *Traveling Man.*

Sonny Jurgenson was one of the premier quarterbacks in the NFL in the '60s and '70s. Calm and collected, with a lasar beam for an arm, Jurgenson knew how to lead a team to victory. Sonny was also was well acquainted with the curriculum of losing. Like many quarterbacks he basked in effusive praise from the press when the Washington Redskins won, and was mercilessly crucified by the same when they lost. When asked how he managed the ups and downs, he reflected, "I have learned every week you are either in the penthouse or the outhouse." This is a lesson that the prophet Elijah would appreciate.

The View from the Mountaintop

Mount Carmel represented the crowning achievement of Elijah's prophetic career. In his finest hour, God's spokesman to the northern kingdom had just routed the prophets of Baal evidenced by the LORD's consumption of his Elijah's sacrifice. Subsequent to this sign of divine favor, Elijah ordered the seizure and execution of the queen's prophets. At the apex, the prophet's poll numbers rose exponentially after his prayer for rain brought a three-and-one-half year drought to a screeching halt. After miraculously winning a marathon footrace with wicked King Ahab's chariot to the Syrian capital Jezreel, Elijah was riding high. Perhaps he thought now things would be different. Maybe he surmised that Ephraim (Israel), would once and for all, sever her idolatrous ties with Baal.

Jezebels Revere Their Emotions as the Voice of God

Rather than making a spiritual U-turn, Jezebel doubled down on evil. She executed the prophets of Yahweh and made a veiled threat to execute Elijah the day after his great victory. Modern Jezebels follow suit. Consider the following:

–   A female mayor of a major city charges police officers with crimes, declaring them guilty before being proven innocent. They are later acquitted and the mayor is summarily disgraced.
–   Another female mayor of a major US city, publicly castigates police officers for following their rules of engagement in apprehending a dangerous criminal who threatened their life.
–   A prominent female pastor displays public contempt for evangelical pastors for praying in Jesus's name and quoting the Bible.

–   Jezebels Threaten Men Causing Them to Fear

On the heels of Elijah's rousing victory came the indisputable lowlight of his life. Elijah's dreams of national revival were shattered with a singular vengeful missile launched from the lips of a malicious queen. Elijah's miraculous victory on Mount Carmel, culminated in the execution of the prophets of Baal. Yet Jezebel was unmoved by the successes of her nemesis. She sent a messenger to serve the prophet a veiled threat cloaked as a vengeful oath, "So let the gods do to me and more also, if I do not make your life as the life of one of them by tomorrow about this time" (1 Kings 19:2). Elijah's emotions went into a tale-spin in which he begged God to take his life.

What Men Fear Most from Jezebel

If there is one thing men fear from Jezebels, it is their words. Jezebels have a way of butchering men with their tongues causing them to recoil in fear. When Jezebels threaten, flood, belittle, or embarrass their husbands, their husbands will stonewall, separate, and eventually divorce. As a pastor I have known women who publicly air their grievances against their husbands only to have their marriages end badly. Fear is the primary reason why men stonewall in marriage. They do not want their women to butcher their souls. Jezebel's tongue is a weapon leaving a trail of bodies in their wake.

Jezebels Sins Have a Tsunami Effect on Others

Jezebel's life underscores the truth that no one sins in a vacuum. Her negative template of womanhood demonstrates that our sins have a tsunami effect on others. First, her sin infected her husband, the most wicked king in Ephraim's history. If one's choice of a spouse either makes or breaks them, the sins of Jezebel shattered Ahab. She influenced him to worship Baal. He degenerated into a henpecked husband, who caved to the godless desires of his "mean-girl" wife. Just as waters seeks its own level, so husbands often rise or sink to the level of their wives. Secondly, Jezebel's sin wrought havoc on the nation of Israel. Ephraim as Elijah pointed out, waffled between worshipping Baal or Yahweh (1 Kings 18:21). As a consequence, the LORD brought seven years of drought upon the nation. Thirdly, Jezebel's sin led to Jezebel "massacring the prophets of the LORD" (1 Kings 18:4). Fourthly, Jezebel's sin led Elijah, the premier prophet in Israel at the time, to the far edge of despair (1 Kings 19:1–10).

The lesson should not be lost on the Christian woman nor anyone else, sin always churns up a wake of unintended consequences. Positively, godly Sarahs leave a lasting legacy for generations.

Jezebels Traffic in Revenge While Refusing to Forgive

Erstwhile forgiveness expert Lewis Smedes, tells a story of one of his former students, a lovely woman inside and out. As he got to know this woman, he noticed that she was disabled and inquired of her story. She informed her that she was a young actress, married to a young actor. Then one day she got into a serious car accident that left her disabled. Her actor husband struggled to cope with her new normal and eventually abandoned her for another woman. Smedes asked the young woman if she had forgiven her ex-husband. She meekly responded, "I think I have." He further inquired, "Well, how do you know you have forgiven him?" She responded, "I find myself wishing him well."

Jezebel, the idolatrous wicked queen of Samaria, was not a "beautiful loser" who "forgave" her enemies when confronted with defeat. Far from congratulating Elijah on his miraculous victory, she threatened to sever his head from the rest of his body! In other ways, modern Jezebels sport a vengeful spirit.

Hang Them High!

Zeresh, the wife of Haman is a primo example of the Jezebel Syndrome. She was an uncompassionate and vindictive woman, who feasted on revenge and fasted on forgiveness. Zeresh and her husband Haman could be termed a match made in Hell as both suffered from a depraved mind-set. Zeresh and Haman were ambitious, malicious, and downright wicked. It would be safe to assume that Zeresh, not unlike her husband, was immensely egotistical. She reserved no pity for those who offended either her husband or herself and was solely interested in advancing her own agenda. Though the narrative of Esther casts her as a minor character, she nonetheless played a pivotal role in the sinister plot of the Book of Esther. On the day that Mordecai persisted in refusing to bow to Haman, she advised her husband to construct a gallows upon which Mordecai could be impaled. Esther 5:14, "Then his wife Zeresh and all his friends said to him, 'Let a gallows be made, fifty feet high, and in the morning suggest to the king that Mordecai be hanged on it; then go merrily with the king to the banquet."

Though God providentially intervened on behalf of His servant Mordecai, Zeresh mirrors the spiteful and vindictive ways of Jezebel. A blood lust for revenge courses through their character veins. Reciprocity rather than reconciliation is their endgame. Jezebel's represent the worst of the curse of Eve by seeking to dominate men, by killing them!

Jezebels Seek to Dominate Their Husbands through Contempt

Saul had a daughter named Michal. By slaying Goliath, David achieved Rockstar status in Michal's world. Conversely her father Saul, was inflamed with jealous rage toward his future successor. Therefore, he set Michal's dowry at one hundred foreskins of the Philistines (1 Sam. 18:25). Michal was used by God to protect David after Saul plotted to kill him (1 Sam. 19:11–17). Perhaps protecting the future king of Israel through subterfuge was the high watermark of Michal's life.

Compassion for Michal

Michal is a woman who warrants compassion. She was taken from David by her wayfaring father, and given to be the wife of another man (1 Sam. 25:44). David reclaimed his first bride subsequent to the death of Saul and after ascending to the throne. In the interim of being taken from David, she was given to another man, Palti, who loved her and mourned her loss as she was transported to be David's wife (2 Sam. 3:13–16). Perhaps Michal had fallen in love with Palti, and out of love with David. In such cases there is hope for Jezebel just as there is for all people. In the last chapter, the author writes of the redemption and hope that God holds out for Jezebel.

The Tragedy of Michal

Michal's majestic name means, "Who is like God?" It is a name that implies that God is the only God, the true God, who is worthy of praise. He is to set above all false Gods as He alone is to be worshipped. An archangel, "Michael," who dwelt in the court of the Almighty, and a prophet, "Micah," shared names with the same meaning. The irony of Michal is that while her name praises God for His worthiness, her actions failed to follow suit. For after she is returned to David to be his wife, Michal as she witnesses him dance a mighty dance before the LORD in his undergarments. Michal was repulsed by what she considered a vulgar display of worship. Contempt screams from every pore as she witnesses the "lewd spectacle." "Now as the ark came into the City of David, Michal, Saul's daughter, looked through a window and saw King David leaping and whirling before the LORD; and she despised him in her heart" (2 Samuel 6:17).

Michal, her soul simmering with contempt, walks to meet David. Rather than praising her husband for worshipping God in spirit and truth, she seized the opportunity to publicly flog him! Sarcastically she mocks, "How glorious was king of Israel today, uncovering himself today in the eyes of the maids of his servants, as one of the base fellows shamelessly uncovers himself" (2 Sam. 6:20). Among Jezebel, there is an innate tendency to verbally flog others either in person or in private. Jezebel's seek to dominate their husbands through a flood of contempt. God judged Michal for dishonoring David by making her infertile until the day of her death (2 Sam. 6:23).

When They Lose Jezebels Double Down on Vengeance

Elijah's victory embarrassed the queen to the point that she resolved to discard those who publicly or privately humiliated her. Historically, Jezebels when exposed as frauds do not run up the white flag of surrender but double down on vengeance. Much like the Pharaoh of Egypt encountered by Moses, Jezebels would rather cut their losses and harden their hearts, than surrender to God's will.

Jezebel persisted in her vengeful campaign, by murdering three hundred prophets of Yahweh.

Contemporary Jezebels

While Jezebel's servants slayed prophets with swords, today modern Jezebels butcher their enemies with their tongues, through male bashing, false accusations, and contemptuous flooding. They embody the lyric of Bob Seger's song, *Traveling Man.* "Women have come, women have gone. Everyone trying to cage me. Some were so sweet, I barely got free. Others they only enraged me." Jezebels castigate men for their God given role in society.

Delilah: The Original Jezebel?

One of the most enigmatic characters of the Bible was a judge named Samson. Samson was a man upon whom God bestowed abundant favor. His birth was announced by the angel of the LORD (Jesus in pre-incarnate form). He was to be a Nazarite to the LORD who was endowed with supernatural strength. Samson's strength would remain so long as he did not cut his hair. Yet Samson possessed an Achilles heel. Today he would be pegged a womanizer who failed to corral his sexual urges. Though a man anointed by God to judge Israel during a critical season of their history, he routinely acted on his unbridled lusts. On one occasion he brazenly said to his father, "I have seen a woman in Timnah of the daughter of the Philistines, now therefore, get her for me as a wife" (Judges 14:2). In the same conversation he added, "Get her for me for she pleases me well" (Judges 14:3).

Samson's life proves that God works in mysterious ways as his attraction to this strange woman was from the LORD (Judges 14:4). God used Samson's love for foreign women to judge Israel's enemies. Yet eventually, his lust for women triggered his demise. For one woman he eventually loved was a Philistine woman named Delilah (Judges 16:4). Samson met his match with this ancient Jezebel. Delilah provided an opening for the Philistines who up to this point had failed to either capture or kill Samson. The Philistines saw an opportunity to hasten his demise by employing Delilah's deceitful charms to pierce Samson's Achilles heel.

Who Was Delilah?

Delilah was a Philistine woman and Samson's illicit lover. The Philistines bartered with her to connive Samson into divulging the secret of his strength. She agreed to their terms and plotted to divest Samson of his supernatural strength. Initially Samson dutifully guarded his Nazarite vow. In the process, he teased Delilah with three lies regarding the secret of his strength. First, he informed her if she bound him with bowstrings then he would be reduced to the strength of an average man. Secondly, if she bound him with ropes, his supernatural strength would abandon him (Judges 16:8–12). Yet Samson effortlessly snapped the strings and ropes as if cutting through hot butter. Delilah's lamented, "Until now you have mocked me with lies. Tell me what you may be bound with" (Judges 16:13).

Samson attempted one more ruse with Delilah. He informed her that if she wove the locks of his hair in a certain manner his strength would wane. Yet Samson betrayed his word after awaking and pulling out the batten and web from his hair (Judges 16:14).

Jezebel's Manipulative Tactics Trigger the Destructive Choices of Men

While the Bible is clear that every person bears responsibility for their own sin (Ezek. 18:4; 20), it also charges that consorting with evil people provokes bad behavior. Such is the when men attach themselves to Jezebels or in the case of Samson, Delilah. To this end Solomon wrote, "He who walks with wise men will be wise, but a companion of fools will be destroyed" (Prov. 13:20). In this antithetical proverb, Solomon is saying that are friendships can largely determine whether we will make wise or foolish choices as our life unfolds. Whether we will prosper spiritually, or be spiritually and perhaps physically destroyed. In this vein, Samson's association with Delilah led to the loss of his eyes and diminishment of his strength.

Jezebels have a way of turning a good man with high morals into a compromising man who develops sinful habits. Paul warned, "Do not be deceived. Evil company corrupts good habits" (1 Cor. 15:33).

Jezebels Can Drive Men to Despair of Life

Delilah's chronic nagging of Samson drove him to despair of life itself. In Judges 16:15–17 we read, "Then she said to him, 'How can you say, I love you,' when your heart is not with me? You have mocked me these three times, and have not told me where your great strength lies. And it came to pass when she pestered him daily with her words and pressed him, so that her soul was vexed to death, that he told her all his heart."

Delilah pouted. She wept, carped and nagged. In the words of Dr. John Gottman, she "flooded," meaning she incessantly criticized Samson. This author has known men whose wives' chronic expressions of contempt led them to commit suicide. Obviously, such is an unspeakable tragedy, reaping untold heartache for family and friends. The Bible does not endorse nagging. Two proverbs state this truth clearly:

> "Better to dwell in the corner of a house-top, Than in a house shared with a contentious woman." (Proverbs 21:9)

> "A continual dripping on a very rainy day, And a contentious woman are alike." (Proverbs 27:15)

Samson collided broadside with the realism of these proverbs. Though responsible for his foolish choices, truly he was a victim of the Jezebel syndrome. Like the tread on overused tires, Samson was constantly worn down by Delilah's incessant nagging to the point he imagined death to be a more inviting option than living with an interminable nag. This is not to say that Samson was suicidal, yet he was so grieved by Delilah's nagging he wished himself dead.

Consequently, Samson let down his guard, and divulged the secret of his strength. Tragically, his eyes were gourged from their sockets, before he was imprisoned by the Philistines. Delilah had succeeded in her mission of wreaking havoc on one of God's appointed judges.

Delilah Motivated Samson to Violate His Vow

The tipping point of Samson violating his sacred trust of the Nazarite vow, was Delilah's incessant grousing and complaining that "vexed him to death." He finally revealed the secret of his strength which is recorded in Judges 13:5, "No razor has ever come upon my head, for I have been a Nazarite to God from my mother's womb. If I can be shaven, then my strength will leave me, and I shall become weak like any other man."

Jezebels Employ Their Sexuality to Lure Men into Bad Decisions

When Jesus warned the Thyatira church about the Jezebel in their midst, he cited her immoral influence on the church. He inveighs, "who calls herself a prophetess to teach and seduce My servants to commit sexual immorality and eat things sacrificed to idols" (Rev. 2:20). Sexual intrigue is the salacious calling card of Jezebels. The detailed description of the modus operandi of Lady Folly is as timeless as it is graphic. Solomon writes:

> "With her enticing speech she caused him to yield, With her flattering lips she seduced him. Immediately he went after her, as an ox goes to the slaughter, Or as a fool goes to the correction of the stocks, Till an arrow struck his liver. As a bird hastens to the snare, He did not know it would cost his life. Now therefore, listen to me my children; Pay attention to the words of my mouth; Do not let your heart turn aside to her ways, Do not stray into her paths; For she has cast down many wounded, And all who were

slain by her were strong men. Her house is the way to hell, Descending to the chambers of death" (Prov. 7:21–27).

Had Samson penned such words they would have been considered autobiographical. Delilah seduced Samson tragically resulting in his violation of his Nazarite vow. She sensually lured Samson into frolicking in her lap, while softly caressing him and lulling him to sleep. While asleep she called for a man to shave the thick locks of his hair. Her mission objective of decimating Samson's strength was completed. Something she accomplished through nagging and seductive charm.

Contemporary Jezebels and Delilahs

Today the contemporary counterparts of Jezebel and Delilah are legion. In the world of business, Jezebel's flirt, fawn, and claw their way up the corporate ladder. In the media and politics, they flaunt their sexuality to buy influence from powerful men. Years ago, this author read an article featuring an interview of a professional athlete. While this athlete was sexually active, he exercised extreme precaution in selecting women. He said he was very careful to only keep company with women whom he believed did not have a hidden agenda. This young athlete was wise to avoid the Jezebels and Delilahs of his day. He would have been wiser still to abstain from sexual promiscuity altogether!

A Contemporary Jezebel

Ghislaine Maxwell was the girlfriend of Jeffrey Epstein, the most notorious pedophile and sex trafficker in United States history. She worked closely with Epstein in recruiting underage girls for his sex trafficking operation in New Mexico, the Virgin Islands, and on his private jet, the *Lolita Express*. One young woman imprisoned in Epstein's sex ring, confessed that Maxwell was as evil as Epstein, having raped her twenty to thirty times. In July of 2020 in Maxwell was arrested by FBI agents in New Hampshire and charged with crimes that could send her to jail for thirty-five years. Maxwell, Madame Heidi Fleiss, and other Jezebels like them, are examples of modern Jezebels of who according to Jesus tolerate and teach others to commit sexual immorality.

Jezebels Seek After High Profile Servants of God

Solomon writes of the seductress, "For by means of a harlot a man is reduced to a crust of bread; And an adulteress will prey upon his precious life" (Prov. 6:26).

Jezebels prey on powerful men in general and Christian leaders in particular. Neil Anderson opined that relative to spiritual warfare, the Christian is Satan's target and the Christian leader is the bull's-eye. One of the best biblical examples of the above biblical aphorism is Potiphar's wife attempted seduction of a young, handsome, muscular Joseph. Thankfully, in that instance Joseph's high view of God and spiritual fortitude withstood this alluring temptress.

Samson was such a "precious" man whose birth was announced by the Angel of the LORD. The LORD had a special task for Samson. He was strategically chosen by God to judge Israel by flogging the wicked Philistines. True to divine decree, his miraculous displays of strength were extraordinarily stranger than fiction. In spite of his moral dalliances, the LORD used this anointed servant to supernaturally advance His divine agenda. Yet God intended him for more. The legacy of his life could be captured in the immortal words of John Greenleaf Whittier, "Saddest words of tongue or pen, what might have been." As greatly as Samson was used by God, had he not succumbed to Delilah's wily ways, he would have been used to an even greater degree.

Modern Jezebels

Years ago, I heard of a woman who told friends of a pastor whom she admired, "I will have himself as my husband someday." True to her word, she did, proving herself to be a modern Jezebel. In a similar fashion, this writer recalls of reading an anonymous article in a prominent Christian magazine of a woman who lured a pastor into a clandestine affair with her. As in the case of David, this adulterous tryst had "given great cause for the enemies of the LORD to blaspheme" (2 Sam. 12:16), while doing violence to this man's marriage and family.

Delilah's Misconduct Triggers the Failure of God's Servants

Earlier, I cited a story in which he was warned by older ministers that his future wife would either make or break him. Delilah's conduct broke Samson to the point where he succumbed to her deceitful scheme. As a result, the children of Israel suffered increased oppression at the hands of the Philistines. While by the grace of God, Samson's life ended on a high note, he might have been spared death and the gouging out of his eyes had he not succumbed to her deceitful scheming. Whether their name is Jezebel, Zeresh, Delilah, or an unknown commodity, modern Jezebels, are proverbial maneaters. Those who would live a good life, avoid them. In this vein Moses's straight talk to the children of Israel in Deuteronomy 30:19 pulsates with relevance: "I call heaven and earth as witnesses today against you, that I have set before you life and death, blessing and cursing, therefore, choose life, that both you and your descendants may live."

Questions for Reflection

1) Describe an experience in which you were jealous of sister or brother and responded sinfully to the person whom you envied. What steps did you take to address your jealousy?
2) Was there ever a time when you made an idle threat either toward your husband, family member, brother or sister in Christ, that you later judged to be sinful? Explain.
3) Jezebel was an idolatrous queen who worshiped Baal, the "rain god." Idolatry like sin, can take many forms. Some idolatry is religious, other material, some personal, or ideological. One of the more cryptic forms of idolatry is ideological. We tend to worship our own prejudices, opinions,

and worldviews. What category of idolatry have you done battle with in the past or currently struggle against?

4) A universal condition of every person is that wrongs will be committed against them. Though Elijah sinned did not sin against Jezebel, he demonstrated her to be a vindictive, unforgiving, and wicked. What offence was committed against you that you had difficulty forgiving? What was it that empowered you to forgive them?

5) Jezebel is a good example of the fact that no one sins in a vacuum. Jezebel's sin led to the Elijah's severe depression triggering his prayer that for God to mercifully take His life. Has your sin ever contributed to someone sinking into a depressive state?

6) Delilah fits the profile of a Jezebel. One of her notorious traits is that she incessantly nagged Samson to the point that death appeared an inviting prospect. Have you ever fallen into a trap of nagging your husband to the point where he became severely depressed? Suicidal?

7) For women only. Was ever a time when you crossed a line from feminine charm to sensual/sexual manipulation of a man? If so, what steps could you take to avoid falling into this trap next time?

8) Zeresh was another ancient Jezebel who sought revenge upon her enemies. Assuming you *can't* relate to wanting to orchestrate the death of your enemies, have you ever taken measures to hurt a person who offended you? Explain.

9) It has been said that while all of God's children are equally precious, they are not equally strategic. One Christian author has said, "While all Christian leaders have a target on their back, Christian leaders have a bull's-eye!" The Bible says, "an adulteress seeks after precious life" (Prov. 6:26). Has there been a time when you behaved inappropriately towards a Christian leader? If so, what measures did you take to correct your behavior?

JEZEBEL: THE
FALSE ACCUSER

"You shall not bear false witness against your neighbor."
—Exodus 20:16

"By the mouth of two or three witnesses
shall every word be established."
—2 Corinthians 13:1

"Every woman has a right to be believed."
—Hillary Clinton

"A lie travels half-way around the world before
truth has a chance to get its pants on."
—Winston Churchill

Richard Jewell was a security guard whose life's passion was protecting innocent people from would be perpetrators. As a young man, he pursued his passion with the aggressiveness of an NFL linebacker. During the 1996 Summer Olympics, Jewell worked as a security officer when he spotted a suspicious package under a bench and radioed one of the EOD (Explosive Ordnance Device), specialists to investigate. This EOD officer carefully unzipped the bag only to discover three live pipe bombs. Jewell immediately alerted police and helped evacuate the area before the three bombs exploded. The incident claimed the lives of two victims and left another one hundred people injured. Many contended that without Jewell's heroics, the death toll would have climbed exponentially higher. Richard Jewell became a hero to many in the aftermath of the infamous Atlanta Olympics bombing.

Three days later, Kathy Scruggs, a journalist for the *Atlanta Journal*, broke the news that Jewell was under investigation. In the article she contended that Jewell fit the profile of the bomber. While the allegation was baseless, and Jewell eventually exonerated, the damage had already been done, as the trauma of being falsely accused cost him dearly. He died prematurely at the age of forty-four. One disturbing takeaway from Jewell's story is that false accusation kills.

The Trouble with Slander

The story is told of a rabbi who was jealous of a popular fellow rabbi. So jealous in fact that he spread a malicious rumor. The rumor while false, inflicted great damage to the falsely accused and his wife. It ruined their reputation, health, and ministry. The rabbi who was the false accuser also suffered terribly to the point where he not only genuinely repented of his malicious falsehood but journeyed to this rabbi's house and asked his forgiveness. The magnanimous rabbi graciously forgave his false accuser. The penitent younger rabbi asked his senior rabbi if there was anything he could do to rectify the matter. He requested that his former nemesis take a feather pillow and climb a grassy hill where the wind blew strongly. He instructed him to then take a knife and slice one end of the pillow. The sage rabbi requested that his young accuser return to him for further instructions. The younger rabbi did what the man requested and the feathers travelled to the four corners of the earth. When he returned to the old man, his instructions were simple, "Go gather them up." Years ago, while talking to one of my superiors he asserted passionately, "There are no repercussions for the false accuser." He was so right!

Doing the Devil's Work

His name means "slanderer." The Devil is the "accuser of the brethren who accused them before God day and night," and who "deceives the whole world" (Rev. 12:9–10). What should be understood by God's people is that it is possible to do the Devil's work. No less of a prominent member of the early church than Peter became a mouthpiece of this slanderer during a critical juncture in Jesus's ministry. He rebuked Jesus, to the point of shaking Him, for informing His disciples that "He must go to Jerusalem, suffer many things from the chief priests and scribes, and be killed, and be raised again on the third day" (Matt. 16:21). Peter who a moment earlier, Jesus applauded for being a conduit of divinely revealed truth, for accurately identifying Jesus as "the Christ the Son of living God," took Jesus aside and began to rebuke Him proclaiming, "Far be it from You Lord; this shall not happen to You!" (Matt. 16:22). Jesus turned to Peter and rebuked, "Get behind Me Satan! You are an offense to Me. For you are not mindful of the things of God, but the things of men" (Matt. 16:23).

Peter, temporarily was doing the Devil's work. If Satan can influence the Apostle Peter to whom Jesus bequeathed the "keys to the kingdom," he can use anyone. When it comes to slander, Jezebels are an unconventional weapon in his diabolic arsenal. They do the devils work.

The View from the Palace

There once was a king whose palace bordered a farm. The centerpiece of the neighboring farm was a lush vineyard, unfolding into a visual feast. The king's casual glances at his neighbor's farm eventually degenerated into a covetous obsession. One day the king made a generous offer to purchase his neighbor's vineyard for more than fair market value. The kings formal offer is recorded in 1 Kings 21:2, "Give me your vineyard, that I may have it for a vegetable garden, because it is near, next to my house; and for it I will give you a vineyard better than it. Or if it seems good to you, I will give you its worth in money."

His neighbor rejected the king's offer out of hand, explaining, "The LORD forbid that I should give the inheritance of my fathers to you!" (1 Kings 21:3). The vineyard, the neighbor tersely explained, had been in the family for generations. It was an heirloom. To sell it would be to dishonor his father and sully his family tree.

This refusal to sell should have marked the end of negotiations. Yet the king came down with an acute case of the greener vineyard syndrome. Instead of shopping for greener vistas of vineyard, he sunk into a severely depressive funk. If Ahab were a godly king, he would have quickly come to his senses while recalling the last word of the law charging, "You shall not covet your neighbor's house; you shall not covet your neighbor's wife, nor his male servant, nor his female servant, nor his ox, nor his donkey, nor anything that is your neighbor's" (Exodus 20:17). Such a prohibition from the LORD included vineyards. Regrettably, the train of this king's loyalty to God had long ago left the station.

The king became a recluse. He sulked, pouted, and refused to eat until the queen called him on the royal bedsheets. She asked, "Why is your spirit so sullen that you eat no food?" (1 Kings 21:5). The king intimated to the queen the trigger for his royal funk. "He said to her, 'Because I spoke to Naboth the Jezreelite,' and said to him, 'Give me your vineyard for money; or else, if it pleases you, I will give you another vineyard for it.' And he answered, 'I will not give you my vineyard.'" (1 Kings 21:6). But you just didn't say no to Jezebel. She scolded, "You now exercise authority over Israel! Arise, eat food, and let your heart be cheerful; I will give you the vineyard of Naboth the vineyard.'"

In modern parlance, the queen was saying, "Darling, you are the king of Israel! Kings never take no for an answer! Now Baby get out of that bed, shower, eat breakfast and leave the rest to me! We will get that vineyard from Naboth if we have to kill him!"

Jezebel the False Accuser

One of the crowning characteristics of Jezebel is her penchant for falsely accusing others for personal gain. Consistent with Eve's curse, Jezebels seek to dominate men through false accusation. Today it is chic for women to falsely accuse men to get what they want. Such false accusation since as the "weaker vessel" (1 Pet. 3:7), they are readily able to play the victim card. Below is a compendium of such false accusations:

- Brian Banks is falsely accused of rape and served six years in prison before eventually being exonerated after his accuser admitted lying. Banks false accuser was ordered by a judge to pay 2.6 million in damages.
- Julie Swetnick accused Supreme Court Justice Brent Kavanaugh of outsized sexual misconduct during college. After a sex crime investigator and former boyfriend found Christine Blasey Ford's allegations against Brent Kavanaugh to be baseless, Swetnick recanted many of her allegations.
- Late Presidential candidate Herman Cain is falsely accused of extra-marital affairs. Though the allegations are baseless he suspends his Presidential campaign to reduce the emotional toll these false accusations have taken on his family.
- A popular television magnate and radio talk show host is falsely accused of sexual harassment. A network of celebrities from a variety of political persuasions came to his defense knowing that the allegations were false.
- Supreme Court Justice Clarence Thomas is falsely accused by Anita Hill, a former disgruntled employee, of inappropriate sexual remarks which were refuted by her co-workers and Thomas himself. Thomas was confirmed and for nearly three decades served as one of the most highly esteemed Supreme Court justices in US history.
- Longtime Harvard law professor, Alan Dershowitz is falsely accused of having sex with a minor girl who was part of Jeffrey Epstein's prostitution ring. The woman making this charge, was urged by her lawyer to lie about a relationship with Dershowitz, since he worked for Epstein at one time. While Dershowitz was exonerated, his health, retirement, and reputation were severely injured.
- Today there are many Brian Banks, falsely accused of sexual assault, who are currently serving time.

—   Evelyn Farkas was a former Obama administration official who went on national television to urge congressional staffers to gather evidence of alleged collusion between President Trump's 2016 campaign and Russia, saying she knew there was evidence of collusion. Yet that same year on MSNBC she reported, "I was urging my former colleagues, and frankly speaking the people on the Hill… Get as much information as you can, get as much intelligence as you can, before President Obama leaves the administration, because I had a fear that somehow that information would disappear with the senior people who left. So it would be hidden away in the bureaucracy." However, transcripts under oath with congressional investigators reveal Farkas's sworn testimony along with former attorney general Loretta Lynch, and Susan Rice, all testified under oath that they neither had nor had seen or knew of any of evidence of Russian collusion. Their testimony under oath exposed their subsequent accusations and innuendos that the Trump administration had colluded with Russian as blatant lies.

Today a barrage of similar false accusations and innuendos are fired on social media without compunction. Twitter moms post their verdicts like Greek goddesses perched atop Mount Olympus. While posting hearsay and slander at will on Facebook, Instagram, and opinion blogs is not specifically feminine, it is the domain of contemporary Jezebels. While slander and gossip are verbal swill considered gospel to many, both deeply offend the living God. He declares, "The words of a talebearer are like tasty trifles, And they go down into the inmost body" (Prov. 18:8; See also, Prov. 26:22).

Jezebel the Outlaw

Jezebel, the domineering wife of Ahab, decided to take matters into her own hands by seizing Naboth's vineyard. In the process she orchestrated the false accusation and murder of Naboth. In devising a ruse to confiscate his vineyard, she judged herself to be above the law.

Contemporary Jezebels

Contemporary Jezebels follow a similar pattern of misconduct. Sadly, while occasionally tried in the court of public opinion they are rarely prosecuted. One such example is Julie Swetnick, The previously cited false accuser of Supreme Court Justice Brent Kavanaugh. Miss Swetnick is a member of a growing sorority of women who maliciously traffics in false accusations of men. Such false allegations are made easier when there are no legal repercussions for doing so. Solomon correctly asserted, "Because the sentence against an evil work is not executed speedily, therefore, the heart of the sons of men is fully set in them to do evil" (Eccl. 8:11).

Powerful Women Behaving Badly

During the 2016 Presidential campaign, Hillary Clinton, the eventual Democrat party nominee, purchased a spurious Russian dossier to smear her Republican rival Donald Trump. The fabricated dossier led to a bogus three year investigation of President Trump. In addition to purporting that a false document was true, Mrs. Clinton also illegally deleted thirty-three thousand emails, sent classified emails over a private server, signed off on the sale of uranium to Russia while Secretary of State, and fraudulently solicited millions of dollars for the Clinton Foundation. If this was not enough, Mrs. Clinton incessantly lied about all of her misconduct, while simultaneously having the audacity to falsely accuse Donald Trump of Russian collusion. Jezebels traffic in unconscionable illegal behavior without compunction.

A Legacy of False Accusation

Women falsely accusing men is not merely a contemporary fad, but has been with us since the dawn of time. False accusation and blame shifting began in the Garden of Eden and has plagued us ever since. Some may regard false accusations as a cultural trend, others a social pathology. More accurately, it is a by-product of fallen humanity. Jezebel is a classic biblical example of a slanderer. After scolding her cowardly husband, she devised a ruse to acquire the coveted vineyard. Her ploy involved lying, deceit, and false accusation. False witnesses were hired. Naboth was executed. Ahab stealthily seized the treasured heirloom of his nemesis. This disturbing episode of greed and malice offers keen insight into the dysfunction of the Jezebel Syndrome. First, true to the LORD's words to Eve, it highlights the curse of a wife usurping authority over her husband. Secondly, it illustrates the malice that foments from fallen women failing to rise to their high calling as daughters of Sarah. The incidences of false accusation by women are legion.

The Pastor's Biggest Challenge

I have a friend who has been in ministry for over four decades. During that time, he has been an immensely successful pastor, evangelist, and spiritual mentor. God continues to lavish His favor on this brother as he trains men both at home and abroad. He has been happily married to his wife for over forty years. He has grown daughters who adore him. Several years ago, he disclosed to me his biggest challenge in ministry. In exasperation he sighed, "women." Pastors are often called upon to referee church fights between two women or two factions of women.

The Wrath of Jezebel

As a prison chaplain, I encountered similar infighting between female inmates. While it is easy to paint with a broom, the smudge-marks evidencing women's desire to dominate are everywhere, at church, home, in society, and in prisons. Pursuant to the latter, both male and female prison guards will freely admit that it is much harder to provide security in a female prison than in a male prison. The reasons they cite for this phenomenon is that women are more spiteful, scornful, and retributive. Jezebels reserve vitriol for their enemies and enjoy watching them suffer. Sadly, there are many Jezebels who are sentenced to prison, where they cannibalize each other.

Female Rivals and Love Triangles

While attending seminary in Portland, Oregon in the early nineties, I became acquainted with a talented young female skater named Tonya Harding. For a time, this Olympic gold medal contender, was the darling of the Portland metroplex.

Her closest US competitor was a talented young skater by the name of Nancy Kerrigan. Kerrigan, while not as athletic as Harding, was a world class skater whose skill and finesse made her a blue chip gold medal contender. Harding, in an effort to hedge her bets of medaling, instigated a cryptic attack on Kerrigan. She hired two men to assault her American teammate with a billy club. This hate-filled attack injured Kerrigan's knees and placed her hopes of medaling in serious jeopardy. Today, jealous rage fueled by Jezebels due to competitive rivalries and love triangles trigger acts of violence, even premeditated murder.

A View from the Bar

While deployed to Iraq during Operation Iraqi Freedom several years ago, I was conversing with a Marine who while stationed in CONUS (Continental United States), moonlighted as a bouncer. Having never been a bouncer, I asked him what it was like. A follow up question was is it easier to manage the misconduct of men or women? His response was immediate and emphatic. His animated answer resembled, "Women are way worse than men! They scratch and claw with their fingernails, they spit, they cuss. Men you can reason with. But women in the bar scene become far more emotional and irrational. They have fingernails and they will use them!"

Jezebels Attempted Domination in the Political Arena

As I write, the Trump impeachment hearings have concluded. While he was not charged with any indictments, several powerful women continued to champion impeachment. Though she has no evidence of crimes committed, Congressional Speaker of the House,

Nancy Pelosi, admitted in an interview that she had been attempting to impeach President Trump for twenty-two months. A freshman Congresswoman expressed through a profane epithet her vitriol for the forty-fifth President and her intention to impeach him. Since Trump assumed office, one longstanding female representative has been publicly chanting her mantra, "Impeach 45!" This malicious desire to unduly discard a US president is reminiscent of Eve's curse and Jezebel's vengeful spirit.

Vengeance is No Respecter of Genders

Vengeance is hardly gender specific. Men and women both demonstrate their fallenness when they pursue personal power over humble servanthood. In the words of late homiletics professor, Haddon Robinson, [wicked men] "learn their geometry lessons well. They know that the shortest distance between two points is a straight line and it doesn't matter who you have to crawl over to get there!"

While vengeance is baked into the human condition, it is particularly embedded in the DNA of angry women afflicted with the Jezebel Syndrome. It is expressed when a woman would rather harbor grudges than make peace. As we saw in the previous chapter, a desire to dominate men is an unsavory by-product of fallen womanhood. Such domestic and global fallout should elicit the rapt attention of every Christ-follower. This disturbing infiltration of cultural feminism into the ranks of the Christ's body signals a radical return to biblical womanhood. It begs the question, "What does a Christ-centered woman look like?"

Protecting the Falsely Accused

False accusation was judged to be a heinous sin, in the Torah, was grounds for corporal punishment. (Rabbi Daniel Travis, Torah. org). One reason why the Bible categorically condemns false accusation is because it is both heinous and destructive. It's destruction is not limited to the falsely accused but always spills over to the community of the faith. Due to the devastation that may be wrought by the false accuser, protecting the falsely accused is paramount. The Word of God supplies clear instruction. First, the ninth commandment of the Decalogue states, "You shall not bear false witness against your neighbor" (Exodus 20:6). While today it is chic to casually slander one if of a different race, faith group, political party, such false accusation is unwarranted and ultimately will be judged by the Almighty God (Heb. 10:30–31). Secondly, when someone was falsely accused it must be verified by "two or three witnesses" (Num. 35:30; Deut. 17:6; 2 Cor. 13:1). Uncorroborated witnesses singing solo accusatory parts, are to be dismissed as non-credible sources.

The Two or Three Protocol

What can be done to protect the falsely accused? This is an immensely relevant question since the LORD favors the oppressed, downtrodden and innocent. When Paul established a house order for the church he issued a "two or three witnesses" protocol for pastors receiving false accusations. For the future church the Lord Jesus instituted a "two or three" protocol when critical measures in the church are being decided. Jesus instructed His disciples, that prior to the church being informed of an unrepentant sinner, "two or three witnesses" must be present when the believer is confronted with their sin. Moreover, the prayers of these two or three witnesses is what Jesus promises to honor in the restoration of the fallen brother or sister (Matt. 18:15–19). In a similar vein, prophets were to prophecy in the early church only in twos or threes. After one prophet spoke, "two or three others were to judge." This was to avoid a false prophecy being afflicted on the body of Christ. Paul is emphatic about the "two or three prophet protocol" in the local assembly as he emphatically charges, "And the spirit of the prophets are subject to the prophets" (1 Cor. 14:29–32). Furthermore, pastors and elders were not to "accept (welcome) an accusation against an elder except by two or three witnesses" (1 Tim. 5:19).

Since, anyone can falsely accuse another, Paul reiterates the "two or three witnesses," principle in 2 Corinthians 13:1. A prophecy was verified by "two or three" prophets (Apostles such as Paul and

John, as well as elders in the early church were not immune to false accusations, see also 3 John). Therefore, Paul lays down guidelines to protect the falsely accused. He charges, "Do not receive an accusation against an elder except from two or three witnesses." Paul further adds "those who are sinning rebuke in the presence of all that others may fear" (1 Tim. 5:20). Included in the group that is to be rebuked are false accusers as well as any elders found to be sinning on the testimony of two or three witnesses. To prevent any deviation from this protocol, Paul issuing a solemn warning to his young protégé, "I charge you before God and the Lord Jesus Christ and the elect angels that you observe these things without partiality. Do not lay hands on anyone hastily, nor share in other people's sins; keep yourself pure."

Falsely charging an elder with a sin he didn't commit is as serious as overlooking a disqualifying sin of an elder. By prefacing his warning, "before God and the Lord Jesus Christ and the elect angels," Paul is instructing Timothy that any failure to follow this divine protocol for addressing an accusation against an elder will result in an answering to Jesus, the Righteous Judge, at the Judgment seat of Christ (see 2 Tim. 4:1–3). The bottom line is that false accusation is a serious matter to the resurrected Christ, "who will judge the living and the dead at His appearing and kingdom" (4:1).

The Greatest Travesty of Justice

The greatest travesty of justice in history was the crucifixion of Jesus Christ. Preceding this injustice were six illegal trials featuring many false witnesses. While being tried in a kangaroo court, the testimony of a plethora of false witnesses did not agree together. We read in Mark 14:55–56, "Now the chief priests and all the council sought testimony against Jesus to put Him to death, but found none. For many bore false witness against Him, but their testimonies did not agree. Then some rose up and bore false witness against Him saying, 'We heard Him say, 'I will destroy this temple made with hands and within three days I will build another made without hands.' But not even then did their testimony agree."

The Son of God was falsely accused. Solace for the falsely accused is that if the holy, sinless Son of God was falsely accused the false accusation of His servants is par for the course. Though Christ-followers are compelled to endure slander and other forms of persecution, for the sake of His name, this does not condone false accusation under any circumstances. For false accusation tears at the fabric of society, causing it to unravel.

Justice Kavanaugh

Hillary Clinton infamously asserted, "Every woman has a right to be believed." This mantra was oft repeated during the Kavanaugh Senate confirmation hearings after two women who remained silent for approximately three decades, surfaced to allege sexual indiscretions against the then Supreme court nominee. Many in the media and the Democrat party rushed to judgment by believing these women. Yet these women's stories were fraught with inconsistencies, memory lapses, and refuted by fellow classmates of Kavanaugh. Female friends of Kavanaugh defended the honorable justice, testifying that the future judge they knew treated all women with unmitigated respect. In the end the allegations were proven to be outlandishly false. These two women were Christine Blaséy Ford and Julie Swetnick. Swetnick was represented by now convicted felon, Michael Avenatti, now in prison. Swetnick was involved in five other lawsuits in which she made false claims about many things.

Nicolas Sandman

Nicolas Sandman was a fifteen-year-old high school student sporting a "Make America Great Again," ball cap to a Pro-Life rally. Nathan Phillips is a Native American who also attended the pro-life rally. Phillips approached the young Sandman and aggressively began beating a drum within inches of the young man's face. Sandman, sought to diffuse the situation by calmly smiling throughout the incident. The video of the incident went viral. CNN and other media outlets, summarily accused Sandman of taunting Hale, a Vietnam veteran. These outlets ran false stories of Sandman. As a result, Sandman, sued CNN for $250,000,000. He settled with CNN out of court. Representing Sandman was Lin Wood, a libel specialist who represented Richard Jewell, Jon Benet Ramsey's parents, and others discovered to be falsely accused.

False Accusation and the Founders

The Founders fathers recognized that in a free society false accusation by evil men and women would occur. Since false accusation is such a heinous sin, legal reparation possesses biblical warrant. The one exception to this is when one is falsely accused by a brother or sister. In such an instance, "accepting wrong," and "[letting] yourself be cheated," is the apostolic mandate (1 Cor. 6:1–8). In an effort to redress libel, the Founders made provision for men and women to "lawyer up" when they are falsely accused. This is one practical solution to stemming the tide of false allegations of misconduct. Punishing those who commit libel by making them pay with their pocketbook is one way to stem the tide of false allegations.

Brian Banks

Brian Banks, was a talented linebacker from Long Beach, California who after committing to play football at USC was falsely accused of rape in 2002 by fellow student Wanetta Gibson. Banks spent nearly six years in prison and five years on probation before his case was overturned. Banks owes his acquittal to a private investigator named Freddie Parish. Parish, with the use of a hidden camera, recorded Gibson confessing that she lied about Banks raping her when the two were in high school. Thanks to the hidden camera, Parish also had proof that the only reason Gibson didn't want to come forward about the truth was because she didn't want to pay back the $1.5 million settlement won from the Long Beach school district after Banks's conviction.

In an exclusive interview with NBC 4, Parish walked through the steps he took to set the scene for Gibson's confession. Thank the

Lord for Banks acquittal! Tragically, Banks forfeited eleven years of his life which he will never get back. These eleven years could have been spent playing linebacker at USC and in the NFL. Tragically, many of the Wanetta Gibsons of the world go scot free after maligning their victims. A silver lining in the case is Gibson being ordered to return the 1.5 million she was awarded by Long Beach Polytech High School after Banks arrest. While there is forgiveness for the Wanetta Gibsons of the world, they need to be ferreted out as the wicked Jezebels, and duly punished by a fair and lawful system of jurisprudence.

We Can Only Imagine

One can only imagine a world without slander. A world where every slanderous missile must be corroborated by two or three witnesses and false accusers will be duly punished. If politicians were compelled to provide substantial evidence and witnesses for their claims.

Forgiving Jezebel

After Jesus was falsely accused, tried in a kangaroo court, scourged with a cat-of-nine tails, and condemned to die a criminals' death, He cried from the cross, "Father forgive them for they do not know what they are doing?" We too are to forgive the Jezebels in our lives. While Jezebels committing crimes may have to justly pay for their crimes, in the end they must be forgiven. One might ask, if they are forgiven, why then should they suffer for the crimes that they committed? One of the thieves on the cross was forgiven by Christ while he hanged dying for the crimes he committed. So, if Jezebels have committed crimes of libel, they merit retribution for their sins- while still needing to be forgiven.

Jesus speaks of the forgiveness debt His disciples owe others. He taught us to pray, "Forgive us our debts as we forgive our debtors" (Matt. 6:12). Later He gave His disciples a solemn warning of the necessity of "forgiving one another from the heart" (Matt. 18:35). Numbering among those to be forgiven are Jezebels.

Iraqi Gulf War hero, General Norman Schwartkoff once asserted, "It is God's job to forgive our enemies, it is our job to arrange the meeting." With all due respect to the highly decorated General, God begs to differ with his perspective. The commands to for believers to forgive their enemies are replete throughout the Bible. The author of Hebrews puts forgiveness in eternal perspective. The Lord charges in Hebrews 10:38, "Vengeance is mine says the LORD, I will repay,' and again, 'the Lord shall judge His people." If vengeance belongs to God it does not belong to us.

One person recognizing this truth was former prisoner of war Louis Zamperini. Zamperini's plane crashed into the ocean where he survived for forty-seven days before being captured by the Japanese Army. During his incarceration Zamperini was brutally subjected to physical and psychological torture until the end of the war. His chief torturer was an officer with the moniker, "The Bird." Louis suffered PTSD and alcoholism until attending a Billy Graham Crusade where he was gloriously converted. After which the former POW and Olympian returned to the Sugamo Prison in Tokyo, Japan to visit all of his former captors, look them in the eye and assure them he forgave them. In 1997, Louis learned that his chief nemesis the Bird was still alive. He resolved a return visit to Japan to meet him. However, the Bird refused to meet with him. Later in an interview Louis explained his radical forgiveness, "If you don't forgive it will be eating on your soul. Forgiveness must be complete. The only way I can forgive is to pray for them."

Those who would experience God's favor, must practice total forgiveness for the sake of Christ's kingdom.

Questions for Reflection

1) Jezebel maliciously falsely accused Naboth and executed him. Has there ever been a time in your life when you falsely accused someone? What did it cost them? What did it cost you?

2) When you hear a rumor about someone how often do implement Jesus's command, "Do not judge according to appearance, but judge righteous judgment?" (John 7:24).

3) Solomon's warning, "If a man answers a matter before he hears it, it is a folly and a shame to him?" (Prov. 8:13). What measures do you take to avoid pre-judging a person or situation?

4) Has greed, covetousness, or jealousy ever caused you to sin against another person?

5) On a scale of 1–7, assess your personal knowledge of the Bible's teaching regarding false accusation.

    1 2 3 4 5 6 7

6) Paul instructs Timothy to reject accusations against elders unless they are accompanied by "two or three witnesses" (1 Tim. 5:19). Have you ever seen a pastor implement this biblical protocol? Explain.

7) All of us need forgiveness and all Christ-followers are commanded to forgive. Is there anyone who you have refused to forgive? Any Jezebels?

JEZEBEL IN THE BEDROOM

"Let your fountain be blessed, and rejoice with
the wife of your youth, As a loving deer and a
graceful doe, Let her breasts satisfy you at all times;
and always be enraptured with her love."

—Proverbs 5:18–19

"The Christian life has not been tried and found
wanting, It has been found difficult and hardly tried."

—G. K. Chesterton

While a senior in high school, I watched the wedding of Prince Charles and Princess Diana on television. I was moved by the Rector's dramatic reading 1 Corinthians 13. Princess Di was stunningly arrayed in her flowing white wedding gown trailed by a long train fit for a queen. The recitation of this familiar prose profiling Christ-like love was captivating. While a beautiful rhapsody deserving continual meditation, 1 Corinthians 13:1–13 is not the primary biblical passage governing God's design for wedded love. Serious Bible scholars are well aware that the incomparable description of Christ-like love in 1 Corinthians 13 is couched in the context of stern rebuke. For Paul's purpose in penning this expose of Christ-like love was to correct the sinful abuse of the spiritual gifts by the Corinthian church. In sum, he contended to the Corinthians that they were better off expressing love to each other than arrogantly flaunting their spiritual gifts when they assembled for public worship. While this beautiful description of love has broad application to the church of all ages, it is not the primary passage governing bedroom etiquette. The predominant biblical text governing the sexual protocol of the Christian married is 1 Corinthians 7:1–6. So far, the chapters of this book have addressed both Jezebels and Sarahs. In this chapter both Jezebels and Sarah's will be in view as the passage is interpreted and applied.

The Problem with Jezebel in the Bedroom

In his landmark book, *The Naked Communist,* Cleon Skousen, a former FBI employee, outlined over forty-five goals to advance the communist agenda. Below are a few of them:

Goal #40 Discredit the Family as an Institution. Encourage promiscuity and easy divorce.

Goal # 25 Break down cultural standards of morality by promoting pornography in books, magazines, motion pictures, and TV.

Goal # 26 Present homosexuality, degeneracy, and promiscuity as "normal, natural, healthy."

It is beyond frightening that communists in America have succeeded in accomplishing an agenda of casual sex, porn proliferation, divorce, and alternative lifestyles. Needless to say, such a heinous scheme is fueled by the domain of darkness. The mortal enemy stokes the incendiary bonfires of sexual promiscuity while undermining God's design for wedded love in the marriage relationship.

One of the more salient problems presented by Jezebels surfaces in the bedroom. One aspect of Jezebel in the bedroom will be addressed in the chapter, "A View from a Woman Cave." While Jezebels do much violence to their environment through sexual immorality, married Jezebels desecrate the bedroom in another way.

Tales from the Bedroom

A friend in the ministry once told me of a Christian couple who had been blessed with a full quiver of children. After the birth of their final child, the wife emphatically informed her husband that she was no longer interested in sex. My friend reported to me that this was a hardship for the husband who was a devout Christ-follower.

Sarah Eggerichs, the wife of Christian marriage expert, Dr. Emerson Eggerichs, has testified that she has heard many Christian women report the following mantra to their husbands concerning love-making, "I tell my husband, I don't have the time, I don't have the energy, and I don't have the desire." When a Christian wife behaves this way or makes overtures that she retains sovereign authority over her body, she violates God's protocol for sexuality within marriage. Such a protocol is clearly outlined in 1 Corinthians 7:2–6.

The problem with Jezebel in the bedroom is that they violate the primary tenets of wedded love, namely, when they wed, their bodies no longer belong to themselves, but to their spouse. When their husbands initiate sex, they may piously object, "love does not seek its own" (1 Cor. 13:5). There are at least two major problems with applying this verse to married sex. First, one must keep in mind the fundamental Bible study principle that words only have meaning when they are used in their context. In this vain, we must recognize that 1 Corinthians 13:1–13 is a parenthesis in Paul's teaching on the proper deployment of spiritual gifts. This parenthesis is intended to reprove the abuse of spiritual gifts in the Corinthian church. Therefore, each characteristic of Christ-like love corrects a carnal tendency of the Corinthian church. Paul is rebuking those who seek their own edification by flaunting either their gift of tongues, or a pseudo gift of tongues. Secondly, applying this characteristic to Christian lovemaking is akin to a wife saying to her husband at din-nertime, "You are so unloving by desiring food! Do you not know that love doesn't seek its own?!"

Meeting One Another's Needs

Just as food has been designed to satisfy one's appetite at dinner time, so sex is designed to meet the God-given physical needs and desires of married couples. Therefore, it must be noted well that though many well-meaning Christians may vigorously protest the advances of their spouse in the bedroom, giving one's rapt attention to 1 Corinthians 7:1–6 is what God requires. For six chapters earlier Paul explicitly detailed a protocol governing sex for married couples. It is imperative that the married Christian rivet their attention on Paul's instructions to vaccinate themselves against worldly strains of married sex.

Abstinence Gone Wild

The likely birth of unauthorized abstinence was shortly after Adam and Eve partook of the forbidden fruit in the Garden of Eden. In an earlier chapter the curse of Eve was interpreted as "her desire to dominate her husband" (Gen. 3:16). Following this path, the misguided daughters of Eve also seek to dominate is by using sex as an unconventional weapon to rule their husbands. One venue where Jezebel chronically seeks to exert authority over her husband is the bedroom. Since Eve was cast out of the Garden of Eden, wives have employed sex as a manipulative tool to con their husbands into meeting their selfish desires. They do so by using sex as a carrot and a stick for their husbands-a carrot to motivate and a stick to punish. When a wife emotionally abuses her husband in this way, she often tills the soil of marital discord leaving her husband vulnerable to sexual immorality. Marital infidelity and sexual dalliance of every form is often the bitter fruit harvested from a wife's habit of dominating her husband in the bedroom. Today the sin of depriving one's spouse of sexual intimacy has spawned a host of problems in the church and society.

Naked And Not Ashamed: God's Original Design

Prior to the fall we are told that Adam and Eve were "naked and not ashamed" (Gen. 2:25) is highly picturesque in explaining God's design for marriage. First, it signifies, "openness," as in transparency. It also denoted "integrity." This is evident from the Hebrew pun embedded in Genesis 2:25 and Genesis 3:1. The integrity of the first couple's "nakedness" (Heb. Nireem, 2:25) is the very commodity that the "cunning" (Heb. Niroom, 3:1), serpent sought to undermine. Pre-fall Adam and Eve were the most transparent couple in history. They had nothing to hide physically, emotionally, or spiritually. They harbored no secrets nor hid any shame. Secondly, their nakedness denoted total selflessness. As the first couple resided in a state of untested holiness, they possessed no sin nature, nor made any selfish demands. Thirdly, they enjoyed exhilarating sexual relations undiluted by sinful desires. Their pristine relationship was character-

76

ized by mutual love, tenderness, and meticulous care for the needs of the other. The first couple's marriage and sex life was not only *in* Paradise, it *was* paradise! Adam and Eve experienced the best sexual chemistry ever as they were naked and not ashamed!

Naked and Afraid

Fast forward to after the fall. Fear was introduced into their relationship. They were afraid of God, but at times also afraid of each other. They feared that they would not have their needs met. They feared that the other would exploit them for selfish gain. The Garden of Eden once the Paradise of God, became fertile soil for early social pathologies as fear, loneliness, isolation, emptiness, and despair. The fall introduced a myriad of personal insecurities into Adam and Eve's relationship. In short-they were no longer naked and not ashamed, but naked and afraid!

Paradise Lost Versus Paradise Regained

While the fall may tersely be defined as Paradise Lost, God wants the Christ-follower to pursue Paradise Regained. Paradise regained is made possible by the Holy Spirit residing within the believer. Pursuant to this Peter writes in 2 Peter 1:3–4: "As His divine power has given us all things that pertain to life and godliness, through the knowledge of Him who called us by glory and virtue, by which have been given to us exceeding great and precious promises, that through these you might be partakers of the divine nature, having escaped the corruption of the world through lust."

The Christian by virtue of the Holy Spirit has all the spiritual equipment to live this physical life on earth. In a very real sense, she/he is in the position of Nike, "Just do it!" Not only are they able to resist lusts, but they also possess the spiritual capacity to add to the foundation of their faith a network of moral graces including brotherly kindness and love. In this environment they are able reclaim the high ground of paradise regained. In the sexual arena they no longer need to be naked and afraid, but may recover their former pristine status of naked and unashamed.

The Forbidding Problem of Naked and Afraid

The biggest hurdle to reclaiming the holy ground of naked and not ashamed is our fleshly obsession with self. If the believing wife and husband mutually and selflessly submit their bodies to each other, their marital trajectory will be in the direction of naked and not ashamed. Therein lays a forbidding challenge. Today Jezebels have a way of shaming men who in their judgment, initiate sex too often. Piercing remarks not born of God, resemble:

- Sex is all about you isn't it!
- You have a one track mind, sex is all you think about!
- Do you ever think of my needs when you initiate sex?
- I give you enough sex! Now go to sleep!
- We just made love last night!
- I don't feel like having sex with you.
- You only love me for my body!
- I am nothing more than a sex object to you!
- You make me feel like a prostitute!

Married Sex Is Wedded to Integrity, Not Shame

Men are often shamed by their wives for initiating sex so often. Too often, they are made to feel like perverts or lustful playboys when they initiate sex more often than their wives. In this respect, men are told by their wives to have eyes only for them, only have their wives push them away! No wonder in their despair they turn to porn and mistresses. Women in pornography don't judge. Mistresses, for a host of reasons, are eager to meet a man's sexual needs.

As the Christian couple reflects on God's will for their sexual relationship, they do well to ask several questions. First is our approach to sex biblical or cultural? Secondly, did God intend for sex to be a quid quo pro arrangement? Third, what is the Lord's vaccination against sexual immorality? Fourthly and finally, what does God require of us as a married couple?

Love American Style or As God Intended

Early in my career as a chaplain, I partnered with several of my chaplain colleagues in conducting seminars for married servicemembers. During the course of preparing for these seminars, I was given some tapes of a marriage expert speaking at a popular evangelical marriage conference. One of these sessions was on married sex. I noted that this purported Christian expert spoke passionately concerning how married couples are to conduct themselves in the bedroom. Yet he failed to cite 1 Corinthians 7:1–6, the biblical primer of married sex, in his teaching. Ironically, this "Christian" sex expert appealed to secular psychology instead of the Bible teaching on wedded love. It is been my observation that such approaches to sex and the married Christian are all too typical.

Is Married Sex a Quid-Pro-Quo Arrangement?

In recent years, a Latin phrase has been retrieved from the ashheap of history. The phrase is "Quid-Pro-Quo." The phrase literally means, "this for that." Former Vice-President, Joe Biden, was caught on tape recounting his Quid-Pro-Quo arrangement with Ukrainian leaders. Leveraging his august position as the Vice President of the United States, he threatened that he would withhold a billion dollars of funding from Ukraine leaders if a Ukranian prosecutor who was investigating his son was not immediately fired. In a video that went viral, he boasted that they promptly fired the prosecutor within a matter of a few hours.

A Quid-Pro-Quo in the Bedroom

Quid pro quos are seen to be manipulative and unethical. Often, they take place in marriage relationships. As a Navy chaplain, I hear a myriad of personal opinions, many of them not born of God. For instance, one occasion a Sailor opined that Valentines' Day is a form of prostitution. He cynically rhapsodized, "A man takes his wife to her favorite restaurant, buys her flowers, maybe chocolates, watches her favorite movie, then before saying goodnight, she rewards him by surrendering her body to his sexual lusts. Yup! Sounds like prostitution to me!" While such a theory, may give us disturbing pause, it begs the question of whether wedded sex is a quid-quo-pro relationship? While it often appears to be the case, God never intended for it to be such in Christian marriage.

Regrettably, quid-pro-quo is the method of compromise suggested by more than a few Christian counselors. Rather than following the clear teaching of 1 Corinthians 7:1–6, many cite the benefits of an unbiblical quid-pro-quo arrangement. One popular marriage expert tells attendees in his seminar that a wife's withholding sex can motivate her husband to get things done around the house, therefore, her withholding sex is a good thing! Like in the previous example, the purported marriage expert would have done well to consult the Scriptures before opining concerning sexual intimacy.

God's Vaccination for Preventing Sexual Immorality

During COVID-19, medical scientists and epidemiologists toiled feverishly to discover a vaccine in the wake of a national pandemic. Few questioned the propriety of investing billions of dollars and painstaking effort into preventing unnecessary death. In a similar vein, Jesus desires His church spare no expense in implementing His vaccine to inoculate married couples against sexual immorality. While not a disease, sexual immorality greatly offends the sensibilities of a holy God. Therefore, it should not surprise us that God's Word is replete with warnings against sexual immorality. God loathes this sin of the flesh. Therefore, the Christ-follower must give their eager attention to how they can avoid committing this sin. The vaccination against this sin is prescribed by Him in 1 Corinthians 7:1–6.

The Contribution of Sex to Marital Fulfillment

Pursuant to this vaccination, Christian marriage counselor Gary Rosberg has asserted that if a couple is struggling in their marriage one mid-course correction to place their marriage on a positive trajectory is their sexual relationship. Rosburg purports that if a married couple improves their sex life by a mere 10 percent it can have two positive effects on one's marriage. First, it enhances intimacy. Secondly, it imparts hope to the married couple. A Christian wife's attitude toward wedded love is one of the best barometers of whether they are a daughter of Sarah or Jezebel. The below scenario illustrates the power of a godly woman to influence her husband for good.

The Christian Couples Sexual Responsibilities

When answering the question, the Christ-follower must remind themselves that the Bible speaks with absolute authority and relevance. Serving notice of the authority and timeless relevance of the Bible is Paul while writing to his young mentee Timothy. Prior to solemnly charging his pastoral protege to always preach the Word of God (See 2 Timothy 4:1–3), He informed him in 2 Timothy 3:16–17, "All Scripture is given by the inspiration of God, and is profitable for doctrine, for reproof, for correction, for training in righteousness. That the man of God may be complete. Thoroughly equipped to every good work."

The Bible contains the wisdom necessary to address every human challenge known to man. No wonder, David exalted, "Your word is a lamp unto my feet and a light unto my path" (Psalm 119:105). David elsewhere underscores the unquestionable infallibility of God's Word. He assures, "The judgments of the LORD are true and righteous altogether" (Psalm 19:9). Due to the failsafe counsels of God's Word, the Christ-follower has no need to guess whether its teachings are true or false. Moreover, the timeless relevance of the Bible is failsafe. In this respect my professor Jim Andrews was correct while asserting, "We don't *make* the Bible relevant, we *discover* its relevance." My professor was correct. The Bible addresses the topic of married sex like no other, the Christ-follower must carefully examine the text to discover its timeless truths. For through diligent study, the incomparable relevance of the Bible is discovered (2 Tim. 2:15).

It must be said that these are commands rather than suggestions. As It is critical for any church exposed to the virus of post-modern thought, to recognize that the Bible is not a litany of suggestions, but a book of divine imperatives given by an all wise God, who indiscriminately loves His people and longs for them to embrace the fullness of eternal life He intends for them. While God's children sometimes question His plan, they do so to their own peril. One universally practical topic addressed by the Bible is God's design for sex in marriage. Impinging on this topic is God's prescription for curing sexual immorality.

Sexual Intimacy, God's Prescription Curing Marital Infidelity

The Lord supplies a powerful vaccine against marital unfaithfulness. This preventative medicine is discovered in 1 Corinthians 7:1–6. If obeyed, married couples possess the capacity to emerge victoriously over every form of sexual immorality. This includes mental adultery as well as physical immorality. The reason for this is that all sexual temptations are related to one thing, our sex drive. When our sex drive is satisfied, sexual temptation is reduced to a toothless tiger.

How Sex *in* Marriage Can Cure Sexual Immorality

The above statement can be well illustrated by the following scenario. Let's say you love rich, moist, delicious carrot cake. Furthermore, not only do you love carrot cake, but let's say your wife makes the best carrot cake in the world. You take it to work and after consuming a good lunch you eat this rather large slice of delectable dessert your wife has packed for you. After licking the last speck of cream cheese frosting from your fork, you feel completely full and satisfied. You remark to your co-worker, "Man that really hit the spot!" A minute later another co-worker walks into the lounge were you just enjoyed a delicious lunch and a large slice of the world's best carrot cake. She is carrying a plate of freshly baked chocolate chip cookies. You look at them. They look beautiful! They smell wonderful! Your co-worker tells you to help yourself to the cookies as he has plenty. You don't have a bias against chocolate chip cookies, actually you find them quite attractive and mouth watering. But the fact of the matter is you just enjoyed your favorite dessert, and you are not tempted by these good looking, nice smelling cookies. So it is when a husband or wife's sexual appetite has been satisfied.

If It Works in Corinth, It Can Work Anywhere

One might argue that in the first century there were no internet porn sites, no nine hundred phone lines, or "After Dark" programming. Yet from the idolatrous temples where prostitutes were trafficked to the pagan bathhouses, the city of Corinth was a simmering cauldron of sensuality and sexual temptation. The church to which Paul issued this instruction was immersed in a cesspool of debauchery that embraced every brand of sexual immorality. So profuse was the sexual immorality in Corinth that an ancient buzzword "Corinthianize" came to mean "to live a promiscuous life." For to partake in the godless festivities of Corinth was to be baptized in the sewage of sexual sin. Some of the Corinthians believers had been redeemed from the bondage of sexual immorality that was often wedded to pagan idolatry (1 Cor. 6:9–11). As such they could be tempted to revert to their former immoral lifestyle. One young Christian was indulging in incest with his step mother (1 Cor. 5:1–6). It could be compellingly argued that if Paul's strategy for immunizing one's marriage could be effective in a church steeped in a morally decadent swamp, then it could work anywhere!

Celibacy Is Honorable If One Can Control Their Sexual Urges

Paul bottom lines this prescription in 1 Corinthians 7:1–2, "Now concerning the things you wrote to me. It is good for a man not to touch a woman. Nevertheless, to avoid sexual immorality, let every man have his own wife and let every woman have her own husband."

First, Paul assures us of the divine sanction of celibacy. By the euphemism, "touch," he means it is good for a man to remain single while practicing total abstention from all sexual activity. He is not stating that a man can never shake hands or hug a woman to whom he is not married. For "touch" euphemistically references sexual intercourse. Paul is clearly stating that a celibate state is an honorable and good status for a Christian man or woman.

However, Paul quickly issues a disclaimer that marriage is the logical option for "every man" and "every woman to avoid sexual immorality." In this vein, Paul's cardinal rule for resolving doubtful issues applies. In 1 Corinthians 10:23 he rhapsodized, "All things are lawful to me, but all things are not helpful; all things are lawful for me, but not all things edify." Though single celibacy is permissible for Christ-followers, for the vast majority, it is not "helpful" in battling sexual lusts (see also, 1 Cor. 7:9).

Sex within Marriage the Key to Pleasing God

In the subsequent passage, 1 Corinthians 7:3–6, Paul unleashes God's strategy for preventing the onslaught of sexual immorality in all its forms. As Paul's marching orders for Christian marrieds unfolds, it is clear that it is not marriage in and of itself, that is God's cure for sexual immorality, but *sex within marriage*. Paul serves notice of this fact in 1 Corinthians 7:3–4. He commands,

> Let the husband render to his wife the affection due her, and likewise also the wife to her husband. The wife does not have authority over his own body, but the husband does. And likewise, the husband does not have authority over his own body, but the wife does.

Marriage morally sanctioning the total fulfillment of one's sexual desires is the best preventive medicine to immunize one against sexual immorality. However, it is clear from what follows that marriage itself is not the cure, but how one conducts themselves in marriage defeats the demon of sexual immorality. His prescription for avoiding sexual immorality is heterosexual marriage is to continue to drink God's tonic for curing sexual immorality. He commands husbands and wives to relinquish their bodies as a wedding present to either their husband or wife. In doing so, they are attentive to both the command and the needs of their partner. As God-fearing believers, they understand that refusing to scrupulously follow God's manual for marital intimacy is to dishonor Him, by ignoring His commands.

Meet Your Partners' Needs So They Are
Not Tempted to Look Elsewhere

Paul's elixir for acute sexual temptation is for married couples to make love often so that their spouse won't look elsewhere for sexual fulfillment. "Do not deprive one another," is the imperative in this text clearly highlighting the married believers' responsibility in the arena of "married sex." Again, this is Paul's prescription for avoiding sexual immorality (1 Cor. 7:2). As such it must be the central idea navigating the believer's thinking. Paul prescribes a healthy, mutually satisfying sex life as the non-negotiable firewall protecting the believer against marital infidelity. One might object that they know married Christians who commit adultery. To this objection, Bruce Wilkinson contends that *marriage* is not the answer to sexual immorality, but having sex *within* marriage is the answer.

Your Body, a Wedding Present

Julie Slattery in her book, *No More Headaches,* a treatment of the sexual component in marriage, shares of how the Lord began to work in her own marriage in the sexual arena. She says, that many times when she was having her devotions, she felt a strong compulsion from the Lord to go upstairs and initiate sexual relations with her husband. As a Spirit-controlled woman she demonstrated her love for Jesus, by meeting her husband's physical needs. Her experience, while perhaps foreign to many wives, certainly demonstrates the premium God places on sex in the marriage relationship. Slattery's story may seem strange to many women as they have viewed sex through the secular lens of a godless culture. Secular culture, otherwise known as "the Cosmos" ("world," 1 John 2:15–17), purports that a woman retains sovereign ownership of her body. Jezebels contend that from the abortion clinic to the bedroom, their bodies belong exclusively to them. The former who favor abortion, plant the flag of sovereignty over their bodies when they become inconveniently pregnant. The latter, guard their bodies like precious treasure that is off-limits to all, including their husbands.

Paul teaches that your body is a wedding present not only to be unwrapped by their spouse on their wedding night, but every night that your spouse desires to enjoy this gift. Paul writes in 7:3–4, "Let the husband render to his wife the affection due her; and likewise, the wife to her husband."

Paul outlines the "conjugal rights" stipulated by the marriage covenant. Christian marriage is a life-long covenantal relationship fraught with both rights and responsibilities. In 1 Corinthians 7:1–6 Paul issues a series of imperatives regarding married sex. The word "affection," carries an equivalent meaning to the word, "touch," in 7:1. For in both instances Paul is speaking euphemistically. By employing a euphemism Paul is using a milder or indirect word that is viewed as kinder, less offensive, or embarrassing. Euphemisms are in the family of a literary devices known as synecdoche. A synecdoche is a verbal expression in which the part is given for the whole. "Touch," and "affection," are a part of sexual intercourse between a man and a wife. While taken literally the terms "touch," and "affection" might include caressing, fondling, hugging, and kissing, and foreplay, yet much more is intended by Paul. To contend otherwise would be absurd. For the apostle of grace is not commanding married Corinthians couples to oblige their spouse only to the point of foreplay, but to oblige them when they desire sexual intimacy!

A Tale from the Clinic

Sarah Eggerichs tells the story of a nurse named Amanda, who assisted her during a medical checkup. The nurse was married and said that her parents lived approximately ten miles from them. She and her husband's weekend routine included visiting her parents every Sunday afternoon. One Sunday, the nurse reported to

Eggerichs, that she was compelled to call her mother to inform her that they wouldn't be able to make it that Sunday since her husband Mark was in a snit. Her mother asked why her son-in-law was so upset. Amanda suggested, "Oh I suppose it is because we haven't been intimate for six or seven days."

Immediately Amanda's mother scolded, "Amanda, how can you deprive your husband of something that takes so little time and makes him so happy?!" Greatly taken aback by her mother's forwardness, she embarrassingly retorts, "Mother!" Undeterred, Mom proceeded to admonish her to meet her husband's sexual needs.

Amanda then remarked, "You know Sarah, after that conversation I began to realize that I can't think of another married couple that has a better marriage than my mother and father." She continued to cite the reason as her mother's wise initiative in ensuring her husband's sexual needs were met.

The Elephant in the Bedroom

This writer has a friend who is a wonderful brother in Christ. This brother is highly respected by peers and associates alike. Yet for many years he has suffered silently in an emotionally abusive marriage. His wife considers sex a despicable act in which she begrudgingly engages in out of a sense of duty. My friend longs for the affection of a loving partner. When he shares these longings with his wife, she belittles him. This sad story could be retold innumerable times.

Your Body, Your Spouses Rightful Owner

What is the solution to this tragic ending not born of God? It is embedded in the text of 1 Corinthians 7:2–6. It is abundantly clear from both the grammar and the context that Paul is employing the language of obligation in the sexual relationship. As plain as this command reads in English, it is strengthened by the Greek reading of this verse. The word used for "render" is the word, "apodidomai." This word means to "repay, give back, or recompense." The idea of this word in context is that there is mutual payment or "recompense" due to the marriage partner in the sexual arena. This is a word used by Jesus in Luke 14:22 while informing His disciples that their acts of faithfulness will be "repaid at the resurrection of the just." This repayment of making one's availability of one's body is made on the basis of "debt" owed. The word for "due" is the Greek word, "opheilon" means, "duty, debt, obligation." This debt and duty eliminates the option of married couples "defrauding each other." All three of these words serve to upgrade the readers' understanding of Paul's command.

Reporting to "Duty" in the Bedroom

In brief, Paul is stating that the married Christ-follower has a solemn responsibility, or "duty" to meet the physical needs of their spouse. This is the only place in the New Testament where a command of mutual submission is issued to both partners. In 1 Corinthians 7:2–6 Paul outlines the sexual rights and responsibilities of each partner. Clearly implied in Paul's teaching is the idea that each partner possesses the right to have their sexual needs respectively met by their husband or wife.

This is implied by the imperative Paul issues to both the husband and wife. By commanding that "the husband render, to his wife the affection due her," he issues an apostolic (and biblical) mandate that the husband fulfill his wife's sexual needs. The Christian wife is similarly charged, "and likewise also the wife to her husband," verse 3. Paul further elaborates in verse 4, "The wife does not have authority over her own body, but the husband does. And likewise, the husband does not have authority over his own body but the wife does." Paul uses the word, "exousia," meaning, "power," or "authority."

It is arresting to realize that while husbands possess headship in the marriage, God gives them no license to reject the love-making advances of their wives in the bedroom. Sex is the one area of the marriage relationship where the Bible commands *mutual submission*.

Married Sex: A Question of Lordship

While Paul's teaching is not difficult to grasp mentally, as a pastor and military chaplain, it has been my experience that many emotionally wrestle with Paul's teaching. In this respect it must be reminded that any "who name the name of Christ," is not only enjoined to depart from lawlessness, but also take seriously the Bible's teaching (see Romans 8:9). For such adherence is a prerequisite course for "being one of Jesus disciples indeed" (John 8:31–32; 15:7). Sex in this regard is a "Lordship" issue. While there are other biblical strategies for Christ-followers such as Bible memorization, and cultivating a robust relationship with God through prayer, Bible study, accountability with other believers, building safeguards for relating to the opposite gender, and abstinence from all forms of sexual lusts, 1 Corinthians 7 is "the first line of defense" for abstaining from "all forms" of sexual immorality.

One might render Paul's instructions antiquated teachings, and therefore, irrelevant to today's Christian couple. Some might judge Paul's teaching to be out of sync with contemporary legal or individual rights in a free society. However, it is critical for Christian husbands and wives to remember that as the bondservants of Jesus Christ, they possess no rights (see James 1:1; Luke 17:10). This makes obeying God's commands a Lordship issue. In this regard Jesus challenged His disciples, "Why do you call Me Lord, Lord, when you do not do the things, I have commanded you?" (Luke 6:46). Jesus's words to His disciples are extremely poignant, "Likewise, when you have done all those things which you are commanded, say, 'We are unprofitable servants. We have done what is our duty to do" (Luke 17:10).

Furthermore, while it is well to keep in mind that while Christian rights are protected under the first Amendment of the US Constitution, the Christ-follower has a higher law. This law is illustrated in Acts 5:29, "But Peter and the other apostles answered and said, 'We ought to obey God rather than men.'" It is always well for the Christ-follower to keep in mind that their vertical responsibilities to a God supersede their horizontal responsibilities to man.

The Christian Bedroom: A No-Manipulation Zone

Food is used as a manipulative interrogation weapon to extract intel from terrorists on fellow perpetrators. Since potentially thousands of lives are in jeopardy this is seen as a legitimate tactic by many in wartime. Yet it is possible for married couples to employ sex as a weapon and tool to manipulate their partners into giving them what they want. Yet sex was never designed by God as a power tool to control one's partner. For the Apostle Paul serves notice, that if sex is a power play in marriage, the power belongs to the partner initiating sex. For he strictly charges the married couples in Corinth that their body in the sexual arena does not belong to them, but to their spouse. Excuses for failing to meet one's spouses need due to selfishness, ill-will, feigned headaches, and the like, are unauthorized. Such sinful attitudes must be readily addressed in the marriage relationship. Failure to address them not only displeases Christ, but leaves one vulnerable to sexual immorality, 1 Corinthians 7:2.

God's Program for Controlling Lust

Today it is tragic that many Christian programs designed to help men combat lust, ignore God's prescription for avoiding sexual immorality. Not only does God supply His Spirit to battle the enemy of our souls, but He also makes a very practical provision that we may resist the onslaught of sexual immorality. The great news is that a vibrant, mutually selfless sex life can prevent the Christian couple from being forced to endure the heartache of sexually immoral sin. One evangelical taking a non-apologetic approach to the implementation of 1 Corinthians 7:2–6 to control sexual lusts is Bruce Wilkinson. Wilkinson's strong endorsement of God's vaccination against sexual temptation is recorded in his book, *Personal Holiness In Times of Temptation.* He writes,

"I'll never forget talking to a man in a parking lot after a *Personal Holiness Conference.* His marriage had ended in divorce after he committed adultery numerous times and his wife discovered it. He was a broken man, and his eyes filled with tears as he said…if only my wife had believed what the Bible teaches about sex in marriage my life might not be the total wreck it is today. She protected and ruled her body, using it as a carrot or a stick in my life. Oh, I know my committing adultery isn't my wife's fault, it's mine. But if she would have had sex with me more than once a month, this might never have happened. She turned me away hundreds of times in my marriage, until I didn't even bother to risk the pain of rejection again. I looked elsewhere. The amazing thing is, I didn't *want* to go anywhere else, I loved my wife-but she decided if I had sex with another woman it proved I didn't love her. So, she divorced me. I think how my life could have been so different if she had known and believed Scripture."[iv]

Depriving One Another

Paul's married readers as well as contemporary Christ-followers might question if they have any recourse for abstaining from sexual intimacy for a brief period. Paul addresses this question in 7:5–6, "Do not deprive one another except with consent for a time, that you may give yourselves to fasting and prayer; and come together again that Satan does not tempt you for your lack of self-control. But this I say as concession, not as a commandment."

Paul issues a strong imperative clearly censuring any departure from the practice of mutual submission in the sexual relationship of married couples. "Do not deprive one another," is the command clearly accenting the married believer's responsibility in the arena of "married sex." Again, this is Paul's prescription for avoiding sexual immorality, 7:2. As such it must be the central idea navigating the believer's thinking.

This command is every bit as strong as Paul's imperative to "Flee sexual immorality" (1 Cor. 6:18). In this verse Paul serves notice of God's intense dislike for sexual immorality. He explains, "Every sin that a man does is outside the body, but he who commits sexual immorality sins against his own body." Likewise, the sin of defrauding your spouse is a sin against your own body. This is because when marriage occurs between a man and a woman a "one flesh," relationship is consummated (1 Cor. 6:16; Gen. 2:23–24; Matt. 19:4–5). Therefore, the Christian married who deprives their spouse sexual intercourse without consent is sinning against their Lord, their spouse, and their own body.

In a culture that celebrates rugged individualism, defrauding of one's partner is rarely ever perceived as a sin, but rather casually dismissed as one's personal preference. Yet the godly Christ-follower must view sin the way God does. A believer's rights to deprive their husband or wife sexual intimacy are forfeited are the moment they enter into a marriage covenant. At that point the right and privilege of conjugal rights belongs to their partner. While Paul proceeds to elaborate on a believer's right to choose to remain single, he is equally clear that a Christ-follower choosing to marry forfeits these rights.

Abstention *Only* by Mutual Consent

Today in America the legal requirement for engaging in sexual relations is mutual consent. How contrary this is to God's standard pursuant to the married sex! Ironically, while the cultures standard for *having* sex is mutual consent, the only reason given for the Christian *not* having sex is mutual consent. Since the Corinthian church is immersed in a morally promiscuous society, it is understandable that Paul would advocate for strict enforcement of guidelines for marital sex. This is not to say by any means that Paul's intends for these guidelines for sexual intimacy to be relevant solely to the Corinthian church, as they are timelessly intended for the church in every generation. For Paul's commandments for married sex are timeless (see again 2 Tim. 3:15–17).

Procreation, Pleasure, and Prevention

Sex in marriage is intended for procreation, pleasure, and prevention. While Paul's primary objective in 1 Corinthians 7 is prevention, procreation and pleasure are most certainly inferred in the context. In the larger context of 1 Corinthians 7 he mentions children. He clearly states that a healthy (pleasurable) sex life for married couples can greatly diminish the strength of temptations to be unfaithful.

Now Paul offers a concession to this command for one singular purpose and only when two conditions are met. The concession is clearly marked by the word, "except." Paul charges, "except with consent for a time that you may give yourself to fasting in prayer, and come together so Satan does not tempt you for your lack of self-control." The purpose for which a married couple may abstain from normal sexual activity is "that they may give themselves to fasting and prayer" (1 Cor. 7:5). However, a married partner may only abstain from sexual intimacy with their partner if the below two conditions are met:

1) Their partner agrees to this plan to abstain from sexual intimacy for the purpose of them engaging in fasting and prayer;
2) If the first condition is met, they must mutually agree on a time to resume sexual intercourse after this brief period of fasting and prayer.

Should these two conditions go unmet, fasting and prayer is permitted, but abstinence from sexual activity is not.

Sexual Fulfillment: A Need Only a Wife or Husband Should Meet

Years ago, this writer recalls a ministry colleague lamenting of a Christian couple who were not meeting each other's sexual needs. As a result, both simultaneously became enmeshed in adulterous affairs. Paul's rationale for abstinence *only* by mutual consent is the absence of any other morally legitimate options if one or both partners are tempted sexually. For monogamous marriage is the only acceptable context in which the gift of sex is to be enjoyed. The married couple's vulnerability to sexual temptation is the reason why a couple would agree on a time when they would make love. "Lest Satan tempt you for their lack of self-control" (1 Cor. 7:5), Paul explains. Such abstinence makes sense when one considers that the purpose of Paul's writing is to combat sexual temptation in a city known as a simmering cauldron of sexual immorality. Non-consensual abstinence from sexual activity gives Satan license to tempt one or both partners.

Resisting the Tempter's Snare

Increased vulnerability to Satan's trap of sexual temptation is the reason Paul urgently charges that they quickly "come together" (have sexual relations). Paul's tone is one of urgency in 1 Corinthians 7. In the immoral atmosphere of sexploitation of this wicked city, it was imperative that married couples give careful attention to their partners' need. Similarly, in contemporary American culture, the pollution of sexual immorality hovers like a dense fog. In this toxic atmosphere sexual temptations abound. Such temptations are intensified when one partner defrauds another partner of sexual intimacy. Thankfully, God has provided a solution to all forms of sexual immorality. The thick fog of sexual temptation evaporates when Christians embrace God's design for love making.

No wonder the beauty of sexual fulfillment in the marriage relationship is heartily applauded by God (Proverbs 5:18–21; Ecclesiastes 9:9–10; Song of Solomon; Hebrews 13:4). Solomon, writing by God's Spirit concurs with Paul's teaching on the priority of sex in the marriage relationship as a safeguard against sexual temptation. He instructs in Proverbs 5:18–21:

> "Let your fountains be blessed and rejoice with the wife of your youth. As a loving deer and a graceful doe, Let her breasts satisfy you at all times; And *always* be enraptured with her love. For why should you my son be enraptured by an immoral woman. And be embraced in the arms of a seductress? For the ways of man are before the eyes of the LORD and He ponders all his paths." (italics mine). Solomon's beautiful rhapsody on the importance of wedded love is contrasted with the with the wicked machinations of the alluring seductress. Solomon continues,
>
> "For why should you my son, be enraptured by an immoral woman, And be embraced in the arms of a seductress? For the ways of man are

before the eyes of the LORD and He ponders all his paths, His own iniquities entrap the wicked man, and he is caught in the cords of his sin. He shall die for lack of instruction, And in the greatness of his folly he shall go astray."

Solomon's further celebrates the pristine beauty of wedded love by admonishing in Ecclesiastes 9:9,

"Live joyfully with the wife whom you love all the days of your vain life which He has given you under the sun, all your days of vanity: for that is your portion in this life, and in the labor which you perform under the sun."

Here Solomon does not relegate sex to a necessary evil to perpetuate the human race, but a gift to be vigorously enjoyed and celebrated. The author of Hebrews also delights in the beauty of wedded love, contrasting it with the wickedness of sexual immorality. In Hebrews 13:4 he asserts, "Marriage is honorable in all, and the bed undefiled; but fornicators and adulterers God will judge." While issuing a warning against sexual immorality, the author seems to be hinting at the cure for sexual sin, namely the celebration of wedded love. He enjoins his readers to establish a firewall of wedded love to serve as a buffer against such immorality. A driving impetus for sporting a robust sexual relationship in marriage is to prevent sexual immorality!

A Word of Encouragement

While it seems easy for carnal believers to dismiss God's injunctions regarding conjugal rights, they do so to their own peril. For serious consequences await those who breezily brush aside God's commands for sexual purity. Specifically, the eternal consequences of giving account of their moral licentiousness at the Judgment seat of Christ. Paul cited the price of such indifference as loss of rewards including disinheritance in the eternal reign of Jesus Christ (see 1 Corinthian 6:9–11; Galatians 5:19–21). In addition to the consequence of forfeiture of eternal rewards, Peter serves notice that sexual immorality aggressively militates against the soul of the Christ-follower. He writes in 1 Peter 2:11, "Beloved, I beg you as sojourners and pilgrims, abstain from fleshly lusts which wage war against the soul."

Indulgence in worldly lusts can potentially reek serious damage to the deepest part of the Christ-follower. While God offers grace, forgiveness, restoration and provision for the renewal of one's mind, how much better for the married Christian to follow God's prescription to avoid sexual immorality of any kind? Bruce Wilkinson writes of the more excellent way provided by all-wise and gracious God. He writes,

> "I'll never forget a conversation I had with a friend at one of our Walk Thru the Bible conferences in Phoenix, Arizona. A morning session on sexual immorality had surfaced some intense interest and discussion, and on my way back to my room a long-time friend began walking beside me. 'Bruce,' he told me, 'I just don't know what to tell these younger guys anymore.' 'What do you mean,' I wondered out loud, surprised because he has been discipling men for almost half a century. 'Well,' he continued, looking kind of sheepish, 'some of these guys have real sexual problems-with temptations and immoral things-I don't know what to tell them.' Then after a pause, he added, 'Bruce, I can't identify with all their problems. My wife has always met all my sexual needs, and, well, I just don't' have any frustrations in that area.' I can still remember the impact of his honest and vulnerable words. I stopped right in the middle of the hallway and looked him directly in the eyes. 'You have nailed

the Bible's answer! You are not sexually immoral not only because of your commitment to Christ, but because you have practiced God's perfect plan against temptations to sexual immorality-sex in marriage!'"[v]

In the arena of married sex, a woman either reflects the carnality of Jezebel or the submission of one of the holy women of God. Granted mutual submission is called for in this unique area of a Christian couple's relationship. As this chapter comes to a close, consider the real-to-life journal of a Sarah, who out of love for her God, seeks to satisfy her husband's sexual needs.

Dear Journal,

In the last few months, I have purposed to meet the need my husband describes as his number two need, namely that of sexual fulfillment. Previously, I have resisted meeting this need unless he first meets my needs. I have wanted him to honor me as his wife, care about my needs, my dreams, my desires, and my hurts. When he has done this in the past, I am more open to meeting his sexual needs. However, full disclosure, there are times when he makes a gallant effort in meeting all these needs, yet I still I selfishly insist on meeting my own needs. I suppose this is because to a large degree I have bought into the cultures lie, "every woman has a right to her own body." I must confess that in the past I have viewed my responsibilities as a Christian woman through the lens of cultural feminism rather than biblical truth. In the past I have to confess Lord that I did not ask what You desire for my sexual relationship with my husband, either through Your Word or prayer. Instead I have pursued my own agenda, and selfishly met my own needs. I listened to girlfriends who remarked that they don't have the time, energy, or desire to have sex with their husbands.

I suddenly began to realize that such a view led not to the betterment, but deterioration of my relationship with my husband. I realized that pushing my husband away made him more distant, irritable, and less responsive to my needs. In short, I was not getting what I wanted out of the marriage and neither was he. I began to realize that pursuing my own sexual agenda in marriage was a lose/lose proposition.

I acknowledge these attitudes as sinful, and have resolved by God's grace to correct every attitude not born of Him. I have confessed that resisting my husband's sexual advances has done nothing to improve the quality of our marriage, nor assisted him in overcoming temptation. In the past few months, I have purposed to follow God's prescription for sex in the marriage relationship. In doing this I fully acknowledge that my body belongs to my husband not to me, and vice-versa. I don't usually think of my body as belonging to my husband, but to myself. I suppose I must confess in this respect that in adopting this philosophy, I have listened more to the voices of culture, than to the clear instruction of God's Word.

As a result of listening to the voice of God, rather than the voices of culture, I have a peace that I have not known since early in our marriage when I willingly gave myself to my husband. As a result, I have noticed significant changes in my husband. He is no longer indifferent, but attentive to my needs. Now we talk and commune at a very deep level. In short, our marriage is better than it has ever been! Thank You Lord! Your Word is faithful and true!

Questions for Reflection

1) Have you ever heard a Christian marriage "expert" or counselor offer guidelines for sexual conduct without referencing the Bible? If so, what authority did they appeal to in an effort to support their conclusions?

2) Have you ever been counseled from 1 Corinthians 7 on God's design for married sex?

3) Have you ever used sex as a weapon or manipulative tool to coerce your spouse into giving you what you want? Explain.

4) Our culture and the church both admonish sex by mutual consent. It may be surprising to know that God commands married couples to practice abstention *only* by mutual consent.

   Of the two philosophies of married sex, which have you practiced most prominently in your marriage?

5) One way to affair-proof your marriage is to have a healthy sex life. Have you ever known of a marriage where one partner refused the other of sexual relations in which the deprived partner commenced an affair?

6) Paul commands, not sex by mutual consent, but abstention from sex by mutual consent for the Christian spouse. On a scale of 1–7, rate how often you and your spouse practice abstention from love-making by mutual consent.

   1 2 3 4 5 6 7

7) If you have not been following the Lord's prescription for curing sexual temptation in your spouse, what steps do you plan to take going forward?

8) Christian psychologist, Gary Rosberg asserts that a couple can substantially improve the quality of their marriage if

they improve their sex life by ten percent. If you are married, do you believe Rosberg's theory to be:

True   Sometimes   True Rarely   True False

Circle One.

9) What method do your spouse and you employ to decide
    when and how often to have sex? After having read this
    chapter, do you think your approach is biblical or cultural?
10) If you are a Christian, what Scriptural principles have you
    employed to govern your sex life?
11) At the beginning of this chapter are two stories of wives
    with radically different views on meeting their husbands'
    sexual needs. One wife believes that she no longer is obli-
    gated to meet her husband's needs since she now has what
    she wants, namely, five children. Ergo, she informs her hus-
    band that she will no longer have sexual relations with him.
        The other wife views the meeting of her husband's
    sexual needs as a wise course of action and therefore, spares
    not effort in meeting her husband's sexual needs.
        Which of these two women remind you more of Jezebel?
        Which of these two women remind you more of
    Abraham's wife Sarah?
        Which one of these women remind you more of yourself?
12) When deciding when to have sex with your husband, how
    largely does the idea, "if I don't meet my husband's sexual
    needs, he may be vulnerable to sexual temptation outside
    of our marriage," factor into your thinking? Circle One.

Often   Sometimes   Rarely   Never

13) If you are a Christ-follower, how committed are you to fol-
    lowing Paul's prescription for married sex? (Rate on a scale
    of 1–7, 1 being not committed, 7 being highly committed.).

14) Sex in the marriage relationship is one area where there is to be "mutual submission." On a scale of 1–7 (1 being low, 7 high), assess to what degree you view it that way.

15) Paul commands Christian couples to abstain from sexual relations *only* by mutual consent (1 Cor. 7:5–6). What practical benefits do you see in following this biblical directive?

16) Think back over the married couples you have known in your life who have intimated to you something about their sex life. Among those professing to sport a healthy sex life, were they in your judgment, happier that those lamenting a frustrating sex life.

17) Have you ever known of a husband whose unfaithfulness to his wife was aided and abetted by his wife "depriving" him of sexual intimacy? Explain.

RUTH: A VIRTUOUS WOMAN FOR TROUBLED TIMES

"Integrity is the highest form of loyalty."
—Stephen Covey

"It was the best of times, it was the worst of times."
—Charles Dickens, *A Tale of Two Cities*

She embodied the spirit of the virtuous woman of Proverbs 31. She was kind, diligent, industrious, and loyal. Her dedication to her family, her neighbor, and her God, became well known to all who resided in Bethlehem. Her name meant "friend." She was a loyal friend whose life oozed unrelenting kindness to her mother-in-law who feared disenfranchisement from the Almighty. This woman of renowned virtue, lived during one of the darkest periods of Israel's storied history. The electricity of God's grace transmitted by her demonstrated the accuracy of Dickens immortal line, "It was the best of times, it was the worst of times." Ruth, a daughter of an accursed people, serves as an anti-Jezebel figure. Ruth and Jezebel shared a few similarities. First, they were both women. Secondly, they were both Gentile women. Thirdly, they both descended from pagan idolatrous nations. For all intents and purposes, that is where their similarities end.

A Friend in Troubled Times

Ruth, was true to her name. She was a loyal friend to her mother-in-law, Naomi, to whom she tirelessly displayed kindness. Later, she was to become the daughter-in-law of a famous prostitute who converted to being a wholehearted follower of Yahweh. Unlike Jezebel, Ruth was not a liar and conniver, but a lady of the highest integrity. In her tender relationship with her mother-in-law Naomi, she embodied the words of Stephen Covey, "Integrity is the highest form of loyalty." She spoke the truth in her heart and radiated loyal love, reminiscent of the covenant God who rescued her from idolatry.

Idolatrous Beginnings

We are not told much about her foreign upbringing in the book that bears her name. However, we know that as a Moabitiss, she bore the smudge-mark of a sworn enemy of the Hebrew nation. The Moabites were cursed as a result of refusing the children of Israel passage to the Promised land. This nation of idolaters practiced child sacrifice to the pagan god Chemosh.

It is presumed that Ruth met her husband, Mahlon, due to an act of disobedience from her father-in-law Elimelech. Elimelech, whose name means, "My father is king," failed to live up to his name. For Elimelech trusted in himself rather than the Almighty to provide during this dark episode in Israel's history. Against the law of Moses, he relocated his family to Moab, while the land of Palestine was afflicted with a prolonged famine.

The True God was Not Angry with Ruth

Over the course of time, Mahlon, the oldest son of Ruth and Naomi, took Ruth to be his wife (Ruth 4:10). Given Ruth's spiritual lineage we are not told why she married outside of her people or religion. Perhaps initially it was for the convenience of having a husband provide for her. It may have been due to social pressure to marry and bear children. Yet the narrative reveals that this young

Moabitiss had a higher motive. Ruth observed something in Yahweh that was lacking in Chemosh, the capricious god of the Moabites. It was believed that Chemosh was incensed with the Moabites for them becoming a vassal state of the Hebrew nation. In contrast to the irascible Chemosh, the calling card of Yahweh was His chesed, or "loyal covenantal love" for His people. Rather than the abomination of child sacrifice was the loyal love "chesed" of Yahweh, "My covenant I will not break nor alter the word that is gone out of My lips, Once have I sworn in My holiness, I will not lie to David" (Psalm 89:34–35).

Like her future mother-in-law, Rehab, Ruth witnessed something in Yahweh that drew her to faith in Him. Undoubtedly, she witnessed the kindness of this God in the life of her other mother-in-law, Naomi, whose name meant, "Pleasant."

In any case Ruth, a daughter of an accursed people, became a loyal follower of Adonai, the Almighty God of Israel. As a result, she became highly favored by the LORD. God was not mad at this daughter of an accursed nation, contrarily He was mad about her! It was the kindness of this God that led her to repentance (see Rom. 2:4).

Ruth's Expresses Honorable Loyalty to the LORD and Her Mother-in-Law

Ruth's husband Mahlons's name meant "Sickly." He most likely acquired his name as a result of a congenital illness. After finally succumbing to his birth defect, his widow Ruth was left to fend for herself. After nearly a decade of marriage, she was left a widow. Her mother-in-law, Naomi and sister-in-law, Orpah, were also widowed in the same decade. While Ruth had married into a family who worshipped a "strange" God, she became a believer in that God. Perhaps Naomi had something to do with her desire to worship the true and living God. Maybe her husband Mahlon, sported an extraordinary faith in Yahweh while in throes of his chronic illness, that attracted Ruth to the God of Israel. Given that Ruth was an extraordinarily compassionate woman, she may out of desperate love for her husband, petitioned the God of Israel for his healing. Naomi had become embittered over time. She likely had something to do with her husband abandoning the land of Palestine during the famine. The narrative suggests that she believed that God judged her for her role forsaking God's people and land. When she eventually entered Bethlehem with Ruth, she corrected the townswomen in Ruth 1:20: "Do not call me Naomi; call me Mara, for the Almighty has dealt very bitterly with me. I went out full, and the LORD has brought me home again empty. Why do you call me Naomi, since the LORD has testified against me, and the Almighty has afflicted me?"

A Bitter Homecoming

Naomi believed, that the disciplining hand of the Almighty God had severely afflicted her. Her countenance reflected this inner perspective. When she and Ruth entered the city, the townswomen failed to recognize her. Her disposition had soured. Her testimony was, "I went out full, and the LORD has brought me home again empty." She meant by this, that while she departed Bethlehem with a full house, she returned with a vacant one, due to the death of her husband and two sons. Naomi was no longer in the positive mental attitude mode. So embittered was she admonished the townswomen to address her by the name, "Mara," meaning, "bitter," rather than "Naomi," meaning, "pleasant."

Ruth: God's Gift of Grace

It was this same feeling of despair, that undoubtedly led her to charge both her daughters to return to the land of their birth that they may discover marital rest. She instructed, "Go return each to your mother's house. The LORD deal kindly with you as you have dealt with the dead and me. The LORD grant that each of you may find rest in the house of your husband" (Ruth 1:7–8).

Orpah, took Naomi's advice and kissed her Goodbye. Ruth however, clung tenaciously to her mother-in-law, while issuing a pledge of loyalty to the LORD and Naomi in dramatic prose. She intoned in Ruth 1:16–17: "Entreat me not to leave you, Or to turn back from following after you; For wherever you go, I will go; And wherever you lodge I will lodge; Your people will be my people, And your God, my God. Where you die, I will die, and there I will be buried. The LORD do so to me, and more also, If anything but death parts you and me." Ruth was so sincere in her commitment to Naomi and the LORD that she took a solemn oath to reside with Naomi and worship her God the rest of her life. Should she default on her pledge of loyalty to Naomi and her God, she invited Yahweh to punish her severely, to the point of taking her life. The resolve of Ruth was as strong as that of Abraham's resolve to obey his God in the greatest hour of trauma (Gen. 22), Joshua's resolve to serve the LORD along with his family (Josh. 24:15), and Paul's resolve to press forward to win the prize of Jesus's eternal reward (Phil. 3:10–14).

Ruth had become a true believer in the God of Israel and a gift of God's grace to Naomi. Her faith in her God was inextricably bound to her mother-in-law Naomi. Such faith was expressed in her practice of the great commandment and the golden rule. She demonstrated love for her God (Deut. 6:5; Lev. 19:12–15; Mark 12:31). Ruth's love for Naomi was an evident demonstration of her love for her neighbor.

Ruth Was a Woman Characterized by Tireless Diligence

Diligence is a virtue celebrated by both Paul and Peter in the letters they authored. Peter wrote in 2 Peter 1:5, "Wherefore, giving all diligence, add to your faith virtue." Ruth was a good example of a woman who diligently pursued virtue. Paul charged Timothy in 2 Timothy 2:15, "Study [be diligent] to show yourself approved unto God, for a workman does not need to be ashamed, rightly dividing the word of truth." Ruth toiled tirelessly to gather barley for her and Naomi, until evening (Ruth 2:17). She rested in the house only "She came and has continued from morning until now, though she rested a little while in the house" (Ruth 2:7). At the end of the day she had threshed an ephah of barley. This labor of love for her mother-in-law was enough to feed Naomi and her for a full month!

Ruth the Risk-Taker

As Naomi's story unfolds, the virtuous character of her daughter-in-law comes to fruition. One virtue possessed by Ruth that is often overlooked is her willingness to take risks for the sake of others. It would have been easy for Ruth, a young Moabitiss, to dismiss her responsibility to glean barley for Naomi by citing the dangers of such a venture. There were inherent risks in being a young widow in Israel during the precipitous season of the Judges. Since, "every man did that which was right in their own eyes" (Judges 21:25), she risked being sexually assaulted by the young men who toiled nearby. During this dark era of Israel's history, the men of a certain town raped a young man's concubine all night until she was dead. If this wasn't bad enough, the young man divided his deceased concubine into twelve pieces and mailed her throughout the land of Israel (Judges 19).

Boaz: An Extraordinary Man Living in a Difficult Time

Boaz being a godly man who understood the times rhetorically assured Ruth, "Have I not commanded my young men not to touch you?" (Ruth 2:9). Boaz was speaking euphemistically. By touch he meant sexually assault. He was essentially saying, "I have warned my young men to not lay so much as a finger on you, or make sexual advances toward you. They know well the consequences of disobeying a direct order from me!" While Boaz statement alludes to the dangers of a young woman harvesting the corners of the field, it also highlights Ruth's boldness in doing the right thing. She risked her life for Naomi. Like Peter stepping out of the boat onto the white squalls on the sea of Galilee, Ruth stepped into the treacherous world of ungodly men. She walked by faith and not by sight (2 Cor. 5:7). Sarah's named Ruth risk their lives for others.

Ruth Practiced Pure Religion

James, the half-brother of Jesus, spoke of "pure religion" in James 1:27, "Pure and undefiled religion before God and the Father is this: to visit orphans and widows in their trouble, and to keep oneself unspotted from the world." Though she was a widow, Ruth relieved the affliction of an older widow, namely her daughter-in-law, Naomi. Ruth was both a widow and a compassionate provider for widows. Having made a beautiful declaration of loyalty to God and Naomi, she immediately began "walking the talk." Upon hearing that the LORD had visited Bethlehem with bread, she began to reap the corners of the fields reserved for orphans and widows, so she might provide for her mother-in-law and herself. Her diligence is witnessed in that she gleaned in the fields until evening and threshed all the barley she harvested (Ruth 2:17–18).

Her actions did not escape the notice of Boaz, a close relative of Naomi and a major player in the civic arena of Bethlehem. God designated Boaz as an Eesh Gabor ("mighty man of valor"). After noticing Ruth reaping in his fields, he correctly inquired, "Whose young woman is this?" (Ruth 2:5). His servants gave Ruth Five Star reviews (Ruth 2:6–7). Boaz comforted Ruth pronouncing a benediction on her: "It has been fully reported to me, all that you have done for your mother-in-law since the death of your husband, and how you have left your father and your mother and the land of your birth, and have come to a people whom you did not know before. The Lord repay your work, and a full reward be given you by the LORD God of Israel, under whose wings you have come for refuge" (Ruth 2:11–12). Boaz witnessed Ruth's diligence and pronounced a benediction upon her. The work that he references is Ruth's meticulous and tender care for her mother-in-law. Ruth, like Rehab and the "holy women of God," embodied the spirit of pure religion.

Ruth's Love for Her Mother-in-Law Was Seen in Her Willingness to Wed Boaz

There are several assumptions made in the narrative of Ruth that are up for grabs. Many of these assumptions are more akin to "Hollywood" than the "Holy Word." One assumption is that romantics sparks flew when Boaz first noticed Ruth gleaning in his field. More than likely this affluent "mighty man of valor," was merely demonstrating responsible land ownership by inquiring to whom Ruth belonged. Since this was the time of the Judges in which "every man did that which was right in his own eyes," Ruth was at risk of being assaulted by men (Judges 21:25). Another is that Ruth and Boaz fell deeply in love and couldn't wait to marry. For the narrative of Ruth reveals her to be many years Boaz' junior. He called this young widow, "daughter." Given the age disparity between Boaz and Ruth we might imagine her yearning to marry a man closer to her age (see Ruth 3:10–11). In military parlance, we can neither confirm nor deny such a theory. What is apparent is Ruth's desire to wed Boaz was a tender expression of love for her mother-in-law Naomi.

Ruth's love for Naomi was seen in her compliance with her mother-in-law's creative plan to inform Boaz of her availability to be married as the widow of his near-kinsman, Mahlon. On a given night during this perilous slice of Israel's history known as the time of the Judges, Boaz slept on the threshing floor to protect his barley harvest from being ransacked by thieves.

At Naomi's behest, Ruth concealed her identity with a discreet dress as she passed under the cover of darkness to Boaz' threshing floor. Modesty was of the essence as Ruth uncovered Boaz's feet while he slept, he was awakened by the cool night air. When Boaz awoke, he was startled to find a woman at his feet. After identifying herself, she disclosed to Boaz that he was her near-kinsman and requested that he consider being her and Naomi's kinsman-redeemer. This transaction included marrying Ruth (Ruth 3:9). This levirate marriage practice of that day entailed a brother or near kinsman marrying their close relative's brother (Lev. 25:47–55). This custom is introduced in the narrative of Judah's daughter-in-law, Tamar. It entailed a brother (near relative) marrying a sister-in-law for the purpose of raising up a descendant to the deceased. Ruth, following such a custom, intimated her desire to be married to Boaz. This mighty man of valor reciprocated his willingness to be her kinsman-redeemer. Though foreign to many, such was a wholly appropriate gesture in the Hebrew culture. Boaz's desire to honor Ruth's request was fueled by her eminent virtue. Ruth's praiseworthiness is seen in the tribute Boaz paid to her in Ruth 3:10–11:

> Then he said, 'Blessed are you of the LORD, my daughter! For you have shown more kindness at the end than at the beginning, in that you did not go after young men, whether poor or rich. And now my daughter, do not fear, I will do for you all that you request, for all the people of my town know that you are a virtuous woman.

Ruth had swiftly won the hearts of the townspeople of Bethlehem by her beautiful deeds. The crowning jewel of her reputation as a virtuous woman was her meticulous care for Naomi. In conjunction with this labor of love, was her refusal to pursue a husband, either rich or poor. Boaz was obviously impressed with this young foreign woman and resolved to honor her request to be redeemed (married), so he might raise of up children to Elimelech and Naomi may leave a posterity upon whom the LORD could pour His favor. Ruth's conduct embodied the spirit of Peter's command in 1 Peter 2:12, "Let your beautiful deeds be made known before the Gentiles, that they may by your good works which they shall behold, glorify God in the day of visitation."

Though Ruth displayed her beautiful works primarily before the Jews, they were no less beautiful!

Ruth Walked by Faith Rather Than Sight

The Apostle Paul writing in 2 Corinthians 5:7 reflected, "For we walk by faith and not by sight." When he penned these words under the inspiration of God, perhaps Paul has in his mind's eye the words of the prophet Habakkuk, "But the just shall live by his faith" (Habakkuk 2:4). The prophet during another tumultuous episode in Israel's history was asserting that faith is what the people of God live by. Ruth embarked on an odyssey of faith when she departed Moab leaving behind her family, religion, and way of life. This is what Ruth did in forsaking her upbringing, her religion, and her land, to pursue the LORD. Ruth demonstrated herself to be a woman of faith. Her walk with God bears some resemblance to Abraham's who left his family to follow God to a strange land with which he had no family, or prior acquaintance. Similarly, Ruth trusted in the God of Israel and sought His refuge (Ruth 2:12).

Ruth's Extraordinary Love Was Praised by Others

Ruth a foreign widow, who became a believer in Adonai, was praised by the Jewish townswomen.

"Then the women said to Naomi, 'Blessed be the LORD who has not left you this day without a close relative; and may his name be famous in Israel! And may he be to you a restorer of life and a nourisher of your old age; for your daughter-in-law who loves you who is better to you than seven sons, has borne him" (Ruth 4:13–16).

High praise indeed! Ruth resembled the virtuous woman of Proverbs 31 of whom it is said, "She watches over the ways of her household, And does not eat the bread of idleness. Her children rise up and call her blessed; her husband also, and he praises her; Many daughters have done well, But you excel them all. Charm is deceitful, beauty is vain, but a woman who fears the LORD shall be praised. Give her the fruit of her hands. And let her own works praise her in the gates" (Proverbs 31:27–31).

By her loyalty to her mother-in-law, Ruth forfeited the prospect of marrying a young man who could care for her. Ruth selflessly put the needs of others over herself. In caring for her mother-in-law Naomi, Ruth was exhibiting the kind of servant's mentality Paul urges in Philippians 2:3–8:

> Let nothing be done by selfish ambition or conceit, but in lowliness of mind, let each esteem others better than himself. Let each one of you look out not only for his own interests but also the interests of others. Let this mind be in you which was also in Christ Jesus, who being in the

form of God, did not consider it robbery to be equal with God, but made himself of no reputation, taking the form of a bondservant, and coming in the appearance of a man, He humbled Himself and became obedient to the point of death, even the death of the cross.

Ruth perhaps initially waylaid her own plans to care for the basic needs of her widowed mother-in-law when as a widow herself it would have been understandable to serve her own needs. This foreign Sarah was very Christ-like in her servanthood! As a mother in the lineage of Christ, she bore the characteristics of the God-Man, Jesus Christ who came "not to serve, but to be served, and to give His life a ransom for many" (Matt. 20:28; Mark 10:45). Reflective of Ruth's servant mind-set is the naming of their son, Obed, meaning, "servant." Both Ruth and her husband Boaz modeled servanthood.

The LORD Rewards Ruth's Loyalty

Ruth's loyalty was rewarded when God favored her a strategic position in the community of faith. Ruth not only married into one of the most prominent families in Bethlehem, but she became one of four women listed in the genealogy of Jesus Christ. Like the other three women she was a most unlikely candidate for such a distinguished calling, since she was a Moabitiss. One reason why God favored her for with this messianic heritage was His amazing grace. Yet another reason why she merited this august privilege was her incredible loyalty to God and her neighbor. God declared, "The one who honors Me him (her) I will honor" (1 Sam. 2:30). Ruth left a legacy of God's chesed (loyal) love for those whose roots extended beyond the house of Israel. Ruth is a Sarah par-excellence! Blessed are those who follow in her train. She embodies the spirit of Lady Wisdom, as described by Dr. Ron Allen.

Lady Wisdom

"[All] of a sudden there comes something new-something so new we cannot miss it. It is a Woman. The streets are filled with women and men, people are everywhere; but the presence of this woman is felt. Though the early morning is already warm, there is a sense of dynamic warmth and presence in this Woman that reaches out and demands our response. She seems out of place, yet she is unembarrassed. Although she is unattended, no one would confuse her with one of the lurking harlots slumped at the entrance of the alley. This woman is a Lady. Something about her is countercultural. Unquestionably feminine, she nevertheless moves boldly int this man's world of commerce. She stands with no child, is escorted by no husband, and has no father at her side, looking another direction she blushes. She is alone, boldly alone, yet unquestionably proper. Right in the middle of the concourse she takes her stand. People numbed by the business of the world about them take note of her. Simply put, the Lady is the loveliest woman we have ever seen. Then she speaks. In the tumult of this city her voice is heard! The Lady's voice seems to come from another world. It is the voice of an angel. The voice of a god. Sweet, strong, resonant; it is the voice one loves at first hearing. As she speaks, we distinguished her words. It seemed that nothing could surpass her beauty, but when we hear her words, we find them to eclipse even her appearance. Her words are a call: To come to her. To reach out to her. To embrace her. To love her. To receive her gifts. To live with her forever."[vi]

Questions for Reflection

1) Contrast Ruth with Jezebel. In what ways does Ruth represent the polar opposite of Jezebel?

2) The late Steven Covey asserted, "Integrity is the highest form of loyalty." Where do you see this statement reflected in the life of Ruth?

3) One of the crowning jewels of Ruth's life was her love for people. Who are the people whom God has placed in your inner circle whom He is calling you to love?

4) James asserted that "Pure and undefiled religion before God the Father is this: to visit orphans and widows in their affliction and keep oneself unspotted from the world" (James 1:27). How did Ruth express pure religion to those around her?

5) Boaz said of Ruth, "for all the people of the town know that you are a virtuous woman" (Ruth 3:11). Judging from what you know of Proverbs 31, in what ways was Ruth virtuous?

6) Solomon posited in Proverbs 27:17, "Iron sharpens iron, so a man [woman] sharpens the countenance of his friend." How could the story of Ruth sharpen your life making you a more virtuous woman?

ESTHER: A WOMAN OF EXTRAORDINARY COURAGE

"There is hardly anyone who will give themselves
up for a righteous cause. Stand up for what you
believe in, even if you are standing alone."
—Sophie Scholl

"If you want to test a man's character, give him power."
—Abraham Lincoln

In 1942 Sophie Scholl was a twenty-year old, Christian woman living in Nazi Germany. A biology and philosophy major at the University of Munich, she had heard about the atrocities of the Nazi War machine and joined her brother Hans in an anti-Nazi society known as the White Rose. They fought against the Third Reich and Hitler by writing and distributing thousands of pamphlets around Germany to undermine fascism and totalitarianism. Since she was a devout Christian, she used Bible verses and philosophical arguments to undermine the Nazi government. Among other things, the pamphlets read, "Our current state is a dictatorship of evil. We know that already, I hear you object, and we don't need you to reproach us for it yet again. But I ask you if you know that, then why don't you act? Why do you tolerate these rulers gradually robbing you in public and in private, of one right after another, until one day nothing, absolutely nothing, remains but the machinery of the state, under the command of criminals and drunkards?"[vii]

Early in 1943 she was arrested for her involvement in the White Rose, including the authoring and distribution of leaflets, One such leaflet read, "Every word that Hitlers speaks is a lie. When he says "peace," he means "war." On February 22, 1943 she was beheaded for treason at the age of 21. Previously she had written in her diary, "There is hardly anyone who will give themselves up for a righteous cause. Stand up for what you believe in, even if you are standing alone."[viii]

In ancient Persia, there was a young orphan who like Sophie Scholl, stood for what she believed. This young woman's name was Hadessah. History knows her as Esther and her story is recorded in a book of the Bible that bears her name.

A Tale of Two Women

Analyzed from one perspective, the Book of Esther is a tale of two women. The actions of both women were used by God to accomplish His will. The first woman said, "No," the second, "Yes." The first woman was a beautiful queen named Vashti. Her husband was the world emperor during the reign of the Persian empire. He was the son of Darius (Cyrus), who knew and loved the prophet Daniel. Xerxes was an intemperate man who whipped the Hellespont River 120 times after a storm ravaged the Persian fleet. One time for each ship that was destroyed. Over the course of time, Xerxes held a banquet for his governors and local magistrates presiding over 120 provinces. The banquet lasted an incredible 180 days. He capped off this long caucus with a weeklong grand finale of feasting by imbibing in fine wine. Xerxes apparent motivation for treating his officials to extravagant feasting was to ingratiate them to himself. He evidently subscribed to the "If you touch a heart, they will lend a hand" philosophy of life. Securing loyalty and political capital was important to the king, since a menacing Greek war machine nation lurked dangerously in the shadows of the empire.

While his appointed officials were totally sauced, Xerxes summoned his lovely queen Vashti to partake in the festivities. This was an unusual request since the banquet hall was lined with the ancient equivalent of drunken businessmen. When Vashti received the summons, she was dutifully entertaining the wives of the provincial ruling officials, a role befitting the wife of a monarch. What was inappropriate was for her to dignify a testosterone saturated party filled with lustful, inebriated, and entitled rulers. This would be as out of place as Queen Elizabeth enduring catcalls from drunken patrons at a Gentlemen's Club. The cultural ambience of this ancient Persian bazaar might call for Vashti to disrobe amid the leering throng of intoxicated men. As a self-respecting woman, such a request, even in a sexually promiscuous male dominated pagan culture, was beyond the pale. Vashti steadfastly refused.

Vashti's telling the king to put it in park, was no small breach of protocol. Rather her rebellion represented a serious violation of the canons of Persian political correctness. The crowd sobered up immediately. The king's advisors strongly urged Xerxes to take swift action in making a public example of Vashti. Xerxes did. Vashti was deposed by the king to prevent a budding feminist movement from blossoming in the empire. Vashti's dismissal paved the way for Xerxes to select another queen. This queens name was Hadessah. Hadessah means, "myrtle, bride, star." Hadessah was destined to be a bride not only because she was interminably gorgeous, but because God had a plan for this young orphan.

Losing Her Name, Not Her Identity

Similar to Daniel, Hananiah, Mishael, and Azariah, Hadessah's name was changed to one that praised a pagan god. A major purpose of this name change was to indoctrinate foreign captives into the Babylonian or Persian culture. The king gave her a Persian name, Esther, most likely praising the Persian goddess, "Ishtar." Esther 2:7 reads, "the young woman [Esther] was lovely and beautiful." Esther made a ravishing queen, an incomparable blend of stunning beauty and feminine charm. She was Miss Universe and Miss Congeniality all rolled into one. She gained incredible favor with Xerxes who selected her to replace Vashti as his new queen. Esther's endowment of such physical, social, and intellectual attributes was wedded to divine purpose. The Lord had created her to preserve God's people from an impending holocaust.

Esther's Unusual Task

It may seem curiously strange for a young Jewess to marry a pagan king. Yet Xerxes choice of Esther as queen was by divine appointment rather than sheer coincidence. For the providence of God permeates the narrative of the book of Esther. As it is often said, though God's name occurs nowhere in the Book of Esther, His presence is everywhere felt. One way the LORD's providential presence is palpably felt was by His innately gifting Esther with exquisite beauty and grace. For such God given endowments captured the king's attention.

Yet Esther was much more than a stunning beauty. For the sovereign LORD assigned the upbringing of young orphan to her godly Jewish cousin Mordecai (Esther 2:7). In this paternal role, Mordecai undoubtedly instilled in his younger cousin a love for Yahweh and the Mosaic Law. Esther did not forsake her heritage when she was violently torn from the land of Israel. She understood the Abrahamic Covenant and God's promise of land, seed, and blessing. Mordecai made sure that she understood the unique role and glorious future God had planned for His chosen people Israel (Jer. 29:10–12). She understood from King David, that Yahweh, the God of the covenant, would keep His oath to faithfully keep His promises to the Jews (Psalm 89:34–35). The upshot was Esther never forsook either her heritage as a young Jewess.

Solomon wrote, "The king's heart is in the hand of the LORD, Like the rivers of water; He turns it wherever He wishes" (Prov. 21:1). Sometimes God uses people to turn the hearts of kings. For Xerxes, God employed Esther. This was her unusual task. Her elevation to queen of Persia was by divine appointment. It was orchestrated by God, rather than Xerxes, who like his father Cyrus, was merely the instrument of divine providence. Esther's divine appointment was not for her, but for the purpose of advancing the LORD's agenda. For behind the scenes God, not Xerxes, was calling the shots in the Persian empire, making the royal court the instruments of His sovereign will.

Satan's Double Agent

When God is at work, the enemy simultaneously plots. Satan's front-man executing his diabolic schemes was a man named Haman. Haman's deep cover was that of a key adviser in Xerxes court. This evil pawn of the enemy was drunk with power. As he passed by the city gates on his daily commute to and from the palace, he insisted that the prominent men of the city bow to him. However, there was one prominent Jew who adamantly refused to give Haman his "due." You guessed it, his name was Mordecai, the legal guardian of the queen. Mordecai's unwavering resolve to not genuflect to the wicked emissary of Satan's domain was indicative of his loyalty to his God. Bowing to this sworn enemy of the Jews was akin to worshipping idols and rendering homage to Satan. Over time, Haman became so incensed that he devised a heinous plot to exterminate the Jews from Persia.

God's Man at God's Place at God's Time

In contrast to Haman, was Mordecai, Esther's guardian was God's man in God's place, at God's time. Prior to his promotion by Xerxes, God providentially assigned him to the gates of Susa, the veritable Wallstreet of the Persian empire. God sovereignly orchestrated his unveiling of a plot to assassinate the king. God employed Mordecai to implement His masterplan to rescue the Jews from a holocaust. After learning of the plot, Mordecai immediately notified Esther through messengers. Esther relayed the message to the appropriate personnel. The conspirators were executed and Mordecai's role in uncovering the plot was providentially recorded in the king's minutes. God later employed this royal log to inform the king of Mordecai's heroics and rescue him from Haman's evil plot.

Mordecai's role as an adviser to Queen Esther was reprised when he uncovered another plot by wicked Haman to exterminate the Jews from the empire. He communicated this diabolic scheme to Esther through messengers. Initially the queen was reluctant to take action. She answered in Esther 4:11–12: "All the king's servants and the people of the king's provinces know that any man or woman who goes into the inner court to the king, who has been called, he has but one law: put all to death, except to the one to whom the king holds out the golden scepter, that he may live. Yet I myself have not been called to go into the king in these thirty days."

Apparently, Esther had temporarily lost sight of God's sovereign appointment of her as queen. She needed Mordecai to provide insight on her non-exemption status and the key role God had ordained for her. He responds to the queen in Esther 4:13–14: "Do not think in your heart that you will escape in the king's palace any more than all the other Jews. For if you remain completely silent at this time, relief and deliverance will arise for the Jews from another place, but you and your father's house will perish. Yet who knows whether you have come to the kingdom for such a time as this?"

Through a messenger, Mordecai, engaged in straight talk with Esther. Peering deep into her soul, he warned that her status as queen was no insurance policy that the king would spare her life amid Haman's ambitious campaign to exterminate the Jews. Yet as a God-fearing Jew, Mordecai expresses confidence that God will either use Esther or someone else to spare the nation. This is not wishful thinking on Mordecai's part. This is what the Lord promised for His people throughout the Old Testament (see Genesis 12:1–3; 2 Samuel 7:12–16; Jeremiah 31:30–34).

Why Not You?

Then he encourages Esther by strongly suggesting that God had sovereignly engineered her ascension to queen so she might rescue Israel, from the precipice of national ruin. This was to be Esther's magnum opus. It was her shining moment for which she was born. Mordecai's injection of reality into the crisis stirred Esther to action. She responded again through messengers in 4:16–17: "Go gather all the Jews who are present in Shushan, and fast for me; neither eat nor drink for three days, night or day. My maids and me will fast likewise. And so I will go to the king which is against the law; and if I perish, I perish!"

Esther Committed Herself to a Cause Bigger Than Herself

Esther was as bold as she was beautiful. Though momentarily resembling a meandering stream by opting for the path of least resistance, at Mordecai's behest, she quickly recovered to risk her life by entering the court of Xerxes. Her resolution in the face of this scandalous ethnic cleansing pogrom was clear, "If I perish, I perish!" This was the queen's new mantra moored to the pier of dauntless courage. In the words of Moses, Esther was "strong and courageous" (Josh 1:9). Demonstrating the courage of her convictions she recognized that there are causes transcending our temporary life on earth. One of those causes was a willingness to die so others may live. She understood the significance of Jesus's words, "Greater love has no man than this, that a man lay down his life for his friends" (John 15:13). Esther believed there was a fate worse than death, namely, leading a dishonorable life. Somehow, she recognized that life resembles a wet bar of soap in that the tighter you grip it, the faster is slides through your fingers. As a result, Esther committed herself to a cause bigger than herself.

Ironically, if Esther had defaulted to cowardice, death would have been her likely plight. Thankfully, her words and actions echoed Jesus's charge in Matthew 16:24–26: "If anyone desires to come after Me, let him deny himself, and take up his cross, and follow Me. For whoever desires to save his life shall lose it, but whoever loses his life for may sake will find it. For what profit is it to a man if he gains the whole world and lose his soul? Or what will a man give in exchange for his soul?" Though Esther lived before Jesus was born in Bethlehem's manger, she met the essential qualifications of being a member of Jesus's inner circle. For she was willing to "lose her life in this world." Similar to Moses who was lauded for "choosing rather to suffer affliction with the people of God than to enjoy the passing pleasures of sin, esteeming the reproach of Christ greater riches than the treasures of Egypt, for he looked to the reward" (Heb. 9:24–26), Esther bravely took her stand with God's people. Just as Moses could have chosen to ignore his heritage as the son of Hebrew slaves, so Esther could have forsaken her pedigree as an orphaned Jewess. Such a temptation may have been very acute in Esther's case. Esther chose to be God's woman, in God's place at God's time.

Her spiritual moxie in committing herself to a cause bigger than herself resembled that of the Apostle Paul. For in another era Paul also was willing to risk his life to save the nation of Israel from national catastrophe, while bringing about national repentance (see Acts 20–26; Romans 9–11). While others sought to dissuade him from going to Jerusalem, he declared, "But none of those things moved me. Neither do I count my life as dear to myself. But that I might finish my course with joy and the ministry that I have received from the Lord Jesus, to testify of the gospel of the grace of God" (Acts 20:24).

Esther Knew Her God

Knowing God is the benchmark for success in God's eternal kingdom. Pursuant to this Jeremiah wrote in Jeremiah 9:23–24, "Let not the wise man glory in his wisdom, Let not the mighty man glory in his might, Nor let the rich man glory in his riches; But let him who glories glory in this, That he understands and knows Me, That I am the LORD, exercising lovingkindness, judgment and righteousness in all the earth. For in these things I delight,' says the LORD."

The intimate knowledge of God is the main objective of the Christian life. In this regard Jesus petitioned the Father in His high priestly prayer, "And this is eternal life, that they may know You, the only true God and Jesus Christ whom You have sent" (John 17:3). What Jesus is praying in the context of John's gospel is that His disciples experience that "abundant life" that He came to provide for them through His sacrificial death for them (John 10:10–11). Jesus paved the way for receiving the gift of eternal life through the cross. This eternal life is not merely the "sweet, by and by in the sky when we die," but a quality of life involving being on intimate footing with the Son of God. Knowing Christ is the flagship priority of the kingdom. In the case of Esther and all of God's children, it is also the key to answered prayer.

Esther acted in faith and courage because like Abraham and Sarah, she knew her God. She knew that he was a God of goodness who faithfully keeps His promises. Daniel prophesied, "the people who know their God will be strong and do mighty exploits" (Dan. 11:32). Esther embodied this prophesy. She performed mighty exploits. J. I. Packer in his book, *Keeping In Step With the Spirit*, writes of models of sanctification. The model he embraces is encapsulated in the mantra, "Trust God and get going." Esther embodied this mantra with her bold actions towards Xerxes.

Esther's Answered Prayer Was Rooted in Knowing God

The priority of knowing God is made abundantly clear by Jesus to His disciples in the Upper Room discourse. Jesus instructed His disciples in John 15:5, "I am the vine you are the branches, he who abides in Me and I in him, the same brings forth much fruit. For without Me you can do nothing." The language employed by Jesus relative to the vine and the branches speaks not to their organic union with Christ (the fact that they are justified), but the practical intimate relationship His disciples can have with the Savior. The phrase, "in Me," references the practical personal relationship the disciples have with Jesus. Jesus commanded His disciples, "abide in Me" (John 15:4–10). Peter, one of Jesus's closest disciples speaks of this same intimacy in his final statement to the church in 2 Peter 3:18, "But grow in grace and in the knowledge of our Lord and Savior Jesus Christ."

Knowing God Is All about Connectivity

Connectivity is a buzzword possessing universal currency in today's cybernetic age. Without connectivity one has no capacity to search the internet or engage in a myriad of cybernetic activities. Yet with strong connectivity or Wi Fi, the possibilities for connectivity the possibilities seem endless. In a similar vein, the spiritual dynamic of "abiding in Christ," is one of being properly connected to the Savior. The word abide is the Greek word, "meno," means, "to continue, to remain, to abide, dwell, or persevere." All of these words reflect Jesus's meaning of meno in John 15. The same is true for the phrase, "in Me" which denotes dependency and intimacy.

As Jesus's disciples remain intimately connected to their Savior, depending on Him through prayer, and obeying His commands, empowers them to produce a bumper crop of fruit. This fruit consists of love, answered prayer, and optimal joy (John 13:33–35; 15:5–13). Relative to answered prayer, Jesus instructed, "If you abide in Me and My words abide in you, you will ask what you will and it will be done for you" (John 15:7). Esther and Mordecai, were Old Testament saints who remained properly connected to their God through prayer and dependence. As a result, God showed up, showed off, by answering their prayers with aplomb.

Esther Do Not Hoard Power But Used Her Positional Authority to Serve Others

History has perennially witnessed the abuse and manipulation of people in the corridors of power. Yet godly women and men view their God appointed authority as a tool to serve rather than a club to bludgeon. A few years ago, a godly colleague of this writer gave him a copy of his philosophy of ministry. Though this brother had achieved a senior rank in the Navy, the tone of his philosophy of ministry was not one of domineering authority but one of humble servanthood. In his document he made it abundantly clear that while he had achieved senior status in the Chaplain Corps, rank was merely a vehicle given to him by God to serve others.

If You Want to Test a Woman's Character, Give Her Power

Abraham Lincoln said, "If you want to test a man's character give him power." The same could be said if you wanted to test a woman's character. Esther passed the test of character with flying colors. Rather than being addicted to her own significance, she considered the welfare of her "subjects."

Lincoln's statement is true when applied to Jezebel. Power exposed the wicked heart of the godless queen. Esther's ascension to power revealed her to be the anti-Jezebel. For while Jezebel, like wicked Haman and his wife Zeresh, had no regard for human life, Esther was willing to die to save her countrymen.

Esther Was Willing to Lose Herself to a Cause Bigger than Herself

Sophie Scholl lost herself in the cause of warning her fellow Germans of Hitler's evil schemes. She forfeited her life as a result of her courage actions. Sophie Scholl's love for her Savior and her countrymen, compelled her to make the ultimate sacrifice. Esther similarly demonstrates her authentic love for her kinspeople when she tearfully prostrated herself before the king: "Now Esther spoke again to the king, fell down at his feet, and implored him with tears to counteract the evil of Haman the Agagite, and the scheme with he had devised against the Jews" (Esther 8:3).

Esther did not shed alligator tears. Far from expressing disingenuousness, her weeping and obeisance before the king was born of love for her kinsmen. Like Ruth, Esther displayed the humble mind-set championed by Jesus of putting the needs of others above one's own needs (Philippians 2:3–5). Many in positions of authority often wield their power in self-serving ways. However, Esther was willing to leverage her power to serve the best interest of others. Jesus is of course the premier model of utilizing power to benefit others. Peter declared of Jesus's substitutionary atonement, "For Christ also suffered for our sins, the just for the unjust, that He might bring us to God, being put to death in the flesh but made alive by the Spirit" (1 Pet. 3:18). Such a sacrifice of one's life is the greatest expression of love. Pursuant to this Jesus stated, "Greater love has no man than this, that a man lay down His life for His friends" (John 15:13).

What made Esther's steely resolve so impressive, was that barring divine intervention, she risked certain death. Her statement was not overdrawn. Xerxes father, Darius, toiled through the night to change the law of the Medes and Persians, in an effort to deliver Daniel from the mouth of lions. While he failed to rescue Daniel by changing the law, God intervened to save Daniel's life (Dan. 6:13–23). Esther undoubtedly had heard of the LORD's deliverance of the aged Daniel occurring a generation earlier. Knowing the recent history of God's deliverance of Daniel, Shadrach, Meshach, and Abednego, had undoubtedly strengthened the sinews of Esther's faith. The modeling by these mighty men of God infused not only faith but Godly character into Esther's spiritual spine.

Esther Believed in the Power of Prayer

Interlaced with Esther's declaration that she would risk her own life to save her people, was her commitment to fast for three days and nights. For the devout Jew, earnest prayer was interwoven with fasting. Esther undoubtedly purposely neglected to mention prayer to conceal hers and Mordecai's identity as Jews (see Esther 2:20).

Esther, like the Apostle Paul and James, the Lord's brother, believed in the power of prayer to move the hand of God. James wrote definitively, "The effective fervent prayer of a righteous man accomplishes much" (James 5:17). Esther would have uttered a hearty Amen to this statement of truth! Paul also confidently asserted both to the Philippians church and Philemon that God's prayers would deliver him from prison (see Phil. 1:19; Philemon 22). By believing in the power of prayer to move the hand of God, she was demonstrating her utter dependence upon God.

Esther a Woman Who Depended on God

Prayer and dependence on God go together like peas and carrots. Esther by virtue of fasting and praying for three days, demonstrated extraordinary dependence on the LORD. While he prophesies to the southern kingdom of Judah, Jeremiah warns of the danger of trusting in oneself. He solemnly intones in Jeremiah 17:5–7:

> Thus says the LORD, Cursed is the man
> who trusts in man And makes the flesh his
> strength, Whose heart departs from the LORD,

For he shall be like a shrub in the desert, And shall not see when good comes, But shall inherit the parched places in the wilderness, in a salt land which is not inhabited.

Conversely, he charges in Jeremiah 17:7–9:

> "Blessed is the man who trusts in the LORD, And whose hope is the LORD, And whose hope is the LORD. For he shall be like a tree planted by the waters, Which spreads out its roots by the river, And will not fear when heat comes; But its leaf will be green, And will not be anxious in the year of drought, Nor will cease from yielding fruit. The heart is deceitful above all things and desperately wicked who can know it?"

In verse 9, Jeremiah warns of the hearts natural bent toward self-deceit when one resolves to trust in themselves rather than God. Far better to anchor our hope and trust in Him. Through prayer and fasting, commanding her maidservants to join her in seeking the face of God, and by instructing Mordecai to charge all the Jews to fast, Esther displayed stalwart dependence on the LORD. The posture of her heart is reminiscent of Jesus's words to His disciples in the upper room, "I am the Vine, you are the branches, he who abides in Me and I in him, bears much fruit, for without Me you can do nothing" (John 15:5).

Esther was not a self-styled woman majoring in rugged individualism. She refused to trust her charm, beauty, powers of feminine persuasion, or ingenuity, to save the day. She understood that any efforts to save Israel apart from God's help, would be futile. Her pious devotion to fast and pray embodied the spirit of Proverbs 3:5–6, "Trust in the LORD with all your heart, And lean not on your own understanding; In all your ways acknowledge Him, And He shall direct your paths."

Esther Sported a Non-Survivalist Mind-Set

Today we live in a survivalist culture. We want to survive professionally, financially, reputationally, and personally. In the ebb and flow of our lives, our will to survive influences virtually every choice we make. To many, survival is more important than being ethically virtuous or biblically correct. While at first blush, survival seems noble, in many cases it is borne of cowardice. In some instances, our survivalist instincts collide broadside with our mandate to follow Christ. In such instances, surviving degenerates into the malaise of moral and ethical compromise.

Esther and Mordecai along with the great saints of the Bible operated on the following basic principle, "I do not have to survive." My observation in the last thirty years of ministry is that Christians make survival the ivory tower and endgame of their lives. Survival like money is amoral, it neither good nor evil until a motive is assigned. Survival can be sinful if it is marshaled to a refusal to follow Christ *anywhere* He leads us and to sacrifice *anything* for His name's sake. Jesus charged wanna-be disciples of their willingness to "lose their lives that they may gain their souls" (Matthew 16:24–25; Mark 8:34–38). Those who make survival the endgame of their lives risk moral and ethical compromise and forfeit eternal rewards.

Jesus calls Christ-followers to "hate their life in this world." Indeed, the way of the cross is paved with the sharp stones of suffering and sometimes death. Jesus followers are called to die to many things including ungodly desires, personal acclaim, self-ambition, and dreams not borne of Him. Sometimes they are called to forfeit their physical lives. Though a glittering career as queen of Persia may have been unfolding for Esther, she was willing to sacrifice everything to fulfill God's purpose for elevating her to royalty.

For people like Esther, Mordecai, Daniel, Shadrach, Meschach, and Abednego, and the apostles, displeasing God was not an option, but willingness to forfeit her life for the sake of others was essential. In this respect Esther resembled the Nathan Hale of the nation of Israel. While on the American side of the Revolutionary War, he was captured at the tender age of twenty-one and sentenced to be hanged for spying. Before he was hanged, he made a famous declaration, "I regret that I only have one life to give for my country!" This beautiful, winsome, and gifted young lady, not unlike Nathan Hale, potentially had much of her life ahead of her. She might have escaped the attempted holocaust if she remained quiet concerning her ethnicity. Yet she was willing to sacrifice everything, including her life, for the sake of rescuing the Jewish nation from the precipice of destruction. Esther, like Moses, she was "willing to suffer affliction with the people of God than to enjoy the pleasures of sin for a season" (Heb. 11:25).

Esther Expressed Loyalty to God by Speaking Truth to Power

Godly women and men speak truth to power out of love for God and their neighbor. Esther joined an elite company of saints featuring John the Baptizer, Stephen, Daniel, Jeremiah, Isaiah, Elijah, Nathan, Azariah, Hanani, Micaiah, who spoke boldly spoke truth to power. They did this as their vertical allegiances to God transcended their horizontal allegiances to men. By doing so they demonstrated loyalty to God over loyalty to men. Esther was strategically appointed by God to be queen over Persia. In that role she risked her life on multiple occasions by entering the king's court contrary to the law of the Medes and the Persians. (Esther 5:2 8:3). The first time she entered was to request an audience with the king to inform the king of Haman's devious plot to wipe her people off the face of the earth.

At the second banquet at which she requested the presence of the king she revealed the heinous plot devised by Haman. When she had the opportunity, Esther begged the king to cease and desist this devious plot to exterminate the Jews. She pleaded, "If I have found favor in your sight, O king, and if it pleases the king, let my life be given me at my petition, and my people at my request. For we have been sold, my people and I, to be destroyed, to be killed, and to be annihilated. Had we been sold as male and female slaves, I would have held my tongue, although the enemy could not compensate for the king's loss" (Esther 7:3–4).

God Answers Esther's Prayers, And Honors Her Faith

While Xerxes had expressed favor to Esther, it is entirely possible that he could have turned on a dime after she identified herself as a Jew. Given Xerxes irascible personality, he might have felt deeply betrayed by Esther refusing to disclose her pedigree when she was interviewed for the position of queen (Esther 2:20). Yet risking her own death was a risk Esther was willing to take. The king was not only sympathetic with Esther, but incensed at Haman! He fumed, "Who is he, and where is he, who would dare presume in his heart to do such a thing?"

While Haman was present, she unabashedly revealed, "The adversary and enemy is this wicked Haman!" (Esther 7:6). Later, Esther boldly requested that Haman's sons be hanged (Esther 9:13).

Speaking truth to power for John the Baptizer, led to decapitation. Stephen was rewarded for his boldness by being stoned to death. Jewish tradition contends that Manasseh, the wicked king of Judah, ordered the God-inspired prophet Isaiah be shoved in a log and sawn in half. Jeremiah was tossed into a pit of "quicksand" and left to die until he was rescued. Hanani, was imprisoned by Asa after prophesying God's judgment for the king's failure to trust God during a looming national catastrophe. Micaiah, prophesied of Ahab's defeat, was imprisoned by the wicked king. Needless to say, speaking truth to power doesn't always result in a happy ending.

Service Born of Love

Irina Ratsushinskaya, was a Russian woman imprisoned in the former Soviet Union prior to the end of the Cold War. As a Christian poet and writer, she was accused of being a Soviet dissident and was incarcerated in a women's prison in Siberia. She served three years of a seven year sentence in brutally harsh conditions which included time in the "small zone" specially designed to torture dissidents. In her memoir, *Grey is the Color of Hope*, Irina speaks of the selfless sacrifice made by prisoners when one of their number was placed in solitary confinement. Solitary confinement in that environment was both physically and psychologically tortuous. Yet solitary confinement though brutal, was limited to a maximum of fifteen consecutive days. However, while the sadist guards loosely observed this rule, they had a cruel habit of releasing the inmates for a mere solitary hour before returning them for another fifteen days. In an effort to curtail this torturous practice, Irina and her fellow inmates would declare a hunger strike during the time a fellow prisoner was in solitary confinement. This would force the hand of the prison administrators, discouraging them from abusing the prisoners in this manner. This display of Christ-like love was rewarded by all of the women surviving the prison camp.

This courageous woman served as a vivid illustration of Jesus' words of someone who "hated [her] life in this world," but was willing to find it in the next. Biblical history records the story of a young Jewish woman who like Irina Ratsushinskaya was willing to sacrifice her own life to save the life of others. This woman is best known as Esther.

Like Sophie Scholl, Irina Ratsushinskaya, and the holy women of God before her, Esther committed herself to a cause bigger than herself. Like Moses she was willing to forfeit her own life and a comfortable existence so others might live. As a result, she left a legacy of being far more than an elegant queen. Esther merits praise as a holy woman of God. One who embodied the spirit of Proverbs 31:30: "Charm is deceitful, beauty is vain, but a woman who fears the LORD shall be praised."

My former professor and friend, Jim Andrews, prayed a prayer that exemplifies the courageous faith of Esther. Below is the prayer that my mentor prayed on a daily basis:

THE UNCONDITIONAL PRAYER OF
THE UTTERLY SERIOUS

Lord God my singular ambition in life,
is to magnify your son
I don't care how you fit me into your plan
You may spend me as You please,
I place no conditions on your arrangements
You set the terms of my service,
My only prayer is that you ordain for my life what-
ever will glorify Christ the most through me,
If my Savior be honored more by my death than
my life,
More in sickness than in health,
More in poverty than in wealth,
More through loneliness than companionship,
More by the appearance of failure than by the
trappings of success,
More by anonymity than notoriety,
Then your design is my desire
Only let me make a difference
(James W. Andrews)

Questions for Reflection

1) An old adage contends, "Beauty is skin deep but ugly goes to the bone." Yet Esther appeared to be as virtuous as she was beautiful. Yet if she had leaned solely on her external beauty, she would likely have relegated herself to an obscure footnote in ancient history. Thankfully, Esther cultivated courage and inner beauty (Esther 2:15–17).

2) If a woman, on a scale of 1–7 (1 being low, 7 being high), assess the priority you give to cultivating inner versus outer beauty.

   1   2   3   4   5   6   7

3) Esther was God's woman, at God's place, at God's time. God has specifically chosen her for the task of being queen of Persia. For what task has God specifically chosen you for?

4) Esther's famous mantra, "If I perish, I perish!" is a declaration of her willingness to die for a cause bigger than herself. As a woman of God, rate your willingness to die for another.

   1   2   3   4   5   6   7

5) Esther's courageous action of going into the presence of the queen did not occur in a vacuum, but flowed out of her deep faith and knowledge of a sovereign God. Daniel prophesying of the Judas and the Maccabees intoned, "But the people who know their God will be strong and do mighty exploits" (Dan. 11:32).

6) On a scale of 1–7, rate how important is knowing God is to you.

   1   2   3   4   5   6   7

   What activities do you engage in to get to know God better.

7) Jeremiah 9:23–24 informs us that if a God-follower boasts in anything they should boast in their knowledge of God. On a scale of 1–7 assess your desire to know God.

   1   2   3   4   5   6   7

8) A primary spiritual discipline Jesus instructed His disciples to engage in was "abiding in Him." Abiding in Christ entails, depending on God through prayer, obedience, loving the body of Christ, and one's neighbor. On a scale of 1–7 assess your desire to abide in Christ.

1   2   3   4   5   6   7

What steps do you intend to take in the future to increase the quality of your connectivity with the Savior?

9) As you contemplate Esther's example, have you ever prayed what my friend Jim Andrews termed, "The Unconditional Prayer of the Utterly Serious?" What benefits could accrue to you personally for praying such a prayer?

THE WARDROBE OF
A GODLY WOMAN

"An excellent wife is a crown to her husband, but she
who causes shame is like rottenness to his bones."

—Proverbs 12:4

"He who finds a wife, finds a good think
and obtains favor from the LORD."

—Proverbs 18:22

Betty Friedan was a twentieth century pioneer in America. Her writings and influence gave birth to the feminist movement and advanced the agenda of the National Organization of Women and Planned Parenthood. Her seminal feminist book, *The Feminine Mystique,* implied that she was a frustrated housewife attempting to assist fellow struggling wives cope with marital strife. In the 1990s it was discovered that she was a radical propagandist for the communist party and a staunch supporter of Stalin. She was an early member of the Communist Party USA. Her goal was to attack traditional biblical womanhood by casting wives as severely oppressed victims of a patriarchal society. By doing this she purposed to promote the dissolution of the family, sexual liberation, and the downgrading of the sanctity of life.[ix] Her agenda was to champion the liberation of women from the Judeo-Christian ethic, through the promulgation of abortion, promiscuity, divorce, homosexuality, etal. Today the smudge marks of her influence are everywhere. The mantle of her godless agenda has been picked up by others while simultaneously wreaking havoc on the American family and society. The ideological wardrobe of

Friedan and her disciples is laced with anti-Christian values. Women such as Hillary Clinton, Alexandria Ocasio-Cortez, Nancy Pelosi, Debbie Stabenow, and Gretchen Whitmer, among many other have been influenced by her lethal ideologies.

Right Thinking Produces Right Living

A universal axiom is that ideas have consequences. Wrong ideas, such as those championed by Betty Friedan and others, promote domestic chaos, mass murder, and global oppression. Conversely, right ideas pulsate with life, joy, divine order, and God's peace. A. W. Tozer asserted, "Right thinking about God will resolve a myriad of practical problems." God has given us a library of right ideas composed of sixty-six volumes.

God's Plan for Women

The Apostle Paul, has much to say about what constitutes a Christ-centered woman than any other New Testament author. Before examining the portrait of a Christ-centered woman, it is necessary to understand the context of the pastoral epistles of the New Testament. In the Apostle Paul's letter to Titus, he exhorts his young protégé to "speak the things which are proper for sound doctrine" (Tit. 2:1). The word, "sound," is the Greek word, hygianouses, from which we derive our English word, "healthy." The teaching of all pastors is to be "healthy," in that it corresponds with biblical teaching concerning Christ and how we are to conduct ourselves as His followers.

Paul charges Titus and all pastors, to champion healthy Christ-centered teaching promoting wholesome fellowship in the body of Christ. The teaching that Titus is to perpetually champion resembles organic food promoting long-term spiritual health, detoxing the Christ-follower from the free radicals of the world, flesh, and the devil. Such healthy doctrine produces the spiritual graces of godliness, heavenly minded-living, and ethical righteousness (Tit. 2:11–13). By employing "hygianouses," Paul is speaking to the permanence of this teaching. The directives which Paul issues to Timothy are not to be viewed as transitory instructions reserved only for the apostolic era, but timelessly relevant to every generation of Christ's church. Paul wants Titus to champion healthy teaching in the church he is called to pastor.

Paul's House Order

In the pastoral letter of 1 Timothy Paul establishes a "house order" for the church of Jesus Christ which is both universal in scope and timeless in duration. The house order represents the standard operating procedure for the church of Jesus Christ in all ages. It is the God-breathed form and function of the church in every generation when it assembles to meet with God and glorify their Savior through corporate worship. The house order of Christ's church transcends cultural values and contemporary fads. Paul serves notice of this house order in a sister pastoral letter of 1 Timothy. He intimates to this young pastor, "These things I write to you, though I hope to come to you shortly; but if I am delayed, I write to so that you may know how you ought to conduct yourself in the house of God, the pillar and ground of the truth" (1 Tim. 3:14–15).

Paul's recitation of an early church's creed in 3:16 is inextricably linked to the house order established throughout the letter. The house order is a divine worship protocol in the solemn assembly when the saints corporately gather to worship God. Pursuant to worship and general conduct, Paul issues commands for both men and women. Compliance with these commands adorns the gospel of Christ with opulent finery. In this way it could be legitimately said to quote Peter, that their "honorable conduct," and "beautiful deeds," may be the agency for the Gentiles "glorifying God in the day of visitation" (1 Pet. 2:12). For this is the way the doctrine of God is adorned is for Christ-followers to surrender themselves to the code of conduct delineated by Paul to Timothy and Titus. Consistent with sound doctrine, Paul issues directives to men and women in the church. In Titus 2:1–5, he charges another pastor and spiritual mentee,

"But as for you speak the things which are proper for sound doctrine: that the older men be sober, reverent, temperate, sound in faith, in love, in patience; the older women likewise, that they be reverent in behavior, not slanderers, not given to much wine, teachers of good things-that they may admonish the younger women to love their husbands, to love their children, to be discreet, chaste, homemakers, good obedient to their own husbands, that the word of God may not be blasphemed."

The Profile of a Godly Woman

Since this is a book about restoring women to God's original design, this chapter will focalize Paul's directives to Titus instructing older women. Paul establishes the profile of godly women and wives. Reading this passage elicits the faces of many saintly women I have been privileged to shepherd and co-laborer. I thank God for the constellation of godly women who embody the spiritual graces of which Paul writes! Reading this passage makes it plain that Paul had an antidote for the Jezebel Syndrome.

The Godly Woman

One by-product of the fall is what some call the insatiability of the female. The theory goes, Eve had Paradise-but she wanted more-more power, more knowledge, more privilege, more dominance. It was Eve's desire for more that triggered the fall. In the spirit of the opening salvo in the classic musical, *Oliver Twist,* we ask, "Please Sir can I have a little bit more?" One crowning signature of the Jezebel syndrome is perpetual dissatisfaction coupled with a desire for more. Paul instructs godly women and men what our discontentment should look like. He informs, "Now godliness with contentment is great gain" (1 Tim. 6:6).

What does a godly woman look like? In answering this question, it must be stated that moral grace of godliness does not envision a crestfallen believer baptized in lemon juice. Rather godliness mimics God-like characteristics. Paul offers a succinct definition of godliness in Ephesians 5:1 when he wrote, "You be imitators of God as dear children." Jesus also gives shape to godliness when He exhorts His disciples, "Therefore, you shall be perfect even as your Father in heaven is perfect" (Matthew 5:48). The godliness Jesus' speaks of likewise imitates the unconditional love of the Father, "who makes the sun to shine on the evil and the good and sends rain on the just and the unjust" (Matthew 5:45). In the context of Jesus' instruction to His disciples He commands them to transcend the conventional love of evil men and women while "loving their enemies, blessing those who curse you, doing good to those who despitefully use you and persecute you" (Matthew 5:44). In essence godliness involves mimicking God's communicable (shared) attributes. These attributes include those mentioned in Peter's matrix of moral graces. It is linked to piety and is the opposite of frivolity that behaves in an irreverent way towards God.

Godliness is a goal to be prized by the Christian woman. It is arresting to consider that there are few things in the world more beautiful to God in the world than a godly woman. Underscoring this is Solomon, "Charm is deceitful, beauty is vain, but a woman who fears the LORD shall be praised" (Proverbs 31:30). The Apostle Paul whose letters Peter studied, marshaled godliness to contentment, proclaiming, "Now godliness with contentment is great gain" (2 Peter 3:15–16; 1 Timothy 6:6).

When on peruses the Psalms and prophetic writings of the Old Testament they learn that marvelous benefits accrue to the eternal account of the godly. For instance, "Those who wait on the LORD will not be disappointed" (Psalm 25:3).

Reverence

A failsafe antidote to the Jezebel Syndrome is reverence. Reverence is a word begging for a direct object. Certainly, the first person a godly wife must demonstrate respect toward is God. Proverbs 31:30 is a favorite verse of this writer championing a woman in whom God delights. In it, Solomon rhapsodizes, "Charm is deceitful, beauty is vain, but a woman who fears the LORD shall be praised." What does the fear of the LORD look like? The wisdom literature gives shape to the fear of the LORD:

The Fear of the LORD Is Wedded to Moral Purity

The fear of the LORD considers sin no trivial matter. In this regard Solomon writes in Proverbs 8:13, "The fear of the LORD is to hate evil, pride, arrogance, and the evil way, and the perverse mouth do I hate." Fearing the Lord entails loving the things God loves and hating those things He hates. The fear of the Lord mirroring the desires of God is supported by comparing 8:13 with Proverbs 6:16–17, "These six things the LORD hates, Yes, seven are an abomination to Him; A proud look, A lying tongue, Hands that shed innocent blood, a heart that devises wicked plans, feet that are swift in running to evil, A false witness who speaks lies, And one who sows discord among brethren." Solomon's catalog of sins encompasses every evil deed either outwardly expressed or internally harbored. Heading the list is pride, the mother of all sins. Arrogance is pride that is visibly displayed, such as a "proud look," one of the seven sins the LORD passionately hates (Prov. 6:17). "The evil way," encompasses immoral sins such as adultery, pre-marital sex, as well as ethical misdeeds, and malicious acts of violence. Verbal sins committed against one's neighbor or those in the community of faith display a deficiency in reverence for the Lord and are extremely grievous to the heart of God.

Paul marshals purity to the fear of the Lord in 2 Corinthians 7:1, "Therefore, having these promises beloved, let us cleanse ourselves from all filthiness of the flesh and spirit, perfecting holiness in the fear of God." In the previous context, Paul charges the Corinthian church to renounce the sins of the sins of a godless culture. While imploring them to pursue holiness he commands, "Do not be unequally yoked together with unbelievers, For what fellowship has righteousness with lawlessness? And what accord has Christ with Belial? Or what part has the believer with an unbeliever? And what agreement has the temple of God with idols? For you are the temple of the living God. As God has said: I will dwell with them And walk among them. I will be there God, And they shall be my people. Therefore, Come out from among them And be separate says the Lord. Do not touch what is unclean, And I will receive you, And you shall be My sons and daughters, Says the LORD Almighty."

The fear of the LORD is a catalyst for a spiritual catharsis. The woman who fears God resists the allure of sinful desires. For while she is in the world, she does not subscribe to worldly mind-sets. As a woman of God, she "hates even the garment defiled by the flesh" (Jude 23). One way she does this is by studying and personalizing the Word of God. Such a mind-set offers rapt attention to Jesus's High Priestly prayer in John 17:17, "Sanctify [set them apart], by Your truth, Your word is truth." By this petition to the Father, Jesus was asking that His disciples distinguish themselves from the wickedness of the cosmos. For this evil system managed by Satan, shares no common values with the kingdom of Christ (John 14:30).

The Fear of the LORD Is the Key to Wisdom and Knowledge

Reverence or the fear of the LORD is an entrée to wisdom and the knowledge of God. Proverbs 9:10 instructs, "The fear of the LORD is the beginning of wisdom, and the knowledge of the Holy One is understanding." Proverbs 1:9 charges, "The fear of the LORD is the beginning of knowledge, but fools despise wisdom and instruction." Fearing God is non-negotiable if a woman is to be godly and please the LORD. Corresponding to this is Psalm 25:14, "The secret of the LORD is with them who fear Him."

The Fear of the LORD involve Reverential Worship

Ecclesiastes 5:1–3 Solomon solemnly outlines a protocol for entering the temple:

> "Walk prudently when you enter the house
> of God; and draw near to hear rather than to give
> the sacrifice of fools, for they do not know that

they do evil. Do not be rash with your mouth, and let not your heart utter anything hastily before God. For God is in heaven, and you on earth; Therefore, let your words be few. For a dream comes through much activity, a fools voice is known by his many words." More will be said about a godly woman who displays reverence in corporate worship in a later chapter."

Fleshing Out Reverence

While fleshing out reverence, three salient examples come to mind. First, Joseph. While in bondage, Joseph was entrusted with everything in his master's house except his wife. This trust was granted due to the LORD being with Joseph and blessing him (see Gen. 39:2–6). Joseph was described as an extremely handsome man who was blessed with a ripped physique. Conversely, Potiphar's wife was a Jezebel who had designs on her husband's young slave. This ancient cougar cast bedroom eyes on Joseph and attempted to seduce him. Joseph, demonstrating outsized reverence for God responded, "How can I do this great wickedness and sin against God?" (Gen. 39:9).

Job

Another Old Testament saint demonstrating the fear of God was Job. The attributes underscoring Job's reverence for God are transferable to women. Job is described as "that man was blameless and upright, one who feared God and shunned evil" (Job 1:1). Job's possessed inside-out integrity as the Hebrew word, "tom" suggests "wholeness." Negatively, he hated evil. This included cursing God or saying anything untoward against the LORD. Positively, it meant Job sincerely worshipped God by scrupulously leaving no spiritual stone unturned. sacrifice. He habitually offered sacrifices while reasoning, "It may be that my sons have sinned and cursed God in their hearts" (Job 1:5).

Anna

Anna was an aged godly widow who demonstrated outsized reverential devotion to the Lord by serving in the temple. Her godly disposition is described in Luke 2:36–38: "Now there was one, Anna, a prophetess, the daughter of Phanuel, of the tribe of Asher. She was of great age, and had lived with her husband seven years from her virginity; and this woman was a widow of about eighty-four years, who did not depart from the temple, but served God with fastings and prayers, night and day. And coming in that instant she gave thanks to the Lord, and spoke of Him to all them who looked for redemption in Jerusalem."

Anna, was a model of godly widowhood. First, she piously devoted her days to prayer and fasting at the temple. Secondly, she served as an evangelist proclaiming the eagerly anticipated arrival of the messiah. As a result, she was greatly rewarded by the Lord for her piety. Anna met the New Testament criteria for a godly widow. For Paul admonished Christian widows to champion like reverence in 1 Timothy 3:11, "Likewise, their wives must be reverent, not slanderers, temperate, faithful in all things."

Peter also endorses God-fearing conduct while writing to those under his care in 1 Peter 3:1–2 he commands, "Wives, likewise, be submissive to your own husbands, that even if some do not obey the word, they without a word may be won by the conduct of their wives, when they observe your chaste conduct accompanied by fear." The "fear" of which Peter speaks is both a reverence for the Lord and a respect for her husband. Certainly, out of reverence for her God, the Christian wife is enjoined in 1 Peter 3:15, "sanctify the Lord God in your hearts and be ready always to give an answer for the reason of the hope that is within you with meekness and fear."

Faithful in All Things

In sum, Paul says that women are to be faithful in all their responsibilities. Christian men and women cannot take a hall pass on the more difficult tasks assigned them. Rather, Paul commands women and wives to examine every area of their lives to ensure they are maintaining faithfulness. Faithfulness headed the apostolic job description (1 Cor. 4:1–2). Moreover, it is the primary condition for the reception of eternal rewards (Matt. 25:21, 23). Older Christian women are likewise expected to exude the quality of faithfulness in their life.

Purity of Speech

In recent years the dignity of godly speech has drastically waned. Words and phrases once considered taboo, are now deemed acceptable fare in everyday conversation. Profanity considered inappropriate for public consumption is no longer censored in the media. Rather it flows freely from the lips of public officials, political pundits, media darlings, even some pastors. Bitter diatribe and hateful epithets which once breached conventional decency, are now embraced as the norm. We have come a long way since Clark Gable uttered a curse word on the silver screen causing many to hastily exit golden era movie houses. Surely, Daniel Patrick Moniyhan's famous phrase, "defining deviancy downward," rings prophetic today. This is true not only in secular society, but also in the church of Jesus Christ. The morning of this writing, I sat close to two Christian men in a coffee shop. At first, I was unsure if they were Christians as they both uttered profanity. How much better would it be if our speech would be an automatic giveaway that we are Christ's disciples!

Wholesome Speech in an Unwholesome World

While the deterioration of speech in the culture should not surprise the Christ-follower, the downgrading of speech in the church should greatly disturb us. One area today where the sins of the culture have become the sins of the church is that of our communication habits. Sadly, some of the offense comes from Christian leaders. A fellow seminary alumnus of this author has been dubbed, "the cussing pastor." Another pastor admitted to his colleagues that his congregation is glad when he can get through a sermon without cussing. Jesus was unapologetic in assessing the weight of our words. He divined in Matthew 12:36, "But I say to you, that for every idle word that men shall speak, they will give an account in the day of judgment. For by your words you will be justified, and by your words you will be condemned."

James, the half-brother of Jesus, honestly assesses the human struggle with speech in James 3:2–3, "For we all stumble in many things, 'If anyone does not stumble in word, he is a perfect man, able to bridle the whole body." Godly men and women strive by God's grace to bring their speech under the control of the Holy Spirit.

Purity of speech includes speaking words of life and restraint in speaking others. Solomon famously wrote, "There is a time to keep silent and a time to speak" (Ecclesiastes 3:7). Suffice it to say, godly women know the times! Positively, they follow the directive of Colossians 4:6, "Let your speech be always with grace, seasoned with salt that you may know how you ought to answer every man." In the vein a godly woman embodies the spirit of one who speaks "fitly spoken words," that are like "apples of gold in settings of silver" (Prov. 25:11).

Godly women also heed Paul's counsel in Godly women take Paul's injunction to the Philippian church seriously, "Do all things without complaining and disputing, that you may become blameless and harmless, children of God without fault in the midst of a crooked and perverse generation among whom you shine as lights in the world" (Phil. 2:14–15). Moreover, they live with the end in view. By God's grace, they take James's words to heart, "Do not complain against each other, for the judge stands before the door" (James 5:9).

The Spiritual Displacement Principle

While a high school physics student, this writer was introduced to the displacement principle which dealt with how water is displaced by the creation of a vacuum. The Apostle Paul in his letters champions a similar principle in which sinful habits are displaced by what theologian Charles Ryrie called, "habits of holiness." Below are a few examples:

> "Therefore, putting away *lying*, 'Let each one *speak truth* with his neighbor." (Eph. 5:25)

> "Let *no corrupt word* proceed out of your mouth, *but what is good* for necessary edification, that it may impart grace to the hearers." (Eph. 4:29, italics mine)

> "Let all bitterness, wrath, anger, clamor, and *evil speaking* be put away from you, with all malice, and be kind to one another, tenderhearted, *forgiving one another*, even as God for Christ's sake forgave you." (Eph. 4:31–32, italics mine)

> "But fornication and all uncleanness or covetousness, let it *not be named* among you, as it is fitting for saints; neither filthiness nor *foolish talking*, nor *course jesting*, which are not fitting, but rather *giving of thanks*." (Eph. 5:3–4, italics mine).

Gossip

Inventor R. T. LeTourneau, has well said that a gossip is like an earthmover, "that moves a lot of dirt and moves it fast!" As Paul establishes the house order for local churches, he addresses the speech of women. He commands that widows resist the impulse to be "gossips and busybodies, saying things they ought not" (1 Tim. 5:15). Rather than trafficking in words of death, godly women follow Paul's lead in speaking words of life-the gospel. (Phil. 2:16). As noted previously a couple areas of unhealthy speech where women habitually struggle is slander and false accusation. Recently, I became acquainted with a woman on a pastoral staff of a prominent church. This woman heard secondhand allegations of a woman being physically abused by her husband. With no confirmation, she presumed guilt rather than innocence, and castigated the husband before knowing the facts. Her impulsivity was proven to be false. Such stories are legion in a culture where it is purported, "every woman has a right to be believed."

Examples of impurity among women are given in 1 Timothy 5:13, "They learn to be idle, wandering about from house to house, and not only idle but also gossips and busybodies, saying things they ought not." One of the identifying marks of contemporary Jezebels is false accusation. False accusation is the twin sister of gossip so characteristic of women who become idle busybodies. Conversely, godly women display wholesome speech patterns that are the opposite of false accusation.

Proverbs 31 one paints a portrait of the virtuous woman as a gracious woman with words of wisdom and kindness dripping from her lips like honey. "She opens her mouth with wisdom, and on her lips is the law of kindness" (Prov. 31:26). In this respect the godly women personalizes the commands concerning speech: "Let your speech always be with grace, seasoned with salt, that you may know how you ought to answer each one." Colossians 4:6. Virtuous women also understand the veracity of Proverbs 17:28, "Even a fool is counted wise when he [she] holds his peace; when he shuts his lips he is considered perceptive."

Practicing the Art of Suspended Judgment

Socrates was a man who championed moral virtue in every arena of his life including what words were launched from his lips. This famous philosopher sought to be a vanguard of wholesome speech for others as well. When someone would come to him with a complaint against another, his habit was to ask them two questions. First, he would ask, "Will what you are about to tell me help me?" Routinely the pupil would respond in the negative. Secondly, the sage philosopher would ask, "Will it help the person you are talking about?" Again, a negative response was typical. Socrates would terminate the conversation by rhetorically asking, "Then I don't need to know about this do I?"

Like Socrates, godly women cultivate the fine art of suspended judgment. In this respect the godly woman takes seriously the command of James 1:19, "let every man [woman] be swift to hear, slow to speak, slow to anger." In keeping with the context of James, a Sarah is careful about spewing malice toward both God and others. Therefore, they seek to master the art of suspended judgment before speaking. Godly women well understand the venomous poison possessed in the six-inch sliver of muscle called the tongue. Again, they internalize the devastating portrait of the tongue painted in James 3:6: "The tongue is a fire, a world of iniquity. The tongue is so set among our members that it defiles the whole body, and sets on fire the course of nature and is set on fire by Hell."

Jezebels Do the Devil's Work

As a career Navy man, I am well acquainted with the tired but true cliché, "loose lips, sink ships." Jezebels also have a habit of speaking evil of others. They do the devil's work through slander and false accusation. They are also addicted to male bashing.

Sinful words cascading from Jezebel's lips poison every facet of their existence while casting a pall on their entire life. Peter similarly informed, "He who will love life and see good days, Let him refrain his tongue from evil, And his [her] lips from speaking guile" (1 Pet. 3:10). The venomous tongue leaves a trail of bodies in its wake. Wise women of God understand the reality of Proverbs 18:21, "Death and life are in the power of the tongue; And those who love it will eat of its fruit."

By employing the law of metonymy (the part for the whole), James has Satan in mind when he references Hell. Sarah's do the Lord's work by cultivating purity of speech. She recognizes that just as Peter's rebuke of Jesus was catalyzed by Satan, all sinful speech patterns emanate from the domain of darkness.

Sarahs Speak Words of Grace and Truth

In an effort to enlist the power of God in controlling their tongues, Godly women can be heard lifting up prayers such as

"Set a guard O LORD before my mouth,
watch over the words of my lips." (Psalm 141:3)

"Let the words of my mouth and the meditation of my heart be acceptable in Your sight O
LORD my strength and my Redeemer." (Psalm
19:14)

Self-Controlled

The Greek word "egkrateian" translated, "self-control" literally means, "out from power." The believer's power to live the Christian life descends from a divine source. Peter writes in 2 Peter 1:3, "As His divine power has given us all things that pertain to life and godliness, through the knowledge of Him who calls us by His glory and virtue." Peter assures that there is no challenge to forbidding for the believer to tackle with God's power. As Peter sets the tone for this truth in 2 Peter 1:3, "According as His divine power has given us all things pertaining to life and godliness, through the knowledge of Him who called us by glory and virtue." Peters serves notice that the indwelling Spirit has supplied all of the spiritual horsepower necessary for the Christ-follower to win every spiritual battle and conquer every sin. Peter's timeless remark in the context of the Lord's deliverance of Lot, Peter timelessly remarks, "the Lord knows how to deliver the godly out of testing, [also "temptation"]" (2 Peter 2:9). Self-control is sourced in the power that God supplies through His Spirit. W. A. Criswell asserted, "We are harnessed to the greatest power in the universe."

Self-control therefore is wedded to the power supplied by God's Spirit to overcome sin. Due to the empowerment of God's Spirit, the believer possesses the capacity for self-control in every situation in which they find themselves (see Romans 8:1–6; 1 Corinthians 10:13; Galatians 5:16). Paul is especially clear in stating that the Christ-follower is provided in every temptation the option of control. After warning the Corinthian church of the sins of ancient Israel leading to the divine discipline of death he assures, "No temptation has overtaken you except that which is common to man; but God is faithful, who will not allow you to be tempted beyond what you are able, but with the temptation will also make a way of escape, that you may be able to bear it" (1 Cor. 10:13).

In every "temptation" God has equipped the Christ-follower with the power to resist the temptation by supplying a way of escape. Often this way of escape is to "flee youthful lusts," and other temptations (2 Timothy 2:22; 1 Timothy 6:11). In the context of 2 Peter 1, the word egkrateian, implies that the believer possesses the capacity to control their evil urges and resist temptations. In this respect, if a Christ-follower protests, "I have a temptation that is outside the boundaries of self-control. It is an addiction I can't control man!" they contradict the clear teaching of God's Word.

Paul similarly underscores this spiritual capacity God gives to believers in Romans 6:12–14. He enjoins, "Therefore, do not let sin reign in your mortal body, that you should obey it and its lusts. And do not present your members as instruments of unrighteousness to sin, but present yourselves to God as being alive from the dead, and your members as instruments of righteousness to God. For sin shall not have dominion over you, for you are not under the law of but under grace."

Both by issuing the command to forbid sin to have "reign in your mortal bodies," and emphatically stating "sin shall not have dominion over you," Paul is serving unequivocal notice that the believer possesses the spiritual fortitude to emerge victorious over sin. He reinforces this ability that has been granted him/her by the new birth in Romans 8:1, "Therefore, there is now therefore, no condemnation to those who are in Christ Jesus, who do not walk according to the flesh, but according to the Spirit." Zane Hodges translates, "no condemnation" as "servitude to sin." In Romans 6–8 Paul emphatically reinforces that the child of God has absolute veto power over the "sin master" to issue an emphatic "NO!" Paul's polemic in Romans 6–8 is summarized in his pithy command to the Galatians, "Walk in the Spirit and you will not fulfill the desires of the flesh" (Gal. 5:16).

Though the power to order one's life through self-control is within the grasp of every believer, the initiation of self-control is the tipping point between success and failure. My mentor Jim Andrews asserted, "Most people do not fail for lack of ability, but for lack of control."

Self-Control Relative to Alcohol

In the New Testament, self-control is often wedded to moderation in the consumption of alcohol. Years ago, I heard a fellow Naval Officer quip, "One glass of wine and my wife will tell you everything!" Self-control in the area of alcohol consumption is an obvious key to controlling one's tongue. Solomon writes, "Wine is a mocker. Strong drink is a brawler. And whoever is led astray by it is not wise" (Prov. 20:1). It is no accident that one characteristic of godly leaders is that they "do not sit long beside their wine" (1 Tim. 3:3; Tit. 1:7). Self-control fueled by God's Spirit is described by Paul as the antithesis of drunkenness. Paul charges, "And do not be drunk with wine in which is dissipation, but be filled with the Holy Spirit" (Eph. 5:18). The word for "dissipation" could be translated, "no salvation." Paul is asserting that while there is never any redemptive value to drunkenness, yielding to the Spirit's control produces a bumper crop of spiritual fruit.

Self-control intersects with every road of discipleship the Christ-follower travels down. James asserted that self-control in the area of the tongue empowers the Christ-follower to "bridle their own body" (James 3:2–3). In the area of their speech women are admonished to be self-controlled. To this end, Paul admonished Timothy for the church not to be charged with the care of younger widows. He warns in 1 Timothy 3:13, "they learn to be idle, wandering from house to house, and not only idle but also gossips and busybodies saying things they ought not." The law of physics, "nature abhors a vacuum," comes into play relative to godly speech. For if a woman is not performing good works by serving others, she will default to idleness, gossip, slander, cynicism, and other of negative speech patterns. More will be said about this throughout the book as the Jezebel largely expresses itself through improper speech.

Another area where self-control is paramount is in their sexual morality. The moral self-control of women is paramount today as pre-marital sex among Christians is pandemic. Older women are to assist younger women in understanding the error of cultural values (Rom. 12:2; 1 John 2:15–17). Moreover, it is incumbent today for older women to mentor their young counterparts on the unintended consequences of sexual promiscuity. One of those consequences, rarely mentioned is the discipline of a loving heavenly Father (Heb. 12:5–11). Godly women must lovingly yet urgently warn their little sisters that sexual sin displeases Christ is a burglar of their joy, takes a costly toll on their psyche, and negatively impacts their future marriage. Younger women are to be admonished to control their sexual impulses out of gratitude for the inexhaustible grace supplied through Jesus Christ death on Calvary's tree (John 1:14–17; Rom. 6:1–3). Like the Apostle Peter, older women must implore, "Beloved, I beg you as sojourners and pilgrims, abstain from fleshly lusts which war against the soul" (1 Pet. 2:11).

Teachers

While teaching is a gift bequeathed by Jesus and the Holy Spirit to members of the church (Eph. 4:11; Rom. 12:7), it is also the responsibility of every member of the body of Christ. For the Great Commission instructing Jesus's disciples to "teach them all to observe all things I have commanded you," applies to every child of God. While this does not assume that all women will formally teach in large groups, godly women are definitely called to teach younger women and children the Word of God. The context of teaching younger women implies that much teaching will take place in small groups or one on one.

The content of the older woman's teaching of another is to be a "teachers of good things" (Tit. 2:4). Saintly older women must be the stewards and couriers of this healthy teaching. In this respect, they must similar to the older men in the church, be "sound in faith" (Tit. 2:2). The grammar denotes, "the faith," speaking of that corpus of truth surrounding Jesus Christ that was once delivered to the saints (Jude 3). In brief, older women should possess a deep knowledge of basic Christian doctrine. They are to be well versed in their understanding of Jesus's identity, saving work, and second coming for the church, et al. They must be well acquainted with the curriculum of the gospel of Christ while harboring no scruples that He is their "Great God and Savior Jesus Christ" (Tit. 2:13).

Teaching Faithful and Able Women

It is within the realm of possibility, that Paul's charge to Timothy to teach "faithful and able men who shall be able to teach others also," includes faithful and able women (2 Tim. 2:2). If so, these faithful women are assigned the task of mentoring younger women. In addition to imparting the Word of God to younger women, the older saintly women in the church must mentor the younger women in the church. Finally, in an effort to properly mentor younger women, it must be kept in mind that older women too must be "sound in faith."

Spiritual Mentors

Topping the older women's mentorship agenda is the priority of mentoring younger Christian women. Paul writes, "that they may admonish the young women to love their husbands" (2:4). It is noteworthy that Paul exhorts Titus to instruct older women to "admonish" younger women to "love their husbands." In this regard, they are commissioned to mentor younger Christian women in loving their children and loving their husbands. The word for "love" is "phileo" meaning, "to have a fond feeling towards." Saintly older women are to teach their younger counterparts how to cultivate affection toward their husbands. The reason Paul employs the word, "phileo" instead of "agape" according to Emerson Eggerichs is that wives are innately hardwired by God to "agape" (unconditionally love) their husbands, however, "liking" (phileo), their husbands is an entirely different matter. Older women are to mentor younger women in striving to have a fond affection for their husbands. In this respect, they fulfill their calling, "with all lowliness, gentleness, with longsuffering, bearing with one another in love" (Eph. 4:2).

Obviously, in the rush and crush of life, it is challenging for a wife to have fond affection for her husband at times. Contrarily, her temptation, as a result of the curse is to rule over her husband (Gen. 3:16). Sarahs by God's grace are to have a fond affection toward their husbands. At this point it is important to note, that the Greek word phileo is used by Paul rather than agape. Since, the domain of wives is the home, it is easy for them to become territorial, cynical, and demanding in their domestic AOR (Area of Operations). This can lead to domestic conflict, such as contempt and dislike for husbands.

Jesus Method of Loving

Late Christian marriage expert, Gary Smalley, asserted that the best strategy to conquer unloving feelings towards one's spouse is to initiate intentional acts of kindness towards them. Smalley contends that such kindness fans the feelings of love. Smalley's contention is consistent with Jesus's teaching on love. Servanthood and love are wedded together by Jesus and the apostles (John 13:17; Acts 20:35; Gal. 5:13; 1 John 3:14–18). Two passages state this clearly,

> "If you know these things, blessed are you if you do them." (John 13:17)

> "It is more blessed to give than to receive." (Acts 20:35)

Whenever we honor either a person, a job, a responsibility, or command, positive feelings follow. This is most certainly true and is consistent with the flawless brand of agape love modeled by Jesus.

Washing the Saints' Feet

Prior to Jesus giving the upper room discourse, the disciples were arguing over who would be the greatest in the kingdom of heaven (Luke 22:24). Such verbal wrangling came on the heels of Christ assuring the disciples that they would be generously rewarded when He returned to establish His kingdom. In Matthew 19:28 Jesus divulged, "Assuredly, I say to you, that in the regeneration, when the Son of Man sits on the throne of His glory, you who have followed Me, will also sit on twelve thrones, judging the twelve tribes of Israel."

While drunk with their own significance, they argued over who would be the "alpha" disciple and sit on Jesus's right and left hands. While this apostolic power play did not please the Son of God, Jesus's treated the disciples with the compassion of unconditional love. After quietly slipping into slaves' clothes, He humbly began to wash the disciples' feet. John, who references himself as "The disciple whom Jesus loved," comments, "Now before the feast of the Passover, when Jesus knew His hour had come that He should depart from this world to the Father, having loved His own who were in the world, He loved them to the end."

While Jesus clearly did not feeling good about the disciples unscripted power grab He lavished agape love on them indiscriminately. This expression of agape love, founded on commitment rather than feelings is a precursor to phileo love (a fond affection).

The Danger of Resisting Sound Doctrine

When I was a teenager, I well remember hearing the tragic news of the Jonestown mass suicide. Charismatic cult leader, Jim Jones, had founded a growing cult that became known as "The Peoples' Temple." A postmortem investigation revealed that Jones's beliefs and conduct continued on a downward trajectory as time unfolded. During the investigation it was discovered that many members of Jones's heretical and immoral cult were women from Bible believing churches. Jonestown is a pungent reminder of what happens when a believer neglects sound doctrine. A thorough grasp of sound doctrine is critical when one considers that women are easily deceived by false teachers inspired by Satan (1 Tim. 2:14; 2 Cor. 11:3). Therefore, Christian women as well as men are compelled to follow the example of the apostles, "Casting down arguments and every high thing that exalts itself against the knowledge of God, bringing every thought into captivity to the obedience of Christ" (2 Cor. 10:5). False beliefs, ideologies, philosophies that do not square with biblical teaching are to be swiftly rejected out of hand. Those mired in such heresies must be hastily rescued. Jude, the half-brother of Jesus implored in Jude 23, "But others save with fear, pull them out of the fire, hating even the garment spotted by the flesh." It is the responsibility of older, godly women to pull back the curtain on such lies.

The Priority of Sound Doctrine

The priority of sound doctrine is important as many today view doctrine and biblical knowledge with a jaundiced eye. Godly women must not treat the Bible as a spiritual smorgasbord where one chooses only the palatable options. For the Bible is not a Persian bazaar of ideas to be embraced or rejected at one's own discretion. Both the hard sayings and "easy sayings," negative and positive must be embraced and taught by the godly woman. Pursuant to this, godly women must well understand that the offence of the gospel must not be removed (Gal. 5:11). They must not retreat from telling "the truth, the whole truth, and nothing but the truth, so help them God."

The above paragraph is extremely important given a fallen tendency of women to view personal sentiments as the voice of God. Both men and women are experts at rationalization. Yet when faced with a crisis, or moral or ethical dilemma, there is an innate tendency for women to default to feelings rather than truth. This leaves them vulnerable to deception (Gen. 3; 2 Cor. 11:2–3; 1 Tim. 2:14). The godly women must persist in consulting the true north compass of God's Word while encouraging younger women to do the same.

The Least of Jesus's Commandments

One component of the Great Commission in Matthew 28:18–20 is "teaching them to observe all things I have commanded you." This mandate hearkens back to what Jesus said in the Sermon on the Mount in Matthew 5:19, "Whoever therefore breaks one of the least of these commandments, and teaches men so, shall be called least in the kingdom of heaven; but whoever does and teaches them, he shall be called great in the kingdom of heaven."

In an effort for godly sisters to mentor their younger sisters in the "whole counsel of God" (Acts 20:27). In this respect, they model for these daughters in the faith the necessity of pursuing practical righteousness in every corner of their lives so they might receive those coveted words, "Well done you good and faithful servant; you were faithful over a few things, I will make you ruler over many things. Enter into the joy of your Lord" (Matt. 25:21, 23).

Profiles in Mentorship

One godly woman spoken of in the New Testament who mentored others was Priscilla. She and her husband Aquila, mentored one of the most strategic evangelists in the apostolic era, a man named Apollos. It was Apollos who Priscilla contributed to Apollos training by "explaining to him the ways of God more perfectly" (Acts 18:26).

Discreet

In contemporary culture discretion is a lost art. In a culture where immorality, sensuality, and free sexual expression are celebrated at every turn, immodesty is rarely questioned. Like the proverbial frog in the kettle, it is easy for Christian women to be seduced by such immodesty. However, the Bible links female discretion to godliness. When Paul established the "house order" of the church in 1 Timothy he instructs Christian women, "in like manner also, that the women adorn themselves in modest apparel, with propriety and moderation, not with braided hair or gold or pearls or costly clothing, but which is proper for women professing godliness with good works" (1 Tim. 2:9–10).

The Power of Discretion

One practical reason for conservative dress in the assembly of the saints is give no opportunity to the enemy to tempt men. While advising his son concerning the seductress who flatters her prey, Solomon charges, "Do not lust after her beauty in your heart, Nor, let her allure you with her eyelids" (Prov. 6:25). Men are urged to passionately ravish the beauty of their wives. Pursuant to this Solomon writes, "as a loving deer and a graceful doe, Let her breasts satisfy you at all times; and always be enraptured with her love" (Prov. 5:19). However, since men by nature are visually oriented, they are easily tempted by the immodest display of skin by their sisters in Christ. Modest dress of the Christian woman accomplishes at least four godly objectives. First, it sets the stage for corporate worship as modest female appearance is the standard set for the corporate worship of women. Secondly, it forces all who engage her to witness her intrinsic godliness, rather than her external beauty. Thirdly, it communicates to all the premium she places on the inner qualities of the heart. In this respect she aligns herself with Lady Wisdom rather than Lady Folly (see Proverbs 8). Fourthly, it conveys to others that her body is reserved solely for her husband as she forsakes all others. Fourthly, modest dress mitigates the potential for young men being tempted to lust after her body.

While a pastoral major in Bible college I was required to read the book, *Dress for Success*. At the time I considered this assignment tedious and unnecessary. Yet godly dress is a practical way for the Christian woman to communicate love to the Lord and the church. Certainly, the discretion of which Paul speaks would apply to discretion in speech as well. In the wisdom literature of the Old Testament the discreet woman is contrasted with the seductress. Lady Wisdom, personified in Proverbs 8 is contrasted with Lady Folly. For the godly Christian woman, Lady Wisdom is to be embraced while Lady Folly is to be shunned.

There is a pressing need today for discretion for both Christian men and women. How it must grieve the heart of God that pre-marital sex is socially acceptable in many Christian circles. The practice of discretion must not only concern how a woman dresses, speaks, relates to the opposite sex, but also in what mental, emotional, and visual exposure she permits herself. Abstaining from salacious romance novels or pornographic movies such as *Fifty Shades of Grey*, are a given. Moreover, the godly woman does well to abstain from literature, social media, or television, condoning immoral lifestyles.

Pure

Purity, or chastity filters through the mind before settling into our behavior. Solomon writes generically in Proverbs 23:7, "As a man thinks in his heart, so is he." The same truth applies to the Christian woman. In light of this timeless truth, the Christian woman does well to personalize Proverbs 4:23, "Keep your heart with all diligence, for out of it proceed the issues of life." The best way to fortify the mind is to control what occupies it. In this respect Paul urges the Philippian believers, "Finally, my brethren, whatever things are true, whatever things are noble, whatever things are just, whatever things are pure, whatever things are lovely, whatever things are of good report, if there is any virtue and if there is anything praiseworthy, think on these things" (Phil. 4:8). To paraphrase the well-worn cliché, "you are what you think!"

Detoxing the Mind of the Free Radicals of Sin

Purity of mind is an exercise in renewal. Paul admonished the Roman believers, "And do not be conformed to this world, but be transformed by the renewing of your mind, that you may prove what is that good, acceptable, and perfect will of God." The imperative is even stronger in the original Greek. Paul emphatically charges, "Stop being conformed to this world!" The sewage of the age has an insidious way of seeping into our souls.

As a Navy Chaplain, I will often seek to access a website necessary to complete administrative tasks. While doing so often a message will appear stating, "Access Denied" when the website is being maintained. Sarahs seek to deny access of worldly perspectives and ideas that militate against the values of Christ's kingdom.

The Beauty of Transformation

Positively, Paul enjoins the Christian woman to "be transformed by the renewing of your mind" (Rom. 12:2). The word, "transformed," is the word, "metamorphosthe," from which we derive the English word, "metamorphosis." Just as a cocoon is transformed into an opulent butterfly, so the Christian woman is to be transformed by the "renewing of their mind." Such renewal of the mind is marshalled to knowledge of God. Paul writes in Colossians 3:8–10:

> "But now you yourselves are to put off all these: anger, wrath, malice, blasphemy, filthy language out of your mouth. Do not lie to one another, since you have put off the old man with his deeds, and have put on the new man who is renewed in knowledge according to the image of Him who created him."

"Putting off" in first century culture had to do with the divesture of clothing. In that day the average person did not enjoy an extensive wardrobe hanging in their closet. Instead they would wear a suit of clothes until they were worn out and in need of replacement. These clothes were not thrown into the laundry, they were thrown away! Therefore, the first step in the metamorphosis of our mind and soul is to detox from the sinful toxins lodged in our spirits. This detoxing of the mind takes place through careful observance of God's Word. To this end Jesus prayed in His high priestly prayer, "Sanctify them through Your truth, Your Word is truth" (John 17:17). In modern parlance Jesus was praying, "Make them holy (distinct) through Bible study."

Another is that worldly debris, like a deadly virus, has infected our souls. Like those at risk of contracting a terminal virus, we spare no expense in taking every necessary precaution. For the Christian life is warfare. In this respect, Peter charged, "Abstain from fleshly lusts which wage war against the soul" (1 Pet. 2:11).

The two primary sources of this knowledge is acquired through heeding biblical teaching and knowledge. Pursuant to the latter David rhapsodized in Psalm 119:9–11: "How can a young man cleanse his way? By taking heed according to Your word. With my whole heart I have sought You; Oh, let me not wander from Your commandments! Your word have I hidden in my heart that I might not sin against You." The same is true for a young woman.

Sexual Purity

One area where the Christian wife is to be pure is in their sexual life. While this may have been obvious in generations past, it bears mentioning in today's promiscuous culture. Today the cultural bar for sexual immorality has been lowered considerably. There are a plethora of reasons for the widespread embrace of immorality of all forms in movies, media, online, and false views of God's grace in the church. Today pre-marital sex among Christian women is pandemic. Fueling this crisis of morality in the church is a breezy indifference to sexual immorality. This writer is acquainted with Christian women who casually dismiss their sexual immorality with the rationale, "I know what I am doing is wrong, but God will forgive me."

Sexual immorality is tolerated in the church to the point where believers unabashedly engaging in such wickedness are permitted to serve in leadership positions. The church in many quarters has taken a "hear no evil, see no evil approach" to judging sexually immoral and alternative lifestyles. This casual looking the other way is costing the church dearly as scores of non-believers discern little difference between the average American Christian and the rank in file non-believer. In this regard Jezebels give non-believers reason to blaspheme.

Christian women are called to rise above the rising tsunami of sexual immorality out of their love for Jesus. While God offers forgiveness for every sin, including sexual sin, mature Christian women are called to be exemplary in word and deed when it comes to controlling their passions. Paul would have older and younger ladies embrace Lady Wisdom (Prov. 8), while resisting the seductive advances of Lady Folly.

Homemakers

In today's American culture, this characteristic of the godly woman is cause for considerable cognitive dissonance-even among non-believing women. Consider the following lament from actress Joanne Woodward:

> "My career has suffered because of the children, and my children have suffered because of my career... I have been torn and have not been able to function fully in either arena. I don't know of one person who does both successfully, and I know a lot of working mothers."[x]

Certainly, being a "homemaker" may not be politically correct, yet it is biblically correct for mothers of young children. Paul's instructs Titus to admonish women to be "keepers at home." He underscores this priority again while describing the role of younger widows in 1 Timothy 5:14. He enjoins, "Therefore, I desire that the younger widows marry, bear children, manage the house..." The phrase "manage" (oikourgous), denotes the rearing of children and tending to matters in the home. She is literally a "house manager" as it relates to tending to the physical and spiritual needs of her children. Paul served notice that this is the domain in which the Christian life toils (1 Tim. 2:15). Her honorable rearing of children is a primary way in which God has ordained that she honor Him. The Lord honored Hannah's prayer for a son, her faithfulness to her vow, and her godly mothering of Samuel (1 Sam. 2:30). Certainly, there is a spiritual component to the wife's home management, namely the spiritual tutoring of her children. In this respect Paul reminded his young understudy Timothy, "When I call to remembrance the genuine faith that is in you, which first dwelt in you, that first dwelt in your grandmother Lois and your mother Eunice, and I am persuaded in you also" (2 Tim. 1:5).

It is obvious that Timothy was mentored by his Jewish mother Eunice who came to faith in Christ (Acts 16:1). Paul continues to praise these two saintly women who nurtured him since the womb, "and that from childhood, you have known the Holy Scriptures, which are able to make you wise for salvation through faith which is in Christ Jesus" (2 Tim. 3:15). As a house manager, the godly wife and mother models the fear of the Lord to her children. Solomon rhapsodizes, "Charm is deceitful, beauty is vain, but a woman who fears the LORD shall be praised" (Prov. 31:30).

Wives Outside the Home

The author's biological parents divorced when he was three. After the divorce, my mother gained primary custody of my older brother and me. My mother, who is a farmer's daughter, and the hardest working woman I have known, worked fulltime to support her two young sons. She did this until she met my legal father a couple years later. In a world where single mothers comprise a large demographic, women work outside the home out of urgent necessity. Under other circumstances, Christian mothers may work to upgrade the family's standard of living. In other instances, women working outside the home appears an economic necessity to compensate for too much month at the end of the money.

Homemakers Outside the Home?

The concept of "homemakers" is often fraught with controversy regarding whether women should be permitted to work outside the home. This phrase has been employed to support legalistic standards for the Christian woman. Yet this phrase does nothing to preclude women working outside the home. When one considers Proverbs 31, there is no prohibition made against the enterprising

Christian women engaging in commerce in the marketplace. While it is this author's view that Paul is not issuing a carte blanche mandate that women not work outside the home, he is establishing a critical domestic priority. This priority is two-fold as it encompasses the spiritual nurture of her children and care for her husband.

Some see the description as "homemakers," as a carte blanche prohibition to the married woman working outside of the home. However, there is nothing in the text hinting at such an imperative. Having said this, it must be quickly added that "homemaker," especially for the younger Christian wife is to be the priority. Certainly, a case could be made that being a "homemaker," is to be a priority, especially when children are in the home. Yet one does well to remember that when interpreting the Bible, they must be as strict as the Bible but not stricter. In this respect one must not commit the error of reading into the text what it does not say.

Proverbs 31 contends for an enterprising wife who is a mother. In Proverbs 31:13–31:

> She seeks wool and flax and willingly works with her hands. She is like the merchant ships, She brings her food from afar. She also arises while it is yet night, And provides food for her household; And a portion for her maidservants. She considers a field and buys it; from the profits she plants a vineyard. She girds herself with strength, And strengthens her arms. She perceives that her merchandise is good, And her lamp does not go out by night. She stretches out her hands to the distaff, and her hand holds the spindle. She extends her hands to the poor, Yes, she reaches out her hands to the needy. She is not afraid of snow for her household, For all her household is clothed with scarlet. She makes tapestry for herself; her clothing is fine linen and purple. Her husband is known in the gates, When he sits among the elders of the land. She makes

linen garments and sells them, And supplies sashes for the merchants. Strength and honor are her clothing; She shall rejoice in time to come. She opens her mouth with wisdom, And on her tongue is the law of kindness. And does not eat the bread of idleness. Her children rise up and call her blessed. Her husband also, and he praises her; Many daughters have done well, But you excel them all. Charm is deceitful, beauty is passing, but a woman who fears the LORD shall be praised. Give her the fruit of her hands, And let her own works praise her in the gates.

This celebrated proverb, paints a portrait of a god-fearing woman who is both a loving wife and mother, and an enterprising woman who contributes to the family income. While she makes her husband and her children her domestic priority, as the Lord leads, she pursues activities that profit both her and her family.

Good

Goodness speaks of both words and deeds. In light of the thankless task of motherhood and being a Christian wife, good acts, not unlike loving deeds, are to be performed unconditionally. Years ago, the author had the privilege of hearing Coach Herman Boone, of *Remember the Titans,* fame speak. Coach Boone who has been applauded for his work in civil rights offered some salient advice to those who weary of doing good. He asserted, "People will judge you for doing good. But don't let that stop you. Just keep on doing good!"

Paul's House Order in 1 Timothy

What good behavior characterizes a godly woman? Paul speaks of the woman's place in the church in 1 Timothy 2:9–11: "In like manner also, that the women adorn themselves in modest apparel, with propriety and moderation, not with braided hair, or plaited gold, or costly clothing, but which is proper for women professing godliness, with good works."

A mosaic of these good works is painted by the Apostle Paul in chapter 5. Paul lists the qualities possessed by a good woman while describing widows in 1 Timothy 5:10. He writes, "well reported of good works; if she has brought up children, if she has lodged strangers, if she has washed the saints' feet, if she had relieved the afflicted, if she has diligently followed every good work." Not unlike, the godly elder or deacon, the saintly widow possesses a good reputation among both believers and non-believers as she is, "well reported of good works." Essentially, the godly woman displays good works in every arena, the home, church, and outside the church. The godly woman is a mentor to her children. She meets the practical needs of the saints-the meaning of "washing the saints' feet." She shows kindness to strangers-the meaning of hospitality.

Servants

Paul's qualification for widows, "if she has washed the saints feet," recalls Jesus washing the disciples' feet in the upper room, prior to His arrest, an obvious reference to servanthood. Certainly, this is precisely what Paul had in mind in listing this qualification for a widow. When Jesus commanded His disciples to follow His lead in washing He used a word translated, "example" which means, "pattern," rather than a replica or blueprint. Far from establishing a rite for the church, Jesus was enjoining His disciples to meet one another's practical needs, just as He had met their needs by washing their feet (see 1 John 3:16–18; Acts 2:44–45). Phoebe was an excellent example of servanthood in the early church. In Romans 16:1 Paul applauds this stellar servant of God, "I commend to you Phoebe our sister, who is a servant of the church in Cenchrea, that you may receive her in the Lord in a manner worthy of the saints, and assist her in whatever business she has need of you; for indeed she has been a helper of many and of myself also."

Subsequent to commending Phoebe, Paul commends a dynamic couple who served him named Priscilla and Aquila. He writes, "Greet

Priscilla and Aquila, my fellow workers in Christ Jesus, who risked their own necks for my life, to whom not only I give thanks, but also all the churches of the Gentiles" (Rom. 16:3–4).

Aquila and Priscilla, like Paul were tentmakers by trade, who met Paul in Corinth (Acts 18:2–3). Perhaps they housed Paul while he resided in Corinth. This dynamic Christian couple, like Phoebe had a reputation for serving. They welcomed Apollos, an anointed first century evangelist, "who knew only of the baptism of John" (Acts 18:25). These precious servants of God lovingly "took him aside and explained to him the way of God more accurately" (Acts 18:26).

Beautifying the Doctrine of God

My Naval career has taken the author many venues both domestically and abroad. One common activity engaged in before a Distinguished Visitor (DV) is scheduled to arrive. During these exercises, Sailors and Marines will paint hulls, police the base grounds for trash, scrub bulkheads (walls) and perform a "round-turn" on their work spaces. We refer to this as "base beautification." Paul charged the church with a beautification project of a much higher order. He commanded Titus to "adorn the doctrine of God in all things" (Tit. 2:10). Elsewhere he commanded the church, "Therefore, whether you eat, or drink, or whatever you do, do all to the glory of God" (1 Cor. 10:31). Similarly, he wrote to the church of Colossae in Colossians 3:23–24:

> And whatever you do, do it heartily, as to the Lord and not to men, knowing that from the Lord you will receive the reward of the inheritance: for you serve the Lord Christ." Bookending this command is Colossians 3:17, "And whatever you do in word or deed, do all in the name of the Lord Jesus, giving thanks to God the Father through Him." Sandwiched between both imperatives is Colossians 3:18, "Wives, submit to your own husbands as it is fitting in the Lord.

Obedience to One's Husband

As part of the adorning process, Paul instructs Titus to exhort older Christian women to "be obedient to their husbands." While considering the responsibilities of the Christian wife, it must be remembered what was stated early in this book namely, that Eve was cursed in desiring to dominate her husband (Gen. 3:15). Therefore, it should be no great surprise that wives bristle at commands to obey and submit to their husbands. Yet the wife's obedience to their husband is always viewed as an act of higher obedience to God and should be viewed as such (Eph. 5:22–24; Col. 3:18). Therefore, wise wives resist the impulse to sport a rebellious posture toward their husband. Rather than recoiling at such a command the godly wife would do well to heed to Paul's general command, "Work out your own salvation with fear and trembling" (Phil. 2:12).

Obedience and the Imitation of Christ

Obedience can be a tough sell when the flesh is involved. It is easy to traffic in rationalizations when it comes to obeying elected officials, human laws, church leaders, parents, and even God. Since immersed in a culture that worships independence and recoils at authority, it is not surprising that obedience and submission repulse many. For many, such a command may appear sadistic if a wife judges her husband a tyrant. Yet an excellent wife recognizes her higher loyalty to the Lord over her husband. In this "submits to her husband as it is fitting in the Lord" (Col. 3:18).

The Preeminent Example of Lordship to Christ

Moreover, a godly wife recognizes that obedience to her husband imitates the example of the Lord Jesus Christ. For Jesus was inherently equal with the Father, He voluntarily submitted Himself to the will of the Father. The author of Hebrews discloses, "Jesus learned obedience by the things which He suffered" (Heb. 5:8). Additionally, Jesus states, "I do not do My own will, but the will of the Father who sent Me" (John 5:30). If the imitation of Jesus and Christ-likeness is the goal of the Christian life, than a wife's obedience to her husband is non-negotiable in areas where sin is not being requested.

The Freedom of Obedience

Obedience is at the heart and soul of discipleship. Jesus charged His disciples, "Why do you call me Lord, Lord, if you do not do the things that I ask?" (Luke 6:46). Failure to obey is to contribute to self-deception and a dying faith. The takeaway for all Christians is that they engage in the beautification of Christ's doctrine, name, and glory through offering rapt attention to all of Christ's commands. In the final analysis, such obedience should not be a burden as it yields the fruit of loving God and one's fellow man. John writes, "For this is the love of God that we keep [obey] His commandments; and His commandments are not burdensome" (1 John 5:3). Conversely, disobedience is a bitter pill leading to a rocky road existence. Solomon speaks volumes when he informs, "Good understanding gains favor, but the way of the unfaithful is hard" (Prov. 13:15).

Emerson Eggerichs, illustrates this critical component of both the husband and wife fulfilling their role toward each other by spinning a scenario of the Judgment Seat of Christ. In this scenario, the Christian wife is tempted to look at her husband, while observing all of his flaws instead of keeping her eyes on the Lord who commanded her. In response, the Lord charges, "Sarah, look at me! Don't look at Emerson, look at me!" The submission of a wife is ultimately to the Lord and not conditioned on one's husband's obedience (Eph. 5:22–24; Col. 3:18–23). Eggerichs similarly makes the point that we ultimately obey all of God's commands as an act of devotion to Him, rather than to others. These are the godly women upon God bestows immeasurable quantities of grace as they, "love our Lord Jesus Christ in sincerity" (Eph. 6:24).

Questions for Reflection

1) Betty Friedan, the mother of American feminism, was no friend of the Judeo-Christian ethic. In what ways does her portrait of womanhood differ with God's?

2) Godly older women are commanded to teach their younger sisters in Christ to "love their husbands and love their children." Whether you are an older or younger Christian wife, how have you modeled this kind of love?

3) The word Paul uses for "love," is phileo, meaning to "have a fond affection." How have you had a fond affection toward towards your husband this week?

4) Another virtue of godly women is self-control. In what aspects of your Christian life do you endeavor to exercise self-control?

5) Older women are to be like Lois, Eunice, Priscilla, and Mary, the mother of Jesus in that they understand sound doctrine. Assess on a scale of 1–7, 7 being high, and 1 being low how well you know sound doctrine.

1 2 3 4 5 6 7

6) Widows are to "wash the saints' feet," meaning serve the needs of their fellow believers. What are some of the ways you have served your brothers and sisters in Christ in the past year?

7) Godly women are to "obey their husbands." In what ways in the past month have you demonstrated this obedience to your husband?

8) In what ways do you teach younger women (perhaps your daughters), to be discreet, morally pure, and homemakers, if they are married?

ABIGAIL: A WOMAN OF GRACE AND WISDOM

"She opens her mouth with wisdom, And
on her tongue is the law of kindness."
—Proverbs 31:26

"Let your speech always be with grace, seasoned with salt,
that you may know how you ought to answer every man."
—Colossians 4:6

In contemporary jargon they would be billed as the proverbial odd couple. He was a loud ruthless drunk who cared for nothing but himself and his vast fortune. She was a gracious and godly woman who was as winsome and beautiful as she was wise. Her husband, Nabal's name meant, "fool." Contrarily, Abigail meant "a father's delight or joy." The Bible does not describe the circumstances forging this unlikely pairing. Yet it does describe Nabal as a notorious fool who was "harsh and evil in his doings" (1 Sam. 25:3). Since he was the descendant of Caleb, a faith-filled man, his deficient character could not be blamed on pedigree.

Yet Abigail was different. She was special. Unique. Godly and wise. The story of Abigail's wisdom and grace is interwoven with the life of her irascible husband. As the owner of vast flocks, he viewed people with a suspicious eye, never giving them the benefit of the doubt. Like an ancient Ebeneezer Scrooge he was always looking to protect his investments while doing the bare minimum for his subordinates. Generosity was not an entry in the dictionary of this card-carrying egomaniac.

Nabal and the Future King

If adversity introduces us to ourselves, Nabal's true character was revealed by his treatment of David, the future king of Israel. While fleeing from Saul, David and his men encountered Nabal's servants. As an elite warrior and commander of Israel's Navy SEALS, David was eminently qualified to protect Nabal's flocks. David therefore, petitioned Nabal to allow him to dwell in his land and receive food in exchange for such protection. The response he received from this churlish man was less than inviting. Nabal treated David as if a rogue outlaw. He responded through David's servants in 1 Samuel 25:10–11, "Who is David, and who is the son of Jesse? There are many servants nowadays who break away each one from his master. Shall I then take that I have killed to my shearers, and give it to men who I do not know are from?"

David's servant's took the message back to David. The future king of Israel was enraged. David was ready to go to war with Nabal and kill him. After dressing in full combat gear, he launched a special operation with four hundred of his Army Rangers to meet Nabal. One can only imagine the bloodshed that would have ensued, if God had not intervened. But He did. His intervention included Abigail, Nabal's charming wife. In the providence of God, one of the young men informed Abigail of her husband's response to David's proposal. This servant gave an accurate assessed the situation in 1 Samuel 25:14–17:

> Look, David sent messengers from the wilderness to greet our master: and he reviled them. But the men were very good to us, and we were not hurt, nor did we miss anything as long as we accompanied them, when we were in the fields. They were like a wall to us both night and day, all the time we were with them keeping the sheep. Now therefore, know and consider what we will do, for harm is determined against our master and against all his household. For he is such a scoundrel that one cannot speak to him.

Nabal's hiring David as his security force was akin to having the A-Team protecting his estate. In the words of the popular song, "Nobody does it better!" Yet Nabal evidently was not impressed with this elite fighting force as he not only took David's company for granted, but insulted them! By so doing he jeopardized the lives of his entire household as David was not in a forgiving mood. In a moment of temporary insanity, the future king of Israel's resolved to massacre all of Nabal's servants (1 Sam. 25:22). David consistently demonstrated a merciful spirit (Psalm 37:11). However, in the case of Nabal, he embraced the philosophy, "mercy is for the weak!"

Abigail had the wise judgment to believe the accurate report of her husband's servant. She quickly made preparations for a feast for David's special forces battalion: "Then Abigail made haste and took two hundred loaves of bread, two skins of wine, five sheep already dressed, five seahs of roasted grain, one hundred clusters of raisons, and two hundred cakes of figs, and loaded them on donkeys. And she said to her servants, 'Go on before me; see, I am coming after you'" (1 Sam. 25:18–19).

Abigail met David and his entourage of men as they were charging downhill. David sweated white hot anger. He was in attack mode. After seeing David, Abigail responded quickly. The story continues, "Now when Abigail saw David she dismounted quickly from the donkey, fell on her face before David, and bowed down to the ground, so she fell at his feet and said: 'On me, my lord, on me let this iniquity be! And please let your maidservant speak in your ears, and hear the words of your maidservant. Please, let my lord regard this scoundrel Nabal. For as his name is, is so is he. Nabal is his name, and folly is with him! But I, your maidservant, did not see the young men of my lord whom you sent. Now therefore, my lord, as the LORD lives and as my soul lives, since the LORD has held you back from coming to bloodshed and from avenging yourself with your own hand, now then, let your enemies and those who seek harm for my lord be as Nabal. And now this present with your maidservant has brought to my lord, let it be given to the young men who follow my lord. Please forgive the trespasses of your maidservant. For the LORD will certainly make for my lord an enduring house, because my lord fights the battles of the LORD, and evil is not found in you throughout your days. Yet a man has risen to pursue you and seek your life, but the life of my lord shall be bound in the bundle of the living with the LORD your God; and the lives of your enemies He shall sling out, as from the pocket of a sling. And it shall come to pass, when the LORD has done for my lord according to all the good He has spoken concerning you, and has appointed you ruler over Israel, that this will be no grief to you, nor offense of heart to my lord, that you have shed blood without cause, or that my lord has avenged himself. But when the LORD has dealt well with my lord, remember your maidservant" (1 Sam. 25:23–31).

David took this unplanned rendezvous as intervention from a good and providential God. He exults in 1 Sam. 25:32–34: "Blessed is the LORD God of Israel, who sent you this day to meet me! And blessed is your advice and blessed are you, because you have kept me this day from avenging myself with my own hand. For indeed as the LORD God of Israel lives, who has kept me back from hurting you, unless you had hurried and come to meet us; surely by morning light no males would have been left to Nabal!"

The Power of a Gracious Woman

Armed with a unique blend of beauty, wisdom, grace, and godliness, Abigail dissuaded David from his mission objective of massacring every male servant in Nabal's household. David's actions followed his words as he accepted Abigail's lavish feast while reassuring her, "Go up in peace to your house. See I have heeded your voice and respected your person" (1 Sam. 25:35). Abigail through her words and actions was he polar opposite of evil queen Jezebel.

Abigail further demonstrated wisdom in refraining from telling Nabal about his gift of food and gracious encounter with David until the morning. After Nabal was no longer drunk but suffering from a heart attack, he reacted to the news not with violence, but a hangover. The LORD claimed his life ten days later.

Abigail Possessed an Unqualified Trust in Her God

In her encounter with David, Abigail invokes the name of the LORD (Yahweh), seven times. These seven uses of God's name speaks to her unqualified trust in God. "As the LORD lives and as your soul lives, as the LORD has held you back from coming to bloodshed and from avenging yourself with your own hand" (25:26). Abigail believed that the LORD was going to providentially prevent David from attacking her husband and the members of their household. Surely Abigail is one of the mighty women of which Peter speaks! (1 Pet. 3:5). While Abigail was a woman who implicitly trusted her God, she did not rest on her laurels waiting for God to act. To cite British theologian J. I. Packer, she didn't "let go and let God," but "trusted God and got going!"

Abigails Are Proactive Rather Than Reactive

While the daughters of Eve in general and Jezebels in particular, are known for ungodly reactivity, Abigail was a model of godly proactivity. She was an Old Testament saint who embodied Paul's command in Philippians 2:12, "work out your own salvation with fear and trembling, for it is God who is at work in you both to will and do of His good pleasure" (Phil. 2:12–13). She was typical of the great saints of history prophesied of by Daniel, "the people who know their God will be strong and carry out great exploits" (Dan. 11:32). This faith-filled woman believed that God had an incredible plan for this future king and it didn't include irrationally slaughtering her husband's household. Whether Abigail had a premonition that David would one day be her husband is uncertain. What is clear is that Abigail had the best interest of everyone affected by the crisis, including her imprudent husband Nabal. Either through divine revelation or knowledge of David's anointing, Abigail's understanding that David would be the future king of Israel is evident from 1 Samuel 25:28, "For the LORD will certainly make for my lord an enduring house, because my lord fights the battles of the LORD." Abigail knew that God had a legacy planned for David that is both unique and eternal! Her prophecy was reiterated in the Davidic covenant of 2 Samuel 7:12–16. The LORD declares in verses 15–16, "But My mercy shall not depart from him, as I took from Saul, whom I removed before you. And your house and your kingdom shall be established forever before you. Your throne shall be established forever."

Abigail also correctly identifies David as "a man after God's own heart," who "fights the battles of the LORD." This phrase is recalls David's faith-filled declaration of dependence on God before he slew Goliath: "Then all the assembly shall know that the LORD does not save with sword and spear; for the battle is the LORD's, and He will give you into our hands (1 Sam. 17:47). Abigail and David were kindred spirits when it came to depending on the LORD. They both knew the secret of their success and the source of their strength!

Abigail understands that Saul is pursuing David with the intention of killing him. She encourages David by assuring him that Saul's efforts will ultimately be thwarted by the Almighty God. She declares, "Yet a man has risen to pursue you and seek your life, but the life of my lord shall be bound in the bundle of the living with the LORD your God," 25:29. Abigail's words demonstrate her unrelenting trust in her God. She never ceases to see the LORD providentially working behind the scenes of life while orchestrating His will for His people. In this respect, she perceived that the LORD's hand of goodness was upon David at every turn (See Ezra 8:18). In the words of Proverbs 3:6, "in all [her] ways she acknowledges Him." As a woman who possesses unqualified trust in her God, she habitually acknowledges His sovereign intervention at every turn of her existence.

Abigail knew instinctively that God would honor His word to David. God had revealed to her the inviolable faithfulness of their covenant keeping God, as extolled in Psalm 89:34–36, "My covenant I will not break, nor alter the thing that is gone forth out of my lips. Once I have sworn by my holiness, I will not lie to David. His seed shall endure forever, And his throne as the sun before Me."

Abigail knew that God's covenant with David was failsafe as it depended on Him and not David. She believed in a God who did not lie but who batted a thousand in keeping His oaths and covenants.

As her speech unfolds Abigail gives further evidence of her faith in the promises of God. "And it shall come to pass, when the LORD has done for my lord according to all the good that He has spoken concerning you, and has appointed you ruler over Israel," 25:30.

Abigail was evidently privy to the fact David had been anointed to be Saul's successor. Whether she received this understanding from the LORD or common knowledge, we are not told. In any case, her words demonstrate faith that God will eventually bring to fruition His plan to make David king. "But when the LORD has dealt well with my lord, then remember your maidservant," 25:31. Instead of leaving her future, and that of Nabal's household to chance, she pleads with David to shower his mercy and grace upon her after the Lord exalts him. After showering David with praise rooted in truth rather than flattery, Abigail appeals to David to treat her with merciful kindness. As a woman of God, she exemplified the spirit of Solomon's admonition, "Trust in the LORD with all of your heart and lean not unto your own understanding. But in all your ways acknowledge Him and He will direct your paths" (Proverbs 3:5–6). Embittered Jezebel's do not trust in themselves do not see Him working behind the scenes of every trauma and trial of faith.

Abigail Knew How to Respond to an Intemperate Man

Abigail had been married to an intemperate man for several years. Therefore, she was well practiced in the fine art of responding to one. She knew how to treat a foolish, self-will man energized by the flesh. A modern psychologist might have diagnosed Nabal as narcissistic socio-path, with borderline personality disorder. God called him a fool. Though spiritually, David was the polar opposite of Nabal, it cannot be denied he was poised to act foolishly on the day Abigail met him. For on the day he met Abigail, he was not having a good day. Up until the moment he rendezvoused with her, he was playing the part of the fool. Undoubtedly, Abigail's experience with Nabal prepared her to address David's need for unconditional respect and encouragement. She knew how to address a man who was deeply offended by another or wounded by his past.

Showing Grace to a Man Wounded by His Past

David had a childhood in which he thought his name was "Shut up!" until he was ten years old. Since he was the youngest son, his older brothers treated him like the runt of the family. He was the Rodney Dangerfield of his own family, "he didn't get any respect." One evidence of this is that David was not even summoned be anointed king until Samuel asked for him. After he was anointed king, they were insanely jealous, judging his motives for visiting them on the battlefield. Yet in spite of David's open wounds and scars, he was a man who deeply loved God. Abigail was to be his completer. As a "holy woman of God," she purposed to show compassion to David and all involved in this volatile situation. She did so by clothing herself with the dress of humble submission, much like Sarah had done centuries earlier.

When she saw David, she dismounted immediately and fell on her face before him. Eight times she referenced him as "my lord." In her appeal to David to spare her husband's household, she referenced herself as "my maidservant," six times.

Jezebel's might have gotten in David's face, calling him a rogue fugitive. They would have made idle threats, reminding him that he was merely a poor shepherd boy while she was a wealthy and powerful queen. Though she did an end run around her husband Nabal to appeal to the better angels of David's nature, she neither disobeyed nor disrespected him referring to him as "my lord," eight times. This was not mere pandering or flattery. For David was assigned by God the moniker, "a man after God's own heart." Moreover, he was anointed at God's behest to be the next king in Israel. Abigail's words cannot be considered trafficking in manipulation. Rather this unique woman of God was a rare blend of truth and courage. She could have permitted her fears to overwhelm her and insulted David for being a renegade. A wanted man. A fugitive from the king and reality. Additionally, she might have claimed her status as the wife of a wealthy landowner. Following this scenario, she might have issued veiled threats to David of men she knew who would declare war on David if he failed to retreat. She did none of these things. Her spiritual intuition was off the meter. Instead of throwing David under the bus, her appeal to him was laced with godly, unconditional respect. Even before David took Abigail to be his wife, she demonstrated the spiritual graces of a godly wife. Though David was outraged at Nabal and foolishly resolved to massacre his nemesis' household in a fit of rage, Abigail took measures to ameliorate his anger.

Abigail Fueled Her Faith by Performing Good Works

James, the half-brother of Christ spoke of the dynamic spiritual relationship between faith and works. While writing to believers, he contends that failure to add good works to one's faith will result in a moribund (dying) faith. A faith that refuses to work will degenerate into a convalescent faith on life support. Abigail, like Abraham and Rehab were "justified before men," respectively by performing good works of obeying God and meeting the practical needs of strangers. While they were already believers through faith in the LORD, they built an unfading legacy by their good works.

Abigail, like all of God's people, strengthen the sinews of their relationship with God by initiating good works towards others. As such she is one of the premier models of godly women who perform good works in the Bible. In the words of the Apostle Paul, she was "well reported for good works" (1 Tim. 5:10). By practicing good works, Abigail resembled Rehab. Her good works constituted showing hospitality to David and his men. By relieving the affliction of David and his men with an abundance of nutrition and comfort food, Abigail became a practitioner of pure religion (James 1:26–28). God has charted out a path of good works that He intends all of His children follow (Eph. 2:10). Abigail aggressively pursued this path. For this she would be greatly rewarded. Regarding the brand of hospitality demonstrated by Abigail Jesus assured, "He who receives a prophet in the name of a prophet shall receive a prophet's reward. And he who receives a righteous man in the name of a righteous man shall receive a righteous man's reward. And whoever gives to one of these little ones a cup of cold water in the name of a disciple, assuredly, I say to you, he shall by no means lose his reward" (Matt. 10:41–42).

The good works Abigail performed would nurture a healthy faith reducing the risk of spiritual atrophy. Similar to Abraham, "faith was working together with his (her in Abigail's case), and by works faith was made perfect" (James 2:22). Abigail forged a mature and resilient faith on the anvil of good works.

Abigail Loved People

Abigail plead with David to not only spare her life but that of all the servants and her obstreperous husband! Arguably, Abigail was putting her life at risk by going to meet David. Yet she like Esther boasted an attitude, "If I perish, I perish!" Like an intrepid warrior, she was willing to put her life on the line, for members of her household. It is noteworthy that she was not risking her life for children, but her servants and an emotionally abusive husband, who was like an albatross around her neck. In this respect one is reminded of John 15:13, "Greater love has no man than this that a man lay down his life for his friends."

Abigail Respected God's Plan

Had Abigail been a Jezebel she would have taken self-preservation measures, and forgotten about her obstreperous husband and servants. She might have also appealed to Nabal's pedigree. For Abigail's husband was a descendant of Caleb, a man of great faith, who along with Joshua, was one of two spies whom God permitting him to enter the promise land and inherit a mountain (Numbers 14; Josh. 14:12–15). Caleb, due to his unshakeable faith in God and courage was a proverbial legend in Israel's storied history. Because of her husband's esteemed pedigree, she might have sported an entitlement posture.

Yet rather than considering herself entitled, Abigail thought of herself as a called woman. Rather than being frantically self-ambitious and driven, she saw herself as merely as a servant at God's divine disposal. In leadership circles, she would be termed a "steward" leader rather than an "owner" leader. Intuitively, she knew that the LORD was with David, and was going to make him king in Israel. In John the Baptizer fashion, her actions said something to the effect, "He must increase, but I must decrease." Abigail not only embraced, but rejoiced in the fact that God was going to make of David's kingdom a lasting legacy. In the words of the Apostle Paul, Abigail, "rejoicing with those who rejoiced and wept with those who wept" (Rom. 12:15).

Abigail Possessed Outsized Powers of Feminine Persuasion

Proverbs 8 personifies wisdom in the form of an elegant lady. Ronald Allen references her as "Lady Wisdom" who cries out to young men in the street to embrace her while forsaking Lady Folly. Abigail, far more than a metaphor, was a flesh and blood template of Lady Wisdom. She was beautiful, gracious, winsome, articulate, God-centered and persuasive. Not unlike Esther, the future queen of Persia, and Ruth, the gracious daughter-in-law of Naomi, God had equipped Abigail with many qualities befitting royalty. She employed her God-given powers of wisdom to divert him off the wrong path and keep him on the straight and narrow. Given that God has decreed monogamy rather than bigamy or polygamy, some have contended that Abigail was the woman God had sovereignly prepared for David following the death of Nabal. Though her marriage to Nabal might be considered an unfortunate if not tragic pairing, God used it spare many of his people from death.

Abigail Demonstrated Extravagant Hospitality

Hospitality is something that God expected from His chosen people, Israel. The LORD enjoined, "You shall neither mistreat a stranger nor oppress him, for you were strangers in the land of Egypt" (Ex. 22:21). Abigail, laboring under great duress, was a model of hospitality. Her hospitable spirit is well illustrated by her encounter with David. The cliché, invoked often during church potlucks and holiday meals, "we had enough food to feed an army," was literally true of Abigail! She went the second mile couriering enough food to David to feed four hundred famished soldiers. The feast Abigail provided would serve the dual purpose of boosting unit morale. The word in David's battalion was that Lady Abigail is as kind as she is beautiful!

Abigail's hospitable spirit was akin to that of Rehab, the prostitute who hid two Hebrew spies in the city of Jericho. Rehab's story is described in James 2:25, "Likewise, was not Rehab he harlot also justified by works when she received the messengers and sent them out another way?" The word translated "received," is the word, "welcomed" and speaks to the hospitality James enjoins to his readers. The Greek word for hospitality means, "to be kind to strangers." Rehab is commended a second time in the New Testament for her hospitality in Hebrews 11:31, "By faith the harlot Rehab did not perish with those who did not believe, when she received the spies with peace."

Hospitality is a moral grace commanded in Hebrews 13:2, "Do not forget to entertain strangers, for by so doing some have unwittingly entertained strangers."

More Than a Trophy Wife

It is obvious from the narrative described in this chapter that Abigail was a woman of grace, beauty, and virtue. Undoubtedly God used these qualities to persuade David as both a man of God and a man. As a man after God's own heart, David had to be impressed with attentiveness to God's presence, plan, and providence. Unlike Jezebel and another one of David's wives, Michal, Abigail concerned herself with the glory of God rather than personal gratification. She is described as one of the most beautiful and winsome women in ancient history, though married to a fool. Abigail was married to a man named Nabal, meaning "fool" during the reign of king Saul. The contrast between this odd couple could not have been more stark. While Abigail was as beautiful as she was wise, Nabal was a ruthless and drunken fool. Abigail was much more than a trophy wife, who solely offered her rich husband the social status of aesthetic beauty. Abigail's wisdom and grace complemented her loveliness. As a virtuous woman, Abigail, "opened her mouth with wisdom, and on her lips was the law of kindness" (Prov. 31:26).

Questions for Reflection

1) Abigail was truly a woman of beauty and grace who exhibited the qualities of a godly woman. One of those qualities was unqualified trust in her God. What strategies have you implemented in your personal walk with God to exhibit such qualities?

2) Abigail was the wife of a wealthy businessman who boasted a host of impressive credentials. Beauty, intelligence, social skills were among her attributes. In spite of her impressive array of assets, perhaps her most impressive was her deep dependence on the LORD and intimate knowledge of Him. Abigail knew her God! On a scale of 1–7 where do you rate on the knowing God scale?

1 2 3 4 5 6 7

3) Abigail was a woman of incredible faith who acknowledged God in all her ways. Rate the quality of your faith in God on a scale of 1–7.

1 2 3 4 5 6 7

4) Many people when they are under duress will think mainly of themselves. Abigail was deeply concerned with her husband's household in addition to her intemperate husband. As a result, she courageously acted on behalf of them. Rate your capacity for acting on behalf of others when under duress.

1 2 3 4 5 6 7

5) Abigail embodied the spirit of the virtuous woman in Proverbs 31:26 in that she was a woman of grace and kindness. What measures do you intentionally demonstrate grace and kindness in your life?

SARAH: A WOMAN OF QUIET SUBMISSION

G. K. Chesterton defined a paradox as a truth standing on its head screaming for attention. A paradox is counter-intuitive and unconventional as at first blush, as it makes little or no sense. It is often iconoclastic as it is disseminated by mavericks who buck the tide of popular culture. Jesus was an iconoclast who trafficked in paradoxes. Below is a compendium of paradoxes cascading from the lips of the Son of God.

"Blessed are the poor in spirit, for theirs is the kingdom of heaven." (Matthew 5:3)

"Blessed are those who mourn for they shall be comforted" (Matthew 5:4)

"Blessed are the meek for they shall inherit the earth." (Matthew 5:5)

"Blessed are those who hunger and thirst for righteousness for they shall be filled." (Matthew 5:6)

"Blessed are the merciful, For they shall obtain mercy." (Matthew 5:7)

"Blessed are those who are persecuted for righteousness' sake, For theirs is the kingdom of heaven." (Matthew 5:10)

Another paradox bearing resemblance with Jesus's beatitudes could be stated, "Blessed are the submissive for they shall get what they want."

The Paradox of Loving/Respecting When You Would Rather Not

If only life was void of conundrums and was easy. Life would be easier if love were conditional rather than unconditional. Life would be simpler if respect was always earned. If we could only love our friends and not our enemies. Oh for a life without paradoxes! Yet this is neither the kind of world God has called us to live in, nor the kind of life we are called to live. Jesus spoke of this dilemma in His most famous sermon.

Jesus taught His disciples in the Sermon on the Mount, "You have heard that it was said, 'You shall love your neighbor and hate your enemy.' But I say to you, love your enemies, bless those who curse you, do good to those who hate you, and pray for those who despitefully use you and persecute you."

Such a commandment must have been a bombshell to those who heard Jesus as they had been subjected to rabbinical schools of thought that our love should be conditional. Jesus then proceeds to offer a rationale for such indiscriminate love in 4:45–48:

> that you may be the sons of your Father in heaven; for He makes the sun to rise on the evil and the good and sends rain on the just and the unjust. For if you love those who love you, what reward have you? Do not even the tax collectors do the same? And if you greet your brethren only, what do you more than others? Do not even the tax collectors do so? Therefore, you shall be perfect, just as your Father in heaven is perfect.

The rationale for loving our enemies makes sense in context. The Lord is speaking to His disciples on the Sermon on the Mount. The word, "disciple" is the Greek word "mathetes," from which we derive our English word, "mathematics." A disciple is a "learner, student, pupil." The etymology of mathetes is rooted in the pedagogical training of rabbis in which rabbinical students mimic their rabbis every movement. The rabbinical students would follow their rabbi on the road, into the restroom, would mimic their mannerisms, would repeat their mantras, teachings, and adopt their moral and ethical instruction. Imitation was the sincerest form of flattery to the ancient rabbinical student. So much so one would know which rabbi, a disciple followed by observing the student's behavior.

As the Son of God, and divine rabbi, Jesus imparts kingdom values that transcend both the laws of man and the leading rabbinical schools of His day. As such, Jesus enjoins His disciples to not only mimic His behavior, but also the character of their Father in heaven. What is the Father's mode of operation? It is to show compassion on both the just and the unjust, the evil and the good.

Mimicking Jesus's Response to Sufferings

In Matthew 5:11 He admonished His disciples, "Blessed are you when they revile and persecute you, and say all kinds of things against you falsely for My name's sake. Rejoice and be exceedingly glad, for great is your reward in heaven, for so persecuted they the prophets who were before you." Jesus, like does not ask anything of His disciples that He is not willing to do. This is clearly illustrated as Jesus gives His final marching orders to His disciples in John 15. He informs in John 15:18–20:

> If the world hates you, you know that it hated Me before it hated you. If you were of the world, the world would love its own. Yet, because you are not of this world, but I chose you out of the world, therefore, the world hates you. Remember the word I said to you, 'A servant is not greater than his master.' If they persecuted Me, they will also persecute you. If they kept My word they will keep yours also.

In 1 Peter 3, one of Jesus's closest disciples urges Christian wives to follow Jesus's example in a way they would rather not.

A Modern-Day Sarah

While a civilian pastor several years ago, it was privileged to shepherd a delightful Christian family. Not only was the husband a man of God who led his family in the word, but his wife and children as well. In a conversation with the wife, she intimated to me a difficult season she had earlier with her husband. This good willed Christian woman, exhorted her husband from the Bible, nagged him, complained to others about his failure to rise to his high calling as a godly husband, and of course prayed for him. This good wife was at her wits end. None of these courses of action seemed to rectify the problem. Then she informed me that one day, the Lord impressed on her spirit that she had failed to do the one thing that the Bible prescribes, namely, practice godly submission. She promptly corrected this omission, by patiently loving and praying for her husband. Soon she began to notice changes in her husband. She joyfully reported to me that the Lord began to work in her husband's heart, transforming him into the man of God he is today. May her tribe increase!

This precious sister's marriage was transformed when she began to implement biblical principles for dealing with a rebellious husband. Her story reminds me of the words of the celebrated British statesman, G. K. Chesterton, "The Christian life has not been tried and found wanting. It has been found difficult and hardly tried." In effect, she was a modern day Sarah.

She was among the most extraordinary women in history. Sarah, the wife of Abraham, was chosen to be the matriarch of God's chosen people, Israel. Ironically, she was infertile until her twilight years. Miraculously, the Lord opened her womb when she was in her early nineties. Prior to this Sarah demonstrated moments of extraordinary faith and obedience. To be sure not all of the episodes of this daughter of Eve were shining moments. For instance, on one occasion she advised her husband Abraham to impregnate her handmaid, so that they may have a son. History continues to bear the scars of this carnal act, borne of the flesh. On another occasion she laughed when the angel informed her husband that she would bring a son into the world the following year. In spite of these lapses of faith during arduous circumstances, Sarah is heralded as a colossal paragon of faith and virtue. Peter writes of her, "For in this manner, in former times, the holy women of God who trusted in God also adorned themselves, being submissive to their own husbands, as Sarah obeyed Abraham, calling him lord, who daughters you are if you do good and are not afraid with any terror." (1 Peter 3:6).

The Princess of Egypt?

Early in story of Abraham and Sarah, the future patriarch of Israel traveled to Egypt. The occasion of his visit was a famine that had afflicted the land. While approaching Egypt's border, he turned to Sarah and made a strange request of the future matriarch of Israel. The request is recorded in Genesis 12:11–13, "Indeed, I know that you are a woman of beautiful countenance. Therefore, it will happen when the Egyptians see you, that they will say, 'This is his wife.' And they will kill me, but let you live. Please say that you are my sister, that it may be well with me for your sake, and that I may live because of you."

Sarah's stunning beauty was of grave concern to Abraham since he knew Egyptian monarchs collected beautiful women like tourists collect travel mugs. Piquing his phobia was the disturbing disregard monarchs exhibited for human life. The future patriarch of the children of Israel reasoned that Pharaoh upon witnessing his wife's beauty would order his death without batting an eyelash. Contrary to the better judgment of faith, Abraham implemented a ploy to prevent this violent scenario from unfolding. Though Abraham is championed as a paragon of faith in the Bible, he suffered bouts of fear and self-reliance.

The narrative continues in verse 14, "So it was when Abraham came into Egypt, that the Egyptians saw the woman and she was very beautiful. The princes of Pharaoh also saw her and commanded her to Pharaoh."

The scouting reports Abraham read on Pharaoh were spot-on accurate. True to form, Pharaoh at the behest of his princes took the patriarch's lovely bride into his harem. As repayment to Abraham, Pharaoh showered him with gifts. In Genesis 12:16 we read, "He [Pharaoh] "treated Abraham well for her [Sarah's] sake. He had sheep, oxen, male donkeys, male and female servants, female donkeys and camels" (Gen. 12:16). Yet Abraham's lapse of faith failed to account for divine intervention. The story continues, "But the LORD plagued Pharaoh and his house with great plagues because of Sarai, Abram's wife. And Pharaoh called Abraham and said, 'What is this you have done to me? Why did you not tell me that she was your wife? Why did you say, 'She is my sister?' I might have taken her as my wife. Now therefore, here is your wife; take her and go your way.' So Pharaoh commanded his men concerning him; and they sent him away, with his wife and all that he had" (Gen. 12:17–20).

Abraham departed Egypt with egg on his face. He was rebuked by a pagan Pharaoh for failing to trust in his God! This reputed man of faith perhaps learned from this and other adversities that God has options of which he had never dreamed, therefore, He merits our implicit trust. Such was the lesson he had learned well by the time God tested the father of Israel with offering his son Issac as a burnt offering (Gen. 22). For by that time Abraham trusted God to intervene and resurrect the ashes of his son if necessary (Heb. 11:17–19).

A Case of Disrespect

As a pastoral major in Bible College, I was required to complete a pastoral internship at a local church. I chose to intern under a pastor who was a gifted preacher, Bible teacher, and counselor. This pastor was well educated, possessing the mental acumen and communication skills to make complex truths plain. He was eminently qualified to successfully lead a church. He was evangelistically passionate, pastoral, and diligent, everything one would want in a pastor.

His wife, similar to her husband was an urbane and articulate woman. In many ways she played perfectly the role of the dutiful pastor's wife. Except for one glaring exception. On more than one occasion I noticed her personal vitriol toward her husband spill over into the public domain. In one instance I recall her angrily labeling him an idiot in front of the singles group. Her insolent diatribe left me to wonder if she berated her husband this way in public, how she treated him in private? Eventually, this gifted, effective servant of God divorced his wife and left the ministry. This pastor's experience recalls the immortal words of John Greenleaf Whittier, "Saddest words of tongue or pen, what might have been!" This woman bore some of the symptoms of the Jezebel Syndrome as she demeaned her husband with a flood of destructive criticism.

The Difference Respect Makes

Emerson Eggerichs and his wife Sarah have made a tremendous impact on marriages since launching, "Love & Respect Ministries." Dr. Eggerichs through his writings and teaching asserts, "Men need respect like they need air to breathe, and women likewise need love like they need air to breathe." Emerson is quick to note, that both love and respect in the marital relationship is to be unconditional.

While unconditional respect may seem counter-intuitive to many as our culture markets the mantra, "respect is earned." Yet respect, like love and forgiveness are unconditional. If respect for the man is not unconditional in the daily rounds of married life, Eggerichs contends that the couple will spin on what he calls "the crazy cycle." The crazy cycle underscores the well worn adage of "doing the same thing over and over again, while expecting a different result." In this environment, Emerson explains, "while the topics change the major issues remain the same." The prosaic reality is that "the issue is not the issue as the issue in marital conflict, the issue is love and respect."

Dr. John Gottman, a clinical psychologist, has arrived at the same conclusion as Eggerichs. Gottman in his clinical practice has observed over two thousand couples interact. By observing them interface for fifteen minutes, he can predict within 91 percent accuracy whether the couples will stay married or file for divorce. He asserts that the salient factors predicting marital success or failure are "love and respect."

Respect: Every Husband's Love Language

Gary Chapman's bestselling book, *The Five Love Languages*, contends that every person possesses love languages that make them feel loved. This author would like to submit that there is a universal love language for men, namely respect. There is a plethora of recent research to underscore this claim. To be sure, there is a distinction that is critical to one's understanding of respect. Imagine a scenario in which a male athlete has a bitter rival for whom no love is lost. Due to past competitions, gamesmanship, trash talking, and perceived cheating, the feeling is mutual. Further envision a sports announcer candidly asks this young athlete an intensely personal question. He probes, "If you had a choice between having your competitor either love or respect you, which would you choose?" Given the nature of men, the choice would be obvious. A man instinctively welcomes the respect of anyone including that of his bitter rivals. Similarly, we don't ask questions like, "Do you love your boss?" Yet a man might assert, "My respect for my boss is so immense, I would follow him anywhere!"

The distinction is also illustrated by a woman saying to her husband, "Hunny, I love you but I just don't respect you." If a wife said such a thing to her husband his spirit would immediately deflate. If she said that to her boyfriend, he may never see her again. Shaunti Feldhahn, also conducted a survey of whether men desire either love or respect more. In her survey she posed the question, "Would you rather be alone and unloved in the world, or loved and disrespected?" Approximately 70 percent of the men she interviewed responded that they would rather be alone and unloved in the world. There is something about the male psyche that repels disrespect.

Sarah: A Biblical Model of Godly Respect

Though God's faithfulness is featured prominently in the narrative, a subtheme is Sarah's heroic quiet faith and godliness. In 1 Peter 3:1–6 we read:

> Wives be submissive to your own husbands, that even if some do not obey the word, may be won by the conduct of their wives, when they observe your chaste conduct accompanied by fear. Do not let your adornment be merely outward-arranging the hair; wearing gold, or putting on of apparel-rather let it be the hidden person of the heart, with the incorruptible beauty of a gentle and quiet spirit, which is very precious in the sight of God. For in this manner, in former times, the holy women of God also adorned themselves, being submissive to their own husbands, as Sarah obeyed Abraham, calling him lord whose daughters you are if you do good and are not afraid with any terror.

While examining this text, the overriding question implied in 1 Peter could be stated, "how does a Christ-follower live in the midst of a world hostile to Christ and those who are His?" The theme could be stated, "Standing strong in the grace of God in the midst of a hostile, godless, and immoral world." Throughout Peter's letter this theme resembles a beautiful mosaic painted with the opulent colors of grace, humility, beautiful deeds, holiness, meekness, and godly submission. All of these moral graces are encapsulated in Peter's injunction in 2:12, "having your conduct honorable among the Gentiles, that when they speak against you as evildoers, they may by your good works which they observe, glorify God in the day of visitation." Paul's statement to the Corinthians agrees with Peter's admonition, "For we are to God the fragrance of Christ, both to those who are being saved and among those who are perishing" (2 Cor. 2:15).

Submission in the Face of Disobedience

Peter generally addresses wives of both non-believing and believing husbands. Peter's mindfulness of both categories is evidenced by the phrase, "even if some do not obey the word" (3:1), implying that the principle of godly submission applies in either case. This is a very relevant point, as some biblical commentators apply Peter's instruction solely to wives with disobedient husbands. While, the context has the wives of "disobedient" husbands in view, women of believing husbands are not excluded from these divine directives. Consistent with the overall theme of his letter, Peter answers the question, "What is the proper godly response to my disobedient husband?"

The Spiritual Discipline of Submission

Peter cuts to the chase when addressing this question in 3:1, "Wives, likewise, be submissive to your husbands, that even if some do not obey the word, they may without a word be won by the conduct of their wives."

The word employed for submission is "hupotasso." It is a military term that means "to arrange in order under." Wives are to arrange themselves under their husband's authority when it is convenient for them to do so, and when it is inconvenient, when they obey or disobey. In every situation except one, they are to quietly submit to their husbands.

What God Thinks of Submission

Suffice it to say, submission is a wildly unpopular topic today causing many to convulse in near apoplectic seizures. Yet it is incumbent upon the perceptive Christ-follower to inquire what God thinks of submission. Below is a brief compendium of verses in which submission is commanded or mentioned.

"Therefore, submit to God. Resist the Devil and he will flee from you." (James 4:7)

"Therefore, *submit* yourselves to every ordinance of man for the Lord's sake, whether to the king as supreme, or to governors, as those who are sent by him for the punishment of evildoers and the praise of those who do good. For this is the will of God, that by doing good you may put to silence the ignorance of foolish men." (1 Peter 2:13–15)

"Let every soul be *subject* to the governing authorities. For there is no authority except from God, and the authorities that exist are appointed by God." (Romans 13:1)

"*Obey* those who have the rule over you, and be *submissive*, for they watch for your souls, as those who must give an account. Let them do it with joy and not with grief, for that would be unprofitable for you." (Hebrews 13:17)

"Remind them to be *subject* to rulers and authorities, to obey, to be ready for every good work." (Titus 3:1)

"Wives, likewise, be *submissive* to your own husbands, that even if some do not obey the word, they without a word, may be won by the conduct of their wives." (1 Peter 3:1)

"Wives *submit* yourselves to your own husbands, as it is fitting in the Lord." (Colossians 3:18)

"Let a woman learn in silence with all *submission*." (1 Timothy 2:11)

"Wives *submit* to your own husbands, as to the Lord. For the husband is the head of the wife, as also Christ is the head of the church; and He is the Savior of the body. Therefore, just as the church is *subject* to Christ, so let the wives be to their husbands in all things." (Ephesians 5:22–24)

Profiles in Submission

As a Navy chaplain for nearly twenty years, I am well acquainted with the curriculum of submission. As one of my former senior chaplains was fond of saying, "No one has more bosses than the chaplain!" How right he was! Military chaplains are special assistants to their Commanding Officers. They submit to their senior chaplains in their chain of influence. They come under the authority of their denominational representatives. Ultimately, they surrender themselves to the higher authority of their Savior and Lord Jesus Christ (Luke 6:46; 17:10). The military infrastructure is designed not to be a culture of inferiority, but of respectful submission and subordination. Anyone who has ever served in the military is well acquainted with the rank infrastructures of the service. Whether on the officer or enlisted side of the house, no one is inherently inferior to anyone else in the military, or in any other enterprise. The rank and file of the military are living illustrations of the Greek word for submission. As previously noted, hupotasso is a military term that means, "to arrange under." In every branch of the military, subordinates subject themselves to the orders of their superiors. It must be noted that senior officers in the Navy, while outranking the junior officers and enlisted servicemembers, are not inherently superior to them. For such a view militates against the image of God in man. It must be stated that they are superior to them in rank, but not in inherent worth. Similarly, the godly wife is to hupotasso her husband, "arrange herself under" him.

The Triune God and Submission

A divine illustration of biblical submission is embodied in the Triune God or Trinity. The Bible teaches that God is One (monotheism). The Great Shema of Deuteronomy 6:4, rhapsodizes, "The LORD our God is one LORD." However, this monotheism does not exclude, but includes other persons of the Trinity. For God subsists in three separate persons, namely, God the Father, God the Son, and God the Holy Spirit (triunity). While the three separate persons of the trinity are co-equal, co-eternal and share the same nature and attributes, they are not separate or demi-gods (polytheism). The co-equality of the Father, Son, and Holy Spirit is illustrated in the Great Commission of Matthew 28:19, Jesus commands His disciples to baptize followers (disciples) "in the name of the Father, and of the Son, and of the Holy Spirit."

As in the case of senior and junior members of military ranks, one is not inherently inferior to another. For as in Matthew 28:19, all three members of the trinity are considered of equal divine worth. Jesus illustrated this clearly in John 10:30 when He intimated, "I and My Father are One." Such truth of equality is also embedded in Jesus's high priestly prayer in John 17. It is repeatedly taught in John's Gospel (John 1:1–18; 14:1–11; 15:1–2). In spite of this inherent equality, the New Testament is unequivocally clear in teaching that Jesus submitted Himself to the will of the Father. In John 8:29 Jesus declared, "The Father has not left Me alone. And I do always those things that please Him." In John 10:28, concerning His life Jesus asserts, "No one takes it from Me. But I lay it down of Myself. I have power to lay it down, and I have power to take it again. This command I have received of My Father." Concerning judgment, Jesus divines, "For the Father judges no one, but has committed all judgment to the Son, that all who should honor the Son just as they honor the Father. He who does not honor the Son does not honor the Father who sent Him" (John 5:22–23). In the latter text in John Jesus's submission to the Father, and equality of the Father are simultaneously acknowledged. Theologians designate such a construct as economic roles of the Trinity. Such roles are witnessed in that "[Jesus] learned obedience (i.e., "submission"), through the things which He suffered" (Heb. 5:8).

The Holy Spirit, likewise is not one scintilla inferior to either the Son or the Father (Matt. 28:19; Acts 5:1–4). Yet the Spirit glorifies both the Father and the Son (John 16). The fact that Paul does not place conditions on the wife's obedience to her husband is telling. It does not speak to inferiority but differing roles.

A Military Analogy

In the military sub-culture provides an excellent illustration of the submission God requires from a wife. Military members understand the rank infrastructure and the chain of command. They take a solemn oath "to protect and defend against all enemies foreign and domestic." Enlisted members of the military also take an oath to obey those in positions of authority over them. However, such an oath is to be understood in the framework of their oath to the United States Constitution. While rarely cited, disobeying an "unlawful order" is implied in the oath. In this respect, a service member may be compelled to disobey an unconstitutional order given by their military superiors.

Submission as to Jesus

Similarly, in the marriage relationship, wives are commanded to submit to their husbands "as it is fitting in the Lord," and "as to the Lord" (Col. 3:18; Eph. 5:22). The natural meaning of "as to the Lord," from the context is "as unto Christ." This evident from Colossians 4:1–2 in which Christian bondservants were enjoined to "Obey in all things your masters according to the flesh, not with eye-service as men-pleasers, but in sincerity of heart, fearing God. And whatever you do, do it heartily *as to the Lord, not to men.*" This meaning mirrors that of the corresponding text in Ephesians 5:22–24: "Wives, *submit* to your own husbands, *as to the Lord.* For the husband is head of the wife, *as also,* Christ is the head of the church; and

He is he Savior of the body. Therefore, *just as* the church is subject to Christ, *so let the wives* be to their own husbands *in everything.*"

In the above passage, it is plain that the husband is cast into the "Christ role" as "head" of the wife. Just as the church is to be subject to Christ *in everything,* so the wife is to be "[subject], *to their own husbands in everything,*"

The Christian recognizes that when they obey their fallen, perhaps unsaved master, they are obeying and reverencing the Lord Jesus Christ. Similarly, when a wife submits to and obeys her unsaved husband, she does it to her Lord and Savior. For these subordinate clauses denote that the Christian wife is to submit to her husband as if she is submitting to Jesus. The exception would be when their husband asks them to do something immoral, unethical, or overtly sinful. The fact that Peter understood such an exception is illustrated in Acts 5:29, "Then Peter and the other apostles answered and said, 'We ought to obey God rather than men.'"

Following in Jesus's Footsteps

In brief, Peter prescribes "quiet submission" as the spiritual cure for a disobedient husband. The prior context offers palpable definition to this biblical directive. Like other New Testament authors, Peter cited Jesus as the premier example of godly conduct. After urging the tribes of sufferings saints to "suffer patiently," and "wrongfully," and perform "good deeds," he directs them to the example of Christ's suffering,

> "For to this you were called, because Christ also suffered for us, leaving us an example, that you should follow in His steps: 'Who committed no sin, Nor was guile found in His mouth' Who when He was reviled, did not revile in return; when He suffered, He did not threaten, but committed Himself to Him who judges righteously; who Himself bore our sins in His own body on a tree, that we, having died to sins, might live for

righteousness-by whose stripes you are healed. For you were like sheep going astray, but have now returned to the Shepherd and Overseer of your souls."

"For to this end you were called. For Christ suffered for us leaving you and example that you should follow in His steps." (1 Pet. 2:21)

The word "example" is a rare word occurring only once in the New Testament. Hupogrammon, literally means, "underwriting." Hiebert posits, "The term literally an 'underwriting,' could refer to a writing or drawing placed under another sheet to be retraced by another sheet by the pupil."[xi]

By employing hypogrammon, Peter denotes an exact blueprint of Christ-like behavior. Peter instructs his readers that Jesus Christ the divine "Shepherd" and "Overseer" of their souls is their premier moral exemplar. His point is that Christ-followers are to diligently mimic the godly response to suffering established by Jesus in the week of His passion. The moral graces delineated by Peter are unmitigated goodness to His enemies characterized by an absence of guile or malice coupled with an unqualified submission to God while suffering wrongs. The aged apostle commands his readers, male and female, to don the same moral graces modeled by the Son of God when in the throes of history's greatest injustice.

The example of Jesus's suffering is the backdrop against which Peter admonishes wives to submit to disobedient husbands. The aged apostle admonishes them to emulate Christ's example of quiet submission in the face of this suffering. By employing the conjunction, "likewise," he is clearly referencing the example of Jesus's sufferings from the previous context. The dimension of Christ's suffering that he highlights is His quiet and reverential suffering. He enjoins Christian wives under his care, to be submissive to their husbands, even in the face of their disobedience.

A Neglected Command

The moral grace that a saintly woman is to pass along to her younger compatriots is seldom championed. Rare is the sermon, Bible study, or Christian symposium in which a wife's obedience to her husband is urged. More popular is an egalitarian view of marriage (equality of authority), in which mutual submission is the norm. However, mutual submission in the marital context is only commanded in the married couples' sexual relationship (1 Cor. 7:1–6). Yet the New Testament is consistent in enjoining women both to obey and submit to their husbands.

Peter commands believing wives, even those suffering a disobedient husband to submit to their husbands in 1 Peter 3:1, "Likewise, wives be submissive to your own husbands, that even if some do not obey the word, they without a word be won by the behavior of their wives." It is clear that Peter issues a directive to all Christian wives to submissively obey their husbands. Lest there be any objection made by wives married to difficult husbands, Peter asserts, "even if some do not obey the word." Even under the most extenuating circumstances, the obedience of Christian wives to their husbands is unqualified. One exception to this rule would be if the wife is being physically abused and her life is endangered. In such a case, separation is both warranted and wise. In such a case of physical endangerment, Jesus's instruction to His disciples would apply to the battered wife, "When they persecute you in one city flee to another" (Matt. 10:23).

Yet it must be kept in mind that Peter's imperatives are couched in the context of Jesus's patient endurance of both the physical and verbal persecution of His assailants while he hung on Calvary's tree. In this vein, Peter it could be confidently allows for other forms of persecution (abuse) such as blasphemy, slander, lying, deceit, ridicule et al. A Christian wife may suffer emotional or verbal abuse from her husband. Yet her response is to be one of quiet submission and unconditional respect (see also, Eph. 5:33). While laboring under such disobedient husbands, the Christian wife is admonished to maintain "the incorruptible beauty of a gentle and quiet spirit, which is in the sight of God of great price" (1 Pet. 3:4). In the face of such a difficult command, Peter was moved by God's Spirit (2 Pet. 1:20–22), to offer additional encouragement to Christian women. In 3:5–6 he underscores, "For in this manner, in former times, the holy women who trusted in God also adorned themselves, being submissive to their own husbands, as Sarah obeyed Abraham, calling him lord, whose daughters are you if you do good and are not afraid with any terror."

Peter cites godly women in general and Sarah in particular as godly women who obeyed their husbands through their extraordinary faith in God. In Sarah's case, her life could have been endangered as she quietly obeyed Abraham by not revealing to Pharaoh that she was his [Abraham's] wife. To this end Walvoord remarks,

> "A woman who wins this kind of victory has a winsome loveliness that comes not from outward adornment but from her inner self, the unfading beauty of a gentle and quiet spirit (cf. 1 Tim. 2:9–11). This adornment of the spirit is of great worth in God's sight. While the world prizes costly clothing and gold jewelry, a woman with a gentle and quiet spirit is precious to God. Peter did not state that women should not wear jewelry and nice clothes, but that Christian women should think of outer attire as the source of genuine beauty."[xii]

In the New Testament the Christian wife is commanded to both obey and submit to their husbands. The two are synonymous acts. While such teaching is not popular today, such actions are key to God's blessing on the wife and her husband. Peter continues, "Sarah obeyed Abraham calling him lord, whose daughters you are if you do good and are not afraid with any terror" (1 Pet. 3:6). While the context and relevance of the above passage will be unpacked elsewhere in this book, it would be well to cite here the synonymous relationship between obedience and submission. The Greek word for obedience is "hypokouo." Etymologically, this compound word is formed from two words. Hupo, means, "under," and akouo, meaning, "listen." The word submission is also a Greek compound, "hupotasso." This word is formed from hupo, "under," and tasso, meaning "to arrange."

Submission—"Ducking and Letting God Hit Your Husband"

While a pastor several years ago, a godly woman in our church called me to inform me that her husband had just returned from a missions trip and had announced his decision to divorce her. The reasons she gave is that he had found himself and also been captivated by a woman with whom he served. I counseled this sister to follow Peter's instruction in 1 Peter 3:1–6. As a woman of the word, she was already familiar with the passage and modeled godly submission in the wake of her husband's disobedience. While her husband refused to discuss the matter with me initially, when a church leader and I visited his wife and he in their home, we witnessed a change of heart. His wife's godly submission coupled with the concern of the church won him over and he pledged to stay married and work on their relationship. What I witnessed from this godly woman was a willingness to resist every temptation to reciprocate her husband's disobedience by assuming an unsubmissive posture. Rather than returning in kind, she returned kindness! This saintly sister, "ducked and let God hit her disobedient husband." In this vein, Paul admonishes,

"If your enemy is hungry, feed him; If he is thirsty, give him a drink; For in so doing you will heap coals of fire on his head and the Lord shall reward you." "Heaping coals of fire on his head," is the biblical equivalent of today's "killing them with kindness." When one does this their Christ-like actions can catalyze change in the difficult person. In short, it may cause them to be convicted, ashamed and bring about repentance in the sinning party. This biblical proverb, is couched in the context of Romans 12:18, "If it be possible, as much as it depends on you, live peaceably with all men." Pursuant to this godly brand of submission, the late Ruth Graham Bell said of her relationship with her husband Billy, "It is my job to love Billy. It is God's job to make him good." (Romans 12:20)

The Reward of Respect

Not unlike in the above real-life scenario, there is a reward in unconditionally respecting one's husband. Perhaps Peter's instruction would have represented a bombshell to Peter's female readers. One may reasonably speculate in the part of them not of God, they would have recoiled at this mandate. Some may have been tempted to brush aside such advice like the bone of a half-eaten chicken. Yet the most thoughtful and saintly would do well to consider what Peter wrote to this precious group of Christian wives in 2 Peter 1:20–22, "knowing this first that no prophecy of the Scripture is of any private interpretation, for prophecy never came by the will of man, but holy men of God spoke as they were moved by the Holy Spirit."

Following this sacred truth, Peter's readers would be forced to acknowledge that the aged apostle was one of the "holy men," so moved to write the sacred Scriptures. Peter previously spoke a sorority of "holy women of God," of which Sarah was a member (1 Pet. 3:5–6). These holy women of God obeyed the "Holy Word," rather than taking their cues from "Hollywood." In doing so they submitted to their husbands under the duress of a disobedient husband. To this end Raymer remarks,

> "Examples of holy women in the Old Testament support Peter's exhortation. Purity of life (v. 2) and a submissive spirit (v. 5) have always been a godly woman's lasting source of beauty and attractiveness. Sarah is chosen as a specific example of a woman who was submissive to her husband. She obeyed Abraham and called him her master. That is she recognized him as the leader and head of her household (Gen. 18:12). Like other holy women of the past, Sarah put her hope in God. This kind of conduct gives women the spiritual heritage of Sarah: you are her daughters is you do what is right and do not give way to fear (ptoesin, "terror" used only here in the

NT). Wives who are fearful (perhaps because of disobeying their husbands) are not putting their full trust in God."[xiii]

The Payoff of Submission

Submission is a powerful change agent able to bring conviction to the husband and the fruit of divine intervention. The wife's submission compels the Lord to act on the persecuted wife's behalf. Someone has well defined submission as "ducking and letting God hit your husband." Peter writes "that even if some do not obey the word they may be won by the conduct of the wives, when they observe your chaste conduct accompanied by fear" (3:1). In the previous chapter, Peter intimated that "beautiful deeds" displayed by the persecuted Christ-follower afford them a powerful incentive for non-believers to trust Christ. The witnessing of such beautiful deeds culminates in the malicious non-believer, trusting Christ and "glorifying God in the day of visitation" (1 Pet. 2:12).

Like metal attaches itself to a magnet, the hostile non-believer is drawn to faith in Christ through the outrageously kind behavior of the godly Christ-follower. One practical context in which these beautiful deeds are displayed is in the marriage relationship. The godly husband is moved to change as he observes the conduct of his submissive wife. Such meek behavior conspiring with the Spirit of God becomes the spiritual elixir healing the disobedient husband's heart. Charles Swindoll calls this, "the silent preaching of a lovely wife."[xiv] Respective to this, the godly wife preaches the gospel without moving her lips! The change begins when the husband "observes" the godly behavior of his wife. The verb suggests a careful study rather than a casual glance. The consistent reverent behavior of the wife ultimately becomes a powerful change agent for the husband. Christian marriage expert, Emerson Eggerichs, remarks of this process that the husband comes under intense conviction as a result of the obedient wife's Christ-like behavior. As a result, the husband may trust Christ, or be compelled to change as a result of the woman's humble and godly disposition.

Sarah's Choice

Peter features Sarah as a paragon of godly submission in the wake of a disobedient husband. Sarah made a choice to obey Abraham in spite of the considerable risk to herself and her family. In doing so, she demonstrated extraordinary faith in her sovereign God. Pharaoh could have had sexual relations with her jeopardizing her status as future matriarch of Israel, or hastening death due to disease. She could have rationalized that the plethora of diseases clinging to the Egyptians warranted social distancing from Pharaoh. It would have been easy for Sarah to reason that her situation was unique, untenable, and therefore obedience was optional. God would understandably issue her a hall pass on this assignment! What would be the harm of declaring this "mission impossible" and reneging on her commitment to submit to Abraham's mandated silence?

Yet Sarah refused to paste a happy face on disobedience. Instead she chose to trust her God. While not saying a word, "She obeyed Abraham, calling him lord" (3:6). Rather than giving Abraham pushback, she launched "operation unconditional respect." The author of Hebrews offers insight to Sarah's submissive spirit when he writes, she "judged Him faithful who had promised" (Heb. 11:11). The writer of Hebrews informs that such faith is a requirement of pleasing God (Heb. 11:6).

Such faith honoring submission not only pleased God but provoked Him to spring into action on her behalf. The Lord intervened by visiting Sarah with a terrible series of plagues (Gen. 12:17). As a result, this pagan monarch rebuked Abraham for deceiving him. He returned Sarah to him, and expelled him from Egypt after showering on him great gifts. Sarah's disobedient husband was disciplined by the Lord and reproved by an unbelieving Pharaoh in response to Sarah's faith in the Lord. In similar fashion, Christian wives daring to commit their disobedient husbands to God, will be like honored.

A Case of Committed Trust

Following the template of the Lord Jesus, godly wives are to mimic their Savior in committing their burden "to Him who judges righteously" (1 Pet. 2:23). In baseball parlance, the Righteous Judge bats a thousand! His ways are failsafe. It behooves all the daughters of Eve to commit themselves to "the Shepherd and Overseer of their souls" (1 Pet. 2:25). Contemporary Sarah's entrust their lives to the Lord. David prescribes trust for those facing evildoers, "Commit your way to the LORD, trust also in Him and He will do it" (Psalm 37:5). He similarly urges, "Cast your burden on the LORD and He will sustain you; He will never permit the righteous to be moved" (Psalm 55:22). First Samuel 2:30 says, "Those who honors Me I will honor, and those who despise Me shall be lightly esteemed." Sarah chose to honor her Lord, by calling Abraham lord. And the Lord rewarded her extravagantly. Moreover, he delivered her from carnal desires of a lustful monarch and the potential trauma that he might have perpetrated on her.

A Case Study in Unconditional Submission

Dr. Wendell Johnston tells of a story when he was a young pastor, he counseled a Christian wife who was desperately attempting to reach her unbelieving husband for Christ. This dear woman would not only verbally "preach" the gospel to her husband, but would also deposit gospel tracts in his lunchbox. She complained to her pastor that her insensitive, non-believing husband would throw them away. Much to her chagrin Dr. Johnston informed her, "I would too if I were him!" He further counselled her to show unconditional love and respect to her husband. When she began to follow this counsel, her husband's hardened posture began to change and he trusted Christ as His Savior.

Hope for Wannabe Sarahs

It is likely that many precious Christian women who love Jesus, may be discouraged by the example of Sarah. Since comparison is often the favorite indoor sport of many Christians, the trigger for such discouragement is likely a failure to measure up. There is an innate tendency to be disillusioned by the high bar of womanhood set by the virtuous woman of Proverbs 31, or the godly example of Sarah. For this reason, it is important to tell what Paul Harvey famously called, "the rest of the story."

The rest of the story is that Sarah while a woman of extraordinary faith, was yet a daughter of Eve. Though she was a princess, she made some critical mistakes in her life. She like her husband Abraham experienced lapses of faith. Like Eve, Sarah sought to dominate her husband Abraham in urging him to have sex with Hagar (Gen. 16). This act of the flesh produced a child who spawned long-standing problems for the patriarchal family and the nation of Israel. Sarah laughed in disbelief when the LORD announced to Abraham that she would bear a son in her old age (Gen. 18:13). Sarah sinned in doubting God could keep his promise due to hers and Abraham's advanced age. Sarah though the matriarch of the children of Israel, was far from perfect. This gives godly Christian wives, who struggle with the curse of Eve, hope.

Yet like Abraham on Mount Moriah, she entrusted her life to the LORD during the most traumatic season of her life. She trusted God when her disobedient husband put her life and sexual purity in jeopardy. She demonstrated herself to be a godly woman of faith when child-bearing appeared humanly impossible. What James wrote of the prophet Elijah, was true of Sarah. Just as "Elijah was a man with a nature like ours," so was Sarah a woman blessed and used by God who possessed a sin nature (see James 5:17).

Sarah's Reward

While submitting to one's disobedient husband may be no simple task, it may nonetheless be a condition for reception of eternal reward. For just as Christian husbands will be greatly rewarded for loving unlovable wives, so wives will be eternally rewarded for submitting to disobedient husbands. Abraham and undoubtedly Sarah both "waited for a city which has foundations, whose builder and maker is God" (Heb. 11:10).

"But not they desire a better, that is a heavenly country, Therefore, God is not ashamed to be called their God, for He has prepared for a city for them" (Heb. 11:16).

Take heart, mighty women of God! Winston Churchill's words have wide currency in a myriad of contexts. "Victory is not final, defeat is not fatal. It is the courage to continue that counts." If you have failed miserably as Sarah did, you are in good company. Hope is not lost! God loves you and can use you in spite of past mistakes. He invites you into the sorority of the "holy women of God."

Questions for Reflection

1) Colossians 3:18 admonishes women to "Submit to their husbands in all things as it is fitting in the Lord." On a scale of 1–7, rate how seriously you take this command?

   1   2   3   4   5   6   7

2) In contemporary parlance, "as it is fitting in the Lord," means "because it is the right thing to do." Rate to what degree you have believed that a wife's submission to her husband in all things is the right thing to do.

   1   2   3   4   5   6   7

3) On a scale of 1–7, seven being high, to what degree do you trust the Lord when confronted with a disobedient husband?

   1   2   3   4   5   6   7

4) Assess how well you exemplify a submissively obedient wife when your husband is "disobedient in word."

1　2　3　4　5　6　7

5) Reflect on the past few years of your life. Assess whether you have placed a greater emphasis on personal appearance or Christ-likeness. Explain.

6) Has there ever been an instance during the course of your marriage in which you submitted to your disobedient husband and God answered your prayer and rewarded you. Explain.

7) Have you ever received advice from others militating against with Peter's prescription for dealing with a disobedient husband? What was it?

MARY: A WOMAN OF EXTRAVAGANT DEVOTION

"Assuredly I say to you, wherever this gospel is preached in the whole world, what this woman has done will also be told a memorial toward her." (Matthew 26:13)

"It is not great talent that God blesses, but great likeness to Jesus Christ." (Robert Murray McCheyne)

"You are as intimate with God as you want to be." (J. Oswald Sanders)

Melissa Henning was a woman in her late teens who contracted stage 3c ovarian cancer. Prior to the diagnosis she fell in love with a gifted young songwriter and singer by the name of Jeremy Camp. Before meeting Jeremy, she fell deeply in love with her Savior and Lord, Jesus Christ. After her diagnosis, God gave Melissa a wonderful gift. He healed her. She and Jeremy married six months later. On their honeymoon, Melissa complained of bloating to her young husband. Much to her and Jeremy's chagrin the cancer had returned with a vengeance. The cancer was inoperable and she died in her early twenties. Janette Henning, Melissa's mother lovingly shares Melissa's moving odyssey of devotion to Jesus in her book, *Melissa: If One Life*. Sometime before she went to be with Jesus she wrote in her journal,

"Jesus Christ, my precious Lord and gracious Savior, thank You. Thank You for pursuing me. Thank You for winning my love by Your true love for me. I know You to be so in love with me, and it's because of that love that I am now so in love with You. Heavenly Father, thank You that You give me the perfect love I've been looking for. Dear God, thank You for loving me so much that You'd continue to forgive and forget all the sins I'd commit that would pull me farther from You. Thank You for throwing them into the sea. I know why the sea is so big!"[xv]

A Case of Hypergamy

Hypergamy is a feminine social dynamic, driving women to romantically pursue an elite brand of man. The cultural trend of hypergamy is fleshed out when women marry men of affluence, power, public acclaim, or outsized potential in their chosen field of endeavor. Some women will marry a man because he is interminably handsome, occupies a position of authority, possesses considerable native intelligence, or boasts a coveted skill. Jezebels frequently bear the rings of hypergamy. There was a first century woman, befriended by Jesus, who like Melissa Camp, sported a far more rigorous ranking system for men. Rather than being a gold-digger, she treasured the jewels of spiritual intimacy with the God-Man above priceless gold. This woman's name was Mary.

A Tale of Two Sisters

During the course of Jesus's earthly ministry, He often dined with two sisters whom He dearly loved. These two sisters reciprocated Jesus's love for them, though in different ways. One was a model servant, a galloping gourmand. The other sister surged off the introspective graph. Mary was an introvert whose spiritual assessment test came back, "Contemplative." Mary cared deeply for the state of her soul. Conversely, whenever Jesus visited with His entourage of disciples, Martha toiled at a frenzied pace in the kitchen preparing a gourmet meal she deemed worthy of the Son of God. Simultaneously, Mary redeemed the time sitting at Jesus's feet absorbing every drop of wisdom cascading from His lips.

Martha's Weakness

It is often remarked of siblings, "They could not be more different!" This certainly was true of Mary and Martha, two sisters who were a study in contrast. Martha, who also loved Jesus, expressed her love for the Savior differently than Mary. Yet this expression caused her to forfeit intimacy with Jesus. This glaring weakness, if left unattended, could sink her ship of faith. Though a Five Star chef, she had a habit of focusing on her gifts more than the Gift-Giver. Had she lived today she would have been diagnosed with Obsessive Compulsive Disorder. For Martha, such a disorder manifested itself in the kitchen. Martha who sported a zero-tolerance policy for "sloth," was not moved by the symbolism of Mary lounging at Jesus's feet. She judged preparing dinner to be a higher priority than having her daily devotions with Jesus. She blurted out, "Lord do you not care that my sister has left me to serve alone?" (Luke 10:41).

One might expect Jesus might sympathetically respond, "Your sister has an excellent point. Serving is important to Me. Mary, we can catch up later. But for now, run along and help Martha prepare dinner." Jesus said nothing of the sort. Conversely, He took Mary's part. He gently reproved, "Martha, Martha, you are troubled and bothered about many things. But Mary has chosen that good part, that shall not be taken away from her" (Luke 10:41–42). In contemporary parlance Jesus was asserting that hot dogs (100 percent beef!), would be fine, filet mignon, however, was overkill.

Martha, though one Jesus deeply loved, was in dire need of a mid-course correction. Jesus' gentle yet firm reproof warranted a realignment of her personal priorities. Martha, in her busyness, unlike her sister, could not be bothered with giving Jesus her undivided attention. For the frenetic pace of her life engulfed her in a hurricane of busyness, which robbed her of precious minutes to linger in the Savior' presence. She needed Jesus to gently remind her that the priority of cultivating spiritual intimacy with her Lord transcended her physical duties of preparing dinner. Simply put, a gourmet dinner was negotiable, communion with the Savior was not! Martha, like her sister, needed a firsthand relationship with the Savior.

A First-Hand Relationship with Jesus

The Greek philosopher Plato opined that in order for one to lead a good life they must order their soul first, then order lives after the same pattern in which they order their souls. Mary did this. She drank deeply at the refreshing spring of intimate knowledge of Jesus Christ. She embodied the words of Peter, "But grow in grace and in the knowledge of our Lord and Savior Jesus Christ" (2 Pet. 3:18). Her reward for having a well ordered inner world was unjust criticism. Mary was often the object of unfair criticism from Judas, but also from her sister Martha. Yet in both instances Jesus defended His deeply devoted female disciple. In both instances her Savior commended her for her devotion. Mary was not content with a mere second hand relationship with the Savior, but one whose waking moments were filled with dynamic devotion. Mary loved Jesus deeply and was reveled in spending time in His presence. In the words of Jesus, she wanted to "dine with Him" (Rev. 3:20). Moreover, the words of the Apostle Paul she desired, "the words of Christ dwell in her richly" (Col. 3:16). Her life is a glowing testimony to the words of J. Oswald Sanders, "You are as intimate with God as you want to be."

The Expulsive Power of a Great New Affection

The secret of intimacy is embodied in a phrase employed by nineteenth century pastor Henry Ward Beecher. The father of the famous author, Harriet Beecher Stowe coined the phrase, "The expulsive power of a great new affection." The phrase is illustrated in the following scenario in which a girl is jilted by her boyfriend. As romantic relationships go, a girlfriend mourns the loss of her boyfriend who "dumps" her for another girl. Despondency ensues. However, the young woman meets another handsome Prince Charming. She falls in love. Her fog of depression is dispelled by the first bright rays of new romance. Her spirits are lifted by the mere prospect of new love sweeping her off her feet. Stardust permeates the atmosphere as her new love interest is larger than life. Her former love becomes a distant memory she files into the archives of forgettable boyfriends. Though she still remembers her old boyfriend he is no longer the focus of her attention. The sparks of new love have both healed her broken heart while flooding it with joy and new purpose. The old hymn says it best: "Turn your eyes upon Jesus, look full in His wonderful face and the things of earth will grow strangely dim, in the light of His glory and grace."

Mary's Extravagant Devotion to Jesus

Fast forward to the end of Jesus's ministry. Jesus was once again visiting Mary, Martha, and their recently resurrected brother Lazarus. A banquet was held in Jesus's honor and Martha was once again serving (John 12:2). John records, "Then Mary took a pound of very costly oil of spikenard, anointed the feet of Jesus, and wiped his feet with her hair and the house was filled with the fragrance of the oil" (John 12:3).

To say Mary's extravagant gift was generous was an understatement. It was stupendous! For there is nothing to indicate that Mary, having been raised in the small fishing village of Bethany, was wealthy. Yet as Judas informs estimates the retail value of this precious oil to be about 6/7 of the average Jews annual salary. Factor into the equation that Mary was not a career woman who enjoyed a lucrative salary. This was an astronomical sum for a woman who was likely a poor fisherman's daughter in the humble village of Bethany! Yet so extraordinary was Mary's devotion to Jesus that she pinched pennies, purchased, and poured this expensive perfume onto the feet of the Savior whom she desperately loved. Mary's sealed her devotion to Jesus by gently drying the oil from Jesus's feet with her hair.

Mary knew what was truly valuable in life. It wasn't a charmingly handsome boyfriend man outfitted in a pinstripe suit, residing in a posh suburb, who drives a $100,000 sports car. It was the God-Man who used a stone for a pillow and the sky for a blanket. Immediately, the betraying thief, Judas Iscariot, first criticized this generous act of extraordinary devotion. He did so by citing the market value of this precious commodity as nearly a year's wages. John in his gospel reveals that Judas ulterior motive for criticizing Mary was that he might steal more money from the money bag used to support Jesus and His disciples. Jesus knowing both Judas's motives and Mary's heart, once again came to her defense commanding, "Let her alone; she has kept this for the day of My burial. For the poor you have with you always, but Me you do not have always" (John 12:7).

Devotion and Duty

Undoubtedly the hours she spent at Jesus's feet afforded her the insight of Jesus's worthiness of this costly vial of perfume. Therefore, where the Savior was involved, she spared no expense. When Judas criticized her for this extravagant act, Jesus defends Mary, applauding her for her insight saying, "Let her alone. She has kept this for the day of her burial. For the poor you have with you always. But Me you do not have always" (John 12:7).

Depth of Knowledge Determines Depth of Devotion

Jeremiah wrote, "Do not let the wise man glory in His wisdom, neither let the mighty man glory in His might, let not the rich man glory in his riches, but let him who glories, glory in this, that he understands and knows Me, that I am the LORD who exercises lovingkindness, and righteousness and justice in all the earth says the LORD" (Jeremiah 9:23–24).

God Loves Extravagant Gifts: A Tale of Two Brothers

Before there were two sisters, there were two brothers named Cain and Abel. Cain brought a garden variety offering that was rejected by the LORD. Abel offered the best of his flocks and the LORD was well pleased with his offering (Gen. 4::1–6). Solomon wrote in Proverbs 3:9–10, "Honor the LORD with your possessions, And with the firstfruits of all your increase; So your barns shall be filled with plenty, and your vats overflow with new wine."

Abel's offering embodies the spirit of these Proverbs. God's pleasure with Abel is expressed in Hebrews 11:4, "By faith Abel offered to God a more excellent sacrifice than Cain, through which he obtained witness that he was righteous, God testifying by his gifts; and through it he being dead still speaks." The LORD honored Abel in his life, legacy, and in eternity, for his loving expression of worship to His God. Though his life was truncated by his murderous brother, his life is an unending testimony to God's declaration in 1 Samuel 2:30, "Far be it from Me; for those who honor Me, I will honor, and those who despise Me shall be lightly esteemed."

Jesus Rewards Those Expressing Generous Devotion to Him

While Jesus previously reproved Martha for her misplaced priority system, in this instance Jesus rewards Mary for her extravagant act of worshipping Him with costly perfume. Matthew's records, "Why do you trouble the woman? For she has done a good work for Me. For you have the poor with you always, but Me you do not have always. For in pouring this fragrant oil on My body, she did it for My burial. Assuredly, I say to you, wherever this gospel is preached in the whole world, what this woman has done will also be told as a memorial to her" (Matt. 26:10–13). Jesus rewarded Mary by promising that her extravagant devotion would endure as an everlasting memorial of her love for the Savior. Not unlike Jesus commendation of the widow's mite, her story is forever etched on the pages of God's Word as a testament of her gratitude for the Savior who was about to die for her sins.

Abiding and Abounding

Mary's extravagant gift to Jesus was connected to her consuming passion to know Him. Mary's act of extravagantly anointing the feet of Jesus was drawn from the well of her deep devotion to the Savior. Abiding and abounding were connected. After this act of extraordinary love for the Savior, Jesus was teaching His disciples in the upper room. John 15:7–8, "If you abide in Me and I abide in you, you will ask what you desire, and it shall be done for you. By this is My Father glorified that you bear much fruit; so you will be My disciples." These same principles applied to all of Jesus's disciples including Mary. Abiding in Christ constituted intimate connection with the Savior and His words that culminates in bearing the pure fruit of love for the Savior and others. In other words, abiding in Christ led to abounding in good works.

Abiding in Christ the Key to Abounding in Good Works

The Apostle Paul at the end of his letter to the Corinthians encourages us to abound in the work of the Lord on the basis of the certain hope of the future resurrection. He admonishes in 1 Corinthians 15:58, "Therefore, my beloved brethren, be steadfast, immoveable, always abounding in the work of the Lord, knowing that your labor is not in vain in the Lord." The connection between "abiding and abounding" is also seen in Paul's letter to the Corinthians. For in 1 Corinthians 16:22 Paul warns of the importance of devotion to Christ, "If anyone does not love the Lord Jesus Christ, let him be accursed. O Lord come!" For Paul loving Christ (abiding) and abounding in Him were inextricably linked.

The Connection between Abiding and Abounding

Mary's devotion leading was such that she both abided and abounded. On the one hand, she dwelt (abided) at Jesus's feet drinking in His divine wisdom. This act of abiding led to her offering expensive perfume to anoint Him for His burial. Flowing from her loving connection to Jesus was an abundance of good works.

Both abiding and abounding are biblical. Jesus instructed His disciples in John 15:5, "I am the Vine you are the branches. He who abides in Me and I in him, bears much fruit. For without Me you can do nothing." Paul serves notice of the importance of persevering in good works in 1 Corinthians 15:58: "Therefore, my beloved brethren, be steadfast, immoveable, always abounding in the work of the Lord, knowing your labor in the Lord is not in vain." In a similar vein, Paul writes to the church of Galatia, "And let us not grow weary while doing good, for in due season we shall reap if we do not lose heart" (Gal. 6:9).

The author of Hebrews also underscores the importance of abounding in good works. He assures, "God is not unjust to forget your work and labor of love which you have shown toward His name, in that you have ministered to the saints and do minister" (Heb. 6:10).

The Importance of Devotion to Christ

In the last book of the Bible Jesus evaluates the works of seven first century churches in what was known as Asia-Minor (modern-day Turkey). The first church he critiques is the church of Ephesus. The star of this faithful church discipled by the Apostle Paul and pastored by Timothy is on an upward trajectory. The church was loaded with good works, giving, sound teaching, and perseverance. Given all the accolades they received from the Lord Jesus, they might have been a going away favorite to win the "church of the year" award. Yet Jesus would have vetoed their nomination. For the Savior solemnly warns them that He has one thing against them, namely, that they have "abandoned their first love" (Rev. 2:4). Jesus had not abandoned them, yet they had abandoned the intimacy that they once enjoyed with their Savior. Their diminishing devotion was reminiscent of the saying, "If God seems far away, guess who moved?" Not Him!

This one offense was so egregious that Jesus urged them to make a spiritual U-turn. He stridently warns them that failure to do so would result in divine judgment. The Savior commands, "Remember therefore, from where you have fallen; repent and do the first works, or else I will come to you quickly and remove your lampstand from its place unless they repent" (Rev. 2:5). By this statement, Jesus was serving notice of His intention to eradicate both the influence and presence of the Ephesian church if they refused to address their problem of listless devotion for the Savior. Such was Jesus's desire that His people be madly in love with Him!

This priority of the Savior is revisited when He critiques the works of the lukewarm church of Laodicea. Their commitment was so nauseating to the Savior that He expressed His disgust by saying, "I vomit you out of My mouth" (Rev. 3:16). After chastising them for their spiritual tepidity, He invites them to intimate fellowship with Himself. He writes in Revelation 3:20, "Behold I stand at the door and knock. If anyone hears My voice and opens the door, I will come into Him and he with Me."

Renewing Your First Love

How does one renew their devotion to the Savior? Jesus says, "Remember therefore, from where you are fallen" (Rev. 2:5). When one abandons their first love, they fall from a great height. For being on intimate footing with the Savior is to enjoy the most elite status in the universe! Occasionally believers express their wistful longing to recover their lost love. Jesus says that the first step to recapturing their first love is recall their early days with the Savior. Like remembering the instant one first fell in love of one's spouse, such reflection is enough to want it back. When one recalls how they loved to pray, witness, and hungered for God's Word and fellowship with God's people, it is enough to want to hit the reset button on one's relationship with Christ.

Repentance

The second step to renewing one's first love is repentance. Jesus continues, "Repent and do the first works" (Rev. 2:5). Repentance is formed from two Greek words that mean, "to have a change of mind." One must have a change of mind concerning how they were living, their neglect for the Savior, spiritual indifference, and false imaginations concerning God. Pursuant to the latter, Paul writes, "Casting down arguments and every high thing that exalts itself against the knowledge of God, bringing every thought into captivity to the obedience of Christ" (2 Cor. 10:5). The Corinthian church had repented of false ideas marketed by Satan's minions who militated against the people of God (2 Cor. 7:9–11). Such repentance denotes the repudiations of false ideas born of the kingdom of darkness, but also a disavowal of false apostle or prophets marketing such lies (2 Cor. 11:13–15).

Distance: Not an Option

When the crew of Apollo 13 was in jeopardy of not surviving the return to earth, Gene Krantz the director of Mission Control in Houston uttered the now famous line, "Failure is not an option!" In a similar vein, Jesus declares to Martha, "distance is not an option!" Stated more positively Jesus is asserting the imperative of intimacy with Him. Conversely, Jesus serves notice that Mary's priority of intimacy with Him was "needful." The word "kreia" translated "needful" denotes "an absolute necessity or imperative." To the Son of God, intimacy with Him was a paramount priority never to be relegated to back burner status.

Eternal Life Is Knowing Jesus

Jesus in the Good Shepherd discourse in John 10 declared, "The thief does not come but to steal, and to kill, and to destroy, I am come that you might have life and that you might have it more abundantly" (John 10:10). The eternal life that Jesus freely offers is more than the sweet by in by, in the sky when we die. It is a quality of life that believers enjoy when they pursue their relationship with Jesus Christ with abandon. Sarahs, like Mary, pursue this abundant life with gusto. This eternal life is embodied by knowing the Father. In His high priestly prayer prayed to the Father, "This is eternal life, that they may know You, the true God, and Jesus Christ Whom You have sent" (John 17:3). Mary knew the value of knowing Christ intimately. Mary's like her gladly proclaim, "That I may know Him and the power of His resurrection and the fellowship of His suffering…" (Phil. 3:10).

Devotion Means Abiding in Christ in Light
of His Any Moment Return

Devotion to Christ means abiding in Jesus in light of His any moment return for the church. John picked up on Jesus's theme of "constantly abiding" in 1 John 2:28. He tenderly charges, "Little children, abide in Christ, so that when He appears, we shall have confidence and not be ashamed before Him at His coming." If one truly loves another, they will take great pains to not displease them. This is true with married couples and is no less true with children. John admonishes his younger believers in the faith as the "beloved children of God," they must reciprocate that love by "purifying themselves, even as Christ is pure" (1 John 3:1–3).

This love for Jesus manifested through intimacy is alluded to by Paul in his letters. He charges, "If anyone does not love the Lord Jesus Christ, let him be accursed. O Lord come!" (1 Corinthians 16:22).

Again, in benedictory fashion Paul reminds the Ephesian church, "Grace be to those who love our Lord Jesus Christ in sincerity" (Ephesians 6:24).

Sincerity in this verse denotes an "undying" love. In both cases Paul is speaking of an authentic love that stands the test of time. Similar to the love cited in 1 Corinthians 16:22, Paul references a persevering love that lives each day in light of the imminent return of Jesus Christ for His church. For these believers, like Mary, Jesus's last word to the church in Revelation 22:12, pulsates with precious relevance, "Behold I am coming quickly, and My reward is with Me, to give to everyone according to his [her] work. I am Alpha and Omega, the Beginning and the End, the First and the Last." Those cultivating the devotion of Mary through abiding and abounding reap to themselves the eternal dividends of being praised and rewarded by their Master. They long to hear the coveted words of their Master, "Well done you good and faithful servants. You have been faithful over a few things I will make you ruler over many, enter into the joy of your Lord!" (Matt. 25:21,23).

Questions for Reflection

1) As a woman of extravagant devotion, Mary anointed Jesus with costly perfume. What gift would you gladly give to the Savior to demonstrate your love for Him?

2) What method do you use to absorb Jesus's words? Personal Bible study? Church attendance? Christian women's conferences? Small group Bible study?

3) Mary was an exemplary woman who abided in Christ. Conversely, her sister Martha abounded in good works. Both are important and should be connected in the Christ-follower. On a scale of 1–7, rate yourself in the area of abiding.

   1   2   3   4   5   6   7

   Rate your abounding in good works.

   1   2   3   4   5   6   7

   What would you like to take to improve in these areas?

4) Solomon wrote, "Honor the LORD with your substance and the firstfruits of your increase" (Prov. 3:9). In what are you giving God your best? What areas could your devotion to the Lord stand improvement?

5) Abel might be designated a male counterpart to Mary through his generous sacrifice to the LORD. Think of a time when you gave your best gift to the Lord Jesus. What was it? Money? Talent? Time?

   Are you planning any offerings to the Lord in the near future?

6) Have you ever abandoned your first love for the Savior? If so, how did you recapture your first love?

THE VIEW FROM A
WOMAN CAVE

"I have perfumed my bed with myrrh, aloes, and
cinnamon. Come let us take our fill of love until the
morning; Let us delight ourselves in love. For my
husband is not home; He has taken a long journey."
—Proverbs 7:18–19

There once were two sisters reared in seedy suburbia. Since their
native city simmered with godless values, both of them dated, fell in
love, and were engaged to unbelieving men. This posed a forbidding
problem for these two sisters since this city was ripe for the judgment
of God. When the Lord judged these cities for their moral bank-
ruptcy, idolatry, and rabid rebellion, both of their fiances were killed.
Mercifully, God spared these sisters along with their father. Though
they emerged physically unscathed from the horrendous judgment
rained on this city, they suffered moral injury. The godless smog of
the city suffocated their souls leaving them spiritually breathless.

Their respective fiances' now dead, they were left to care for
their aging father and mourn the loss of their deceased mother. Since
it was not politically correct to go through life without children, the
sisters opted to improvise. Since no men were in sight, they devised a
plan to intoxicate their father then seduce him. Their objective was to
have their aged father impregnate them so they could be loosed from
the social stigma of infertility. They succeeded in their mission. As
both daughters conceived and gave birth to healthy baby boys. These
baby boys became the progenitors of two wicked nations, namely
Moab and Ammon. As fate would have it, these nations became the

mortal enemies of the people of God. The perceptive reader may recognize this story as coming from the book of Genesis. It is the true story of two girls whose faith was plundered from within and by the immoral culture in ancient Sodom and Gomorrah.

While Lot was not blameless in this incestuous episode, it is beyond the scope of this book to address Lot's issues (hence, the title, *The Jezebel Syndrome*). The incest of Lot's daughters is emblematic of the immoral spirit of Jezebel. Today there is a moral pandemic in the church of Jesus Christ. This pandemic has afflicted young and old alike. Recently, I heard of a sister in Christ who was advised by her fellow sisters to sleep with the man she is dating before marrying him. Their thinking was one has to be certain that they are compatible in the sexual arena if they are going to wed. This sister was disillusioned as these women name the name of Christ! For such daughters of God, the Bible is clear, "Let everyone who names the name of Christ depart from inquity" (2 Tim. 2:19).

A Good Girl Gone Bad

Zoe was reared in a conservative Christian home. Having been first exposed to the Bible in her mother's womb, she can recite verbatim the ten commandments and most of the Sermon on the Mount. Rhetorically speaking, she knows all the verses. Zoe is attractive, vivacious, intelligent, articulate, and charming. Given her stunning appearance and impressive assets, no one was surprised that she caught the eye of Ted, a handsome student athlete with a bright future. They dated, fell in love, and were engaged to be married. After a few months of dating, Zoe and Ted begin having sexual relations. Afterward Zoe is besieged by guilt for indulging in conduct clearly displeasing to her Savior. She experiences, pangs of conscience, the Spirit's grief, and shame for betraying her conservative Christian upbringing, not to mention her Savior and Lord. Compounding her guilt is the prosaic reality that Ted is a not a Christian. How could she be engaged to a man who is obviously not saved? Zoe experiences intense warfare in the deepest part of her soul, knowing God's displeasure with couples being unequally yoked. However, she drowns the voice of God in an ocean of rationalizations. Lying to herself she reasons, "I know what I am doing is wrong, but God will forgive me. After all, God reserves infinite grace for all His children. Jesus died for all of my sins, including my sexual sins. Everything will be okay. God loves me unconditionally, forgives me completely, and sympathizes with my weakness. Therefore, I have nothing to fear. Besides, Ted and I are deeply in love and will marry someday. And when we do, I will take him to church and pray that he gets saved. In the meantime, God will understand and not hold pre-marital sex against us! God never gets angry with His children. After all, He is not mad at us, He is mad about us!" Is Zoe right in her assessment?

An Insightful Conversation

Several years ago, a pastor friend invited me to weigh in on a theological debate that had surfaced between the senior and youth pastor at his church. The disagreement was not over philosophy of ministry but theology. After briefly exchanging pleasantries with this gifted young pastor, he stated his bottom line up front. He informed me that the debated issue was whether God ever gets angry with His children. His senior pastor contended that God does indeed get angry with His children when they sin. He invited me to weigh in with my own perspective.

Much to his chagrin, I explained that the Bible emphatically teaches that God is angry with His children when they willfully indulge in sinful rebellion against Him. While the number of Scriptures expressing this in the Old Testament are legion, I cited Hebrews 10:38 as supporting evidence, "Now the just shall live by faith, But, if anyone draws back, My soul has no pleasure in Him." In this verse the authors employment of the literary device litotes (the expression of an intensified positive statement by a negative), conveys that God will be "very angry" with believers who recant on their faith in Jesus either through apostasy or rebellion. Certainly, God's anger is on display in the prophets. For instance, Habbakuk serves notice, "The LORD is purer eyes than to behold iniquity and cannot bear to look upon lawlessness" (Habakkuk 1:13). Since this conversation nearly two decades ago, this writer has encountered a vast network of sincere believers purporting that God's ire is never raised when His children engage in willful rebellion.

Legalism vs. Libertinism

The experience recalls a year in which this writer was called to minister to a group of people who were recovering from suffering in a spiritually abusive church. These precious saints migrated from a legalistic environment to one with strong libertinism tendencies. In this environment they were repulsed by any teaching that felt either obligatory or uncomfortable. This writer recalls an elder in a church he pastored chastising him for deriving from a biblical text "five obligations" rather than "five encouragements" of a local church. This elder's insistence on a "soft sell" approach to preaching is disturbing in light of the solemn charge Paul makes to Timothy, "I charge you therefore before God and the Lord Jesus Christ, who will judge the living and the dead and His appearing and kingdom. Preach the word!" Be ready in season and out of season. Convince, rebuke, exhort, with all long-suffering and teaching. For the time will come when they will not endure sound doctrine, but according to their own desires, because they have itching ears, they will heap up to themselves teachers; and they will turn away their ears from the truth and be turned to fables." (2 Timothy 4:1–4). Elsewhere Paul admonished his young protégé, "These things command and teach" (1 Timothy 4:11).

What We Think of God

Clearly, Paul was not timid while charging his young protege to not mince words relative the commands of God. Contrarily, "convince, reprove, rebuke, command, and teach," signal a hard rather than soft sell approach to preaching the infallible Word of God. Among other reasons, Paul disclosed that the basis for such unapologetic preaching was an inordinate thirst for false teaching in the church. The apostle of grace charged his young mentee that in the latter days spiritual quacks would dominate the religious landscape, marketing happiness over holiness, sentimentality over sanctification, feel good theology over biblical theology. Many decades ago, C. S. Lewis reflected on the feel-good theology of his day,

> "By the goodness of God nowadays we almost exclusively mean His lovingkindness; and in this we may be right, and by love in this context most of us mean kindness, the desire to see others than ourselves happy. Not happy in this way or just that but happy. What would really satisfy us is a God who said anything we happened to like doing, 'What does it matter so long as they are contented?' We want not so much Father in heaven, but a grandfather-a senile benevolence who, as they say, liked to see young people enjoying themselves, and whose plan for the universe was that it might be truly said at the end of each day, 'a good time was had by all.'"

Since Lewis penned those words over a half century ago, considerably more fog has been diffused concerning God's posture towards His children. While in evangelical circles, many correctly believe that the Father accepts the believer as a result of imputed righteousness, they simultaneously blur the biblical distinction between *imputed* righteousness and *practical* righteousness. God's Word teaches us that both forms of righteousness are important. In this vain, Joe Stowell accurately assesses, "God accepts us just as we are, but He is not satisfied with us just as we are." Satisfaction with one's maturity level is a spiritual dysfunction this writer labels performance confusion.

Is Love All You Need?

While perhaps not a buzzword familiar to many, performance confusion is well illustrated by the following candid confessions of a sincere believer:

> "I spent years focused on meaningless technicalities and powerless traditions of men, trying

to 'do' things or 'be' someone pleasing to God. I couldn't go to sleep without re-living my faults and failures of the day, confessing them (at least all I could remember) to be 'clean' before Him so I could go to sleep…only to wake up the next morning to the never-ending treadmill life men had introduced me to…of trying to do and be pleasing to God…all over again. 'Am I praying enough Lord? Reading my Bible enough? Do I worship You enough? Am I serving enough? Am I giving enough money? Are you pleased with me? Is anything I am doing enough??? If you'll just SHOW ME what you want me to do Lord, whatever it is… I'll promise I'll do it. I really want to know You are pleased with me God.' Then one day He answered my prayer. He SHOWED ME He was pleased with me from the moment He first thought of me (before I was even born) and that my Life was actually conceived 'out of His Love and pleasure! He began to reveal my true Life didn't originate from flesh and blood, or the will or passion of any man…but from the will, passion and joy of Him getting to BE my heavenly Father! I found out I didn't have to 'do' anything to bring joy to my Father's heart, and that He has always been pleased with me…not because of my performance (or lack of it) but just because I was His child, and in His eyes I had always been holy and blameless to Him in His love!"

Just my knowledge of that alone causes me to shout a resounding YES to actively participate in His divine nature with Him and His inheritance for me…and that alone gratifies and pleases Him… to the fullest extent! I go to bed much differently now. Sin is the furthest thing from my mind, because I know it is from His. I fall asleep with tears of joy thinking about all I got to participate in that day…

and how I will once again wake up tomorrow, in Papa's perfect will, His joy and His peace…and who we'll get to go out and Love on and be Jesus to…together as One! As He is, so am I. And I AM having the time of my life!

You are Loved…and were pleasing to your heavenly Father… before you were alive to know it. You belong, and you always have… even before you had the ability to say YES to enjoy it. Just say YES. Just Dive In. That's ALL Papa ever wanted…and the idea of that alone…was, and will always be…pleasing to Him!

Licensed to Sin?

At first blush, the reader may strongly concur with this brother's "enlightened" perspective. For this reflection accurately represents pop theology marketed by many churches. Yet sadly, the musings of this well-meaning brother fail the smell test of biblical scrutiny. Paul's instruction in 2 Corinthians 10:5 is relevant to this brother's rhapsody, "Casting down arguments and every high thing that exalts itself against the knowledge of God and bringing captive every thought to the obedience of Christ."

Sympathetically, one wonders if this brother experienced a "grace breakthrough" that caused him to be loosed from a legalistic pier. While there is merit to being loosed from the shackles of legalism, there is no virtue for one's spiritual pendulum to swing toward libertinism (spiritual license to sin). Even as one wag quipped, "Satan doesn't care which side of the horse you fall off as long as you fall off." In this respect, this brother's spiritual rhapsody fails the acid test of biblical truth. Is God concerned about practical righteousness after one is saved? Is He concerned about our sin? Is it possible to displease Him? Should a Christ-follower be concerned about practical righteousness after they are saved? Is the believer licensed to sin?

The Only Question?

Mystic author, Brennan Manning asserts that he "is utterly convinced that on the day of Judgment the Lord will ask His children only one question. Namely, did you know that I loved you?"[xvi] To believers enamored by "new and improved" ways to interpret the Bible, this perspective may sound appealing. But the question imperative for every Christ-follower to ask is does this perspective stand the scrutiny of Scripture? This chapter will attempt to answer such questions raised by contemporary western evangelicals.

The Payoff of Practical Righteousness

How would Jesus, the Apostle Paul or Peter answer Zoe or the young believer convinced that God had no expectations of him? In the Sermon on the Mount Jesus addresses His disciples. In both the immediate and larger context of Matthew's gospel, He delineates the character of those who will co-reign with Christ. He outlines the righteous conduct of those who will inherit the kingdom of heaven. Through the beatitudes and other teaching in His most famous sermon He informs His followers that righteousness, purity of heart, integrity of speech, sexual purity, forgiveness from the heart, humility, peacemaking, and loving one's enemies will characterize the life of those who will be called greatest in the kingdom of heaven.

Morality and Rewards in the New Testament

Following Jesus's line of thinking is the Apostle Paul in his letters to the Corinthians and Galatians. In 1 Corinthians 5–6, Paul commanded the Corinthian church that they exhibit "tough love" to brothers or sisters who willfully indulged in sexual immorality. He enjoins,

> "I wrote to you in my epistle not to keep company with sexually immoral people, Yet I certainly did not mean with the sexually immoral people of this world, or with the covetous, or extortioners, or idolaters, since then you would need to go out of the world. But now I have written to you not to keep company with any-

one named a brother, who is sexually immoral, or covetousness, or an idolater, or a reviler, or a drunkard, or an extortioner-not even to eat with such a person" (1 Corinthians 5:9–11).

Paul's strict directive not to consort with such classifications of unrepentant sinners was rooted in maintaining the purity of Christ's body (1 Corinthians 5:6–7). As apostle and spiritual father jealous for the bride and body of Christ (2 Corinthians 11:2–3), Paul recoiled at the possibility that his spiritual children might partake in the leaven of sexual immorality, drunkenness, idolatry, et al. In the same context, he offers strong incentive to abstain from such sins and unrepentant brothers themselves. He solemnly rebukes, "Do you not know that the unrighteous will not inherit the kingdom of God? Do not be deceived, neither fornicators, nor idolaters, nor adulterers, nor homosexuals, nor sodomites, nor thieves, nor covetous, nor drunkards, nor revilers, nor extortioners will inherit the kingdom of God" (1 Corinthians 5:9–11).

Some have contended that Paul distinguished between the Corinthian believers he was addressing and non-believers who imbibed in such sins of the flesh. Yet this is absurd in light of what he said earlier in Chapter 5, as one of their own was immersed in an incestuous relationship with his stepmother. The Corinthian believers risked forfeiture of eternal rewards if they indulged in such abominable deeds without repenting (see also, Galatians 5:19–21; 2 Corinthians 7:10–11: Eph 5:2–5). Paul issues the same warning to the Ephesian believers in Ephesians 5:2–5:

> But fornication and all uncleanness or covetousness, let it not be named among you, as it is fitting for saints; neither filthiness, nor foolish talking, nor coarse jesting, which are not fitting, but rather the giving of thanks. For this reason, you know that no fornicator, unclean person, nor covetous man, who is an idolater, has any inheritance in the kingdom of Christ and God.

Again, the eternal destiny of the believer in heaven is not at stake, as Paul outlined the ineffable heavenly blessings bequeathed to the church, including election before the foundation of the world, the adoption of sons, and the sealing of believers with the Holy Spirit of promise, which guarantees their salvation-inheritance (Eph. 1:3–14; 4:30). While the believers' eternal life is never in jeopardy, their reward-inheritance may be forfeited barring repentance from such abhorrent sins. Pursuant to this point, the author of Hebrews who expounds on the believer's reward-inheritance warns, "Marriage is honorable in all and the bed undefiled, but whoremongers and adulterers God will judge" (Hebrews 13:4).

The Children of Israel a Proof of Christ's Dealings with His Church

In 1 Corinthians 10:1–11 the Apostle Paul summarizes some of the most salacious episodes in Israel's storied history. He cites the narrative of Exodus 32:6 in the idolatrous episode of Israel at the base of Mount Sinai, "The people sat down to eat and drink and rose up to play," The Hebrew word, "play," denotes blatant sexual promiscuity. Israel's comingling idolatry with sexual immorality is always viewed by God as a heinous offence (see Revelation 2–3). By citing the ignominy of Israel's idolatrous and salacious behavior, Paul issues two egregious sins of Israel of old. Similarly, the pride of the Corinthian believers compelled them to tolerate a plethora of sinful activities in their midst. Simultaneous to referencing the plagues "the destroyer" (namely God), had leveled against them, he charges in 10:5, "but with most of them God was not well pleased for their bodies were scattered in the wilderness." In the next verse he warns, "Now these things became our examples, to the intent that we should not lust after evil things as they also did" (10:6). Five verses later, he reinforces this idea while adding an additional nuance, "Now all these things happened to them as examples, and they were written for our admonition, upon whom the ends of the ages have come."

When Paul "examples," means, "evidences," or "proofs." By this he is contending that the way God redressed Israel's sin mirrors

His [God's] dealings with the church today. In the wake of God's faithfulness to lovingly judge His church, just as He judged the children of Israel, Paul admonishes the Corinthians who judge themselves to be impervious to spiritual failure, to "take heed lest he fall" (1 Corinthians 10:11), "Flee from idolatry" (10:14). Previously, he urged them to "Flee sexual immorality" (1 Corinthians 6:18). When one considers the severe discipline God inflicted on the children of Israel, it seems preposterous that this same God would be indifferent to sexual immorality in the church. This writer is convinced that a careful reading of the New Testament not only reveals the Lord's antipathy for sin, but also how a believer's persistence in sinful conduct can result in the forfeiture of eternal rewards.

Morality and Ethics in Hebrews

The judgment which the author of Hebrews references, when taken in context, applies to both believers and non-believers. The author had already warned his readers of taking great pains to avoid the sin of that fornicator Esau (Hebrews 12:15–17). Preceding this solemn warning is 12:14, "Pursue peace with all people, and holiness, without which no one will see the Lord." Rather than teaching a works-based justification, a reward of intimacy with Christ is being taught. A beautific vision of God is in view. The author of Hebrews is expressing an idea similar to Jesus's beatitude, "Blessed are the pure in heart for they shall see God." In the larger context of Hebrews 12, the author is saying that God disciplines His children with the purpose of them being "partakers of His holiness," so they may enjoy intimate footing with their God. One outflow of holiness is sexual purity. For in the larger context of this passage we read, "Marriage is honorable in all and the bed undefiled; but fornicators and adulterers God will judge" (Hebrews 13:4).

Is God Ever Displeased with His Children?

His name was David. He was the hero of one of the most famous dramas in Old Testament history. The Bible says that God took David from the sheepfolds of Israel "to shepherd Jacob His people" (Psalm 78:70–71). God's presence and power was with him. The LORD loved David and uniquely blessed him. David cultivated an intimate relationship with His God. During critical decision points in his life, He "strengthened his hand in God" (1 Samuel 30:6). David was dubbed by the LORD, a man after God's own heart and the sweet Psalmist of Israel.

Yet David, like everyone else, was imperfect. In middle age, his relationship with the LORD began to grow stale. Familiarity with the Holy had bred contempt. Success in battle and other kingdom enterprises fostered a spirit of complacency, making him vulnerable to sin and temptation. In the season when kings routinely go to battle, David opted for a staycation at the palace. His poor choice was symptomatic of a spiritual drift factor in David's life. Ultimately it was a choice that culminated in disaster. After rising from a nap on the palace roof, he observed a beautiful woman bathing. His passions ignited, he sent for her and consummated an adulterous affair. Bathsheba, his mistress, soon after disclosed to the king that she was pregnant. In an effort to conceal his affair, and the paternity of their "love child," he summoned Uriah, a warrior in his Army, and Bathsheba's husband. Unable to execute his plot to cover his sin, he concocted a ruse to murder Bathsheba's husband. He succeeded. The casual reader might conclude that God was not angry with David's moral dalliance if it were not for ten words at the end of this dark drama, "But the thing that David had done displeased the LORD" (1 Samuel 11:27). The LORD in His divine displeasure severely disciplined David's sin with sevenfold judgment. God's displeasure with David's wickedness translated into holy anger. The familiar narrative illustrates that God does not greet our sin with a wink and a nod, but that it greatly offends Him. Yet there is hope for Davids and Jezebels.

Zoe: The Rest of the Story

After three months of sinful cohabitation with her boyfriend, Zoe is lovingly confronted about her immoral lifestyle by Priscilla, a godly co-worker. By citing several passages in the Sermon on the

Mount and Paul's epistles, Priscilla informs her that while God loves us unconditionally, He is displeased with us when we willfully rebel. Priscilla further instructs Zoe that leading a Christ-centered, moral and ethical life is a condition to co-heirship with Christ.

Zoe not only repents of her willful immorality, but also begins a Bible study with Priscilla on the Sermon on the Mount. During this Bible study, this daughter of God makes a firm commitment to pursue a life that will lead to her being "called great in the kingdom of heaven" (Matthew 5:19). Zoe was transformed from being a daughter of Jezebel to a daughter of Sarah.

Questions for Reflection

1) Zoe was a Christian who followed the pattern of Jezebel rather than the example of Sarah. While mired in an immoral lifestyle rationalized, "I know what I am doing is wrong, but God will forgive me." Have you ever entertained such thoughts?

2) To what extent do you agree that children of God can be enmeshed in heinous sins like immorality or extortion?

3) At the beginning of this chapter an essay is cited in which a believer purported that God is pleased with His children, no matter what they do. Do you agree with this assessment? Explain.

4) Jesus said, "Blessed are the pure in heart for they shall see God" (Matt 5:8). The author of Hebrews admonished, "Pursue peace with all people, and holiness, without which no one will see the Lord" (Hebrews 12:14). In both of these texts, the reward-inheritance of reigning with and enjoying intimacy with Christ is in view. On a scale of 1–7 assess how much often you have considered personal purity as a condition for eternal rewards?

1   2   3   4   5   6   7

5) God wants all of His children to be assured that by faith they receive the irrevocable gift of eternal life. Yet by reflecting on some of the Scriptures in this chapter, make a list of what kinds of activities displease Him?

6) Paul offers proof that the Lord was both displeased and dealt severely with His children who persisted in ungodly conduct, solemnly warning, "Now these things were our examples that we should not lust after evil things as they also lusted" (1 Corinthians 10:6, 11). Assess to what degree these negative proofs of God's dealings with His people coupled with these solemn warnings incentivize you to live a purer life?

1 2 3 4 5 6 7

JEZEBEL IN THE CHURCH

"If men won't be men, women will."
—Friedrich Neitzche

"Adam was not deceived, but the woman
being deceived was in the transgression."
—1 Timothy 2:14

Several years ago, I became acquainted with a ministry compatriot who pastored a church in the same city. I was impressed with this brother who had been gloriously saved and called by God to labor in His vineyard. However, over the course of time he encountered a woman who declared herself a prophetess. One major prophecy she made to this pastor is that he must divorce his wife and marry her! An affair between my colleague and this self-appointed prophetess ensued. This woman was an example of a contemporary Jezebel. She is reminiscent of the words of the Lord Jesus to the church of Thyatira, "Nevertheless, I have a few things against you, because you allow that woman Jezebel, who calls herself a prophetess, to teach and seduce My servants to commit sexual immorality and eat things sacrificed to idols" (Rev. 2:20).

Testing the Spirit of Jezebels

This contemporary Jezebel, like the ancient wicked queen, convinced one of Lord's choice servants to commit sexual immorality with her. The sheer fact that her teaching contradicted clear biblical prohibitions against sexual immorality and adultery, relegated her to false prophetess status. John's warning in 1 John 4:1 is timely,

"Beloved, do not believe every spirit, but test the spirits, whether they are of God; because many false prophets are gone out into the world." Zanes Hodges comments on this verse,

> "The mention of the Holy Spirit (3:24) causes John to pause for a warning that has been needed in every age of the Christian church. The Christian who possesses the Holy Spirit must not be so naïve as to think that God's Spirit is the only spirit at work in the world. Satan has many spirits who serve him here, as is shown by the fact that many false prophets have gone out into the world."[xvii]

The spirit of which Hodges speaks is the "spirit of Antichrist," and the "spirit of error" (1 John 4:3–4). Jesus originally charged John and the disciples to "test the spirits" of the false prophets. He warned in Matthew 7:16–19:

> Beware of false prophets, who come to you in sheep's clothing, but inwardly they are raven-ous wolves. You will know them by their fruits. Do men gather grapes from thornbushes or figs from thistles? Even so, every tree bears good fruit, but a bad tree bears bad fruit. A good tree cannot bear bad fruit, nor can a bad tree bear good fruit.

The fruit of which Jesus speaks is what they say. For both in the context of Matthew 7 and the parallel passage in Matthew 12, the litmus test for false prophets is their false teachings (see Matt. 12:31–37). This is what Jesus meant when He informed, "Therefore, by their fruits you will know them" (Matt. 7:20). John, following His Lord, admonishes the believers under his care to ensure that the teaching of anyone professing to speak for God correspond with the teachings of Jesus and His apostles by examining what the self-pro-claimed servant of God teaches. John references these teachings as the "doctrine of Christ" (1 John 1:8). Such false prophets or prophetesses failing this test are designated "deceivers and antichrists," who overflow with the "spirit of antichrist" (2 John 7; 1 John 4:3).

The Sin of Jezebel

As previously stated, Jezebel introduced Baal worship to the northern kingdom of Israel. Along with Baal worship, she urged the children of Israel to indulge in sexual immorality and practice child sacrifice. The LORD took such great offence at Ahab and Jezebel's false religion, that He shortly afterward judged them with the Assyrian captivity. The woman Jesus referenced metaphorically as Jezebel trafficked in "the deep things of Satan" (Rev. 2:24). Such abominable teachings were commensurate to what Paul referenced as the "doctrines of demons," that would pervade the church in the latter days (1 Tim. 4:1).

The Backdrop of "Jezebel Nation"

Who was the Jezebel who trafficked in the church of Thyatira? Some believed that she was the wife of a pastor in the church of Thyatira who went rogue. Though this woman's precise identity is unclear, what is clear is her propagation of a heresy greatly offensive to the living Christ. In the city of Thyatira, the trade guilds were governed by the god Apollo. Apollo, who was designated in ancient Greek mythology as, "the son of God," was designated the patron of the guilds. The "union dues" for being a member in good standing in these guilds was to participate in the immoral festivities in the temple of Apollo. The practice of believers accepting this rite of passage to remain a member in good standing with the guild, greatly offended the true Son of God, Jesus Christ. However, the social pressure to breach their loyalty to the living Christ was enormous. For failure to render due homage to Apollo could result in being barred from the trade guild and having your shop in the agora (marketplace) boycotted. Such disenfranchisement could lead to the closing of one's shop and the inability to feed one's family.

Jezebel's Solution

Members in the church of Thyatira were ensnared on the horns of a moral dilemma, do I follow Jesus, or do I cave to the pressure of idolatry to save my business? Jezebel was eager to help them resolve the dilemma. Her solution was to suggest that it was okay to participate in the festivities of the temple, to including eating meat that had been sacrificed to idols and participating in the sexual orgies. Jesus identifies her sin as "to teach and seduce My servants to commit sexual immorality and eat things offered and eat things sacrificed to idols" (Rev. 2:20). John Walvoord underscores the identity of this shadowy character in Thyatira:

> "Jesus's major condemnation of Jezebel was that she was a false prophetess who taught believers to take part in sexual immorality that accompanied pagan religion and to eat food sacrificed to idols. What was acceptable to that local society was abhorred by Christ. Their departure from morality had gone on for some time (v. 21). The church in Thyatira may have first heard the gospel from Lydia, converted through Paul's ministry (Acts 16:14–15). Interestingly now a woman, a self-claimed 'prophetess,' was influencing the church. Her name "Jezebel" suggests that she was corrupting the Thyatira church much like Ahab's wife Jezebel corrupted Israel (1 Kings 16:31–33) Christ promised sudden and immediate judgment, called her sin adultery and promised, that all who follow her would suffer intensely. He also promised, I will strike her children dead, meaning that the suffering would extend also to her followers. The judgment would be so dramatic that all the churches would know that Christ is the One who searches the hearts and the minds."[xviii]

The Importance of Doctrinal Purity

In the first century there was a notorious heretic named Cerinthus. Cerinthus erroneously taught that Jesus was an ordinary man upon whom the Spirit descended at His baptism and departed at His crucifixion. The Apostle John while attending the public bath encountered this notorious "Antichrist." He hastily left the public of bath. Jude, the brother of Jesus, under the inspiration of the Spirit of God, admonished the church in Jude 3–4, "Beloved, while I was very diligent to write to you of our common salvation, I found it necessary to write to you exhorting you to earnestly contend for the faith once delivered to the saints. For certain men have crept in unnoticed, who long ago were marked out for this condemnation, ungodly men, who turned the grace of God into lewdness and deny the only Lord God and our Lord Jesus Christ." Jezebel's heresy attacked the doctrine of Christ, which represented the faith that was once delivered to the saints.

Today's Heresies

Jezebel may have contended that Jesus was not the only way to the Father (John 14:6). While sporting a COEXIST bumper sticker on her chariot, she may have purported that the best version of Christianity was wedded to other world religions. She was the queen of religious syncretism. Like a person feasting at a buffet of religious ideas, Jezebel chose her favorite heretical entrees to the neglect of healthy doctrinal foods she considered less palatable. Jezebel snacked on the meringue of false teaching, while refusing the solid food of Christ-centered teaching. She might have asserted that Jesus did not share equal divine par with the Father, but was inferior to Him. In this vein, she might have viewed Jesus as a demi-god, or divine errand boy when God flung the galaxies into existence. She might have downgraded Jesus in another way by teaching that His divine persona featured both good and evil. Following the infamous first century heretic Cerinthus she might have declared that that Jesus, the Man, and the Christ were two distinct people. Jezebel may have purported that Christ descended on Jesus (the man), at His baptism and departed from Him shortly before His death. Finally, in a Gnostic culture, immorality should be viewed not as sinful, but virtuous since what one does with their physical body is inconsequential. All such doctrines would fail the test of orthodox Christianity and would have righteously angered the living Christ.

Jezebel's Judgment

Just as God's judgment on the northern kingdom of Ephraim was inevitable after the wicked reign of Ahab and Jezebel, so God was ready to judge the Church of Thyatira if they did not repent. Jezebels stubborn refusal to repent invited imminent judgment. Jesus solemnly warned, "Indeed I will cast her into a sickbed, and those who commit adultery with her into great tribulation, unless they repent of their deeds. And I will kill her children with death, and all the churches will know that I am He who searches the minds and hearts. And I will give each one of you according to his works" (Rev. 2:22–23). The present tense of, "will cast" suggests that the process of judging this sect bearing Jezebel's name had already begun.

The Deception of Jezebel

Jezebel majors in deception and minors in truth. Like Lucifer who deceived Eve, though her theology is stained with the veneer of truth, it is composed of the rotted oak of lying deceit. Jezebels market godless philosophies cleverly concealing the age-old lie, that men and women can be gods (Gen. 3:4–5; 2 Thes. 2:11). Such a false ideology was propagated by actress Shirley MacLaine who shamelessly boasted on a beach, "I am god! I am god! I am god!" Today's Jezebels profess that adherents to their heresy will be privy to an esoteric knowledge of God exclusive to those practicing their deception. They persuade others that the simple gospel they have been taught is patently false. They scornfully reject Jesus's claim that faith in Him is the only way to the Father (John 14:6). In short, they have fallen prey to Eve's deception.

Eve's Deception

It is noteworthy, that whenever Eve is mentioned in the Scripture her deception by Satan is simultaneously cited. Writing under the inspiration of God's Spirit, Paul was concerned with the church being deceived by false apostles who specialized in putting the best face on falsehood. These spiritual intruders, following the lead of their Satanic commander, were experts at sleight of hand, sophistry (putting the best face on falsehood), and deceit (2 Cor. 11:13–15). In this heretical atmosphere Paul divulged his heartfelt concern to the Corinthians in 2 Corinthians 11:3, "But I fear, lest somehow as the serpent deceived Eve by his craftiness, so your minds may be corrupted from the simplicity that is in Christ."

Given Paul's concern, careful consideration is warranted for comparing Eve's deception to the Corinthian's deception. For Eve's deception and that of her daughters is one of the primary reasons Paul give for forbidding women to teach in the church. Paul similarly writes in 1 Timothy 2:13, "For Adam was not deceived, but the woman being deceived fell into the transgression."

Adam sinned willfully. Eve was deceived. When the LORD confronted Eve for her sin she admitted, "The serpent deceived me, and I ate" (Gen. 3:13). While Eve's passing the buck of her sin onto Satan was inappropriate, her admission that the serpent deceived her is spot-on accurate. Eve, and her daughters' proclivity toward deception is a primary reason why God has decreed that they not exercise authority over a man, nor teach. The woman's proclivity toward deception is hinted at by Paul in 2 Timothy 3:6–7, "For of this sort are those who creep into households and make captives of gullible women loaded down with sins, led away of various lusts, always learning and never able to come to the knowledge of the truth."

Apostate teachers are able to deceive gullible women due to their vulnerabilities to deception. By offering a rationale for the women's role in the church, based on the fall, Paul is offering keen insight into fallen womanhood. For in the fall, two salient aspects of Eve's sin our observed. First, Eve deception by the serpent highlights her vulnerability to deception. By citing this Paul may be contending that her propensity toward deception is stronger than that of Adams.

Eve's Attempted Domination

Secondly, Eve sinned by usurping the role of Adam. Eve's giving of the fruit to Adam was an expression of domination. While it is true that Adam sinned in accepting and eating of the fruit of the tree, Eve's domination must not be casually dismissed. The woman's domination of the man militated against God's order of creation, which bequeathed Adam with the hierarchical position of headship. Therefore, for Paul to empower women to lead in the church would fuel the curse and run counter-course to the divine order.

Adam's God given position of headship is witnessed through the order of creation, namely, the fact that he was "first formed" (1 Tim. 2:13). One may also contend for Adam's headship as a result of his naming his wife Eve (Gen. 3:20). Therefore, prohibiting the daughters of Eve from ruling in the church appears logical in light of the curse brought about by Eve's usurpation of Adam's authority.

The Man's Authority in the Old Testament

The Old Testament model for leadership is top heavy with male dominance. Whenever women are mentioned in a prophetic role, they are assigned a secondary or tertiary role. Deborah and Miriam are examples of this pattern. Barak's timidity in fulfilling his role as a judge paved the way for Deborah to excel in her role as an associate judge. Yet the narrative of Barak and Deborah demonstrates that this was not God's design. Ironically, Barak is mentioned in the great faith hall of fame in Hebrews 11:32. Miriam, the sister of Moses was afflicted of leprosy for usurping her brother's authority as God's appointed leader of Israel. Feminine leadership of men, flies in the face of the overall biblical theme of the man (andra, "man, husband"), being the authoritative head over his wife. The subordination of the wife to the husband's authority is a theme replete in both the Old and New Testaments. Throughout the Pentateuch (first five books of the Bible), the Hebrew wife's submissive role is often highlighted. In one instance, the husband possesses the "authority" to nullify a vow that his wife makes if he does not approve of such a vow. A father is afforded the same veto power of vows over his daughter (Num. 30:10–15).

In another instance, if a "spirit of jealousy" came over the husband, the wife was subjected to a battery of tests engineered by God to determine whether she had been unfaithful to her husband or was innocent of all charges (Num 5). The rationale for this ancient litmus test ascertaining the wife's fidelity underscores the authoritative God-given role of the husband the marriage relationship. Numbers 5:29 summarizes, "This is the law of jealousy, when a wife, while under her husband's *authority*, goes astray and defiles herself." (italics mine).

The Need for Sound Principles of Interpretation

When approaching the role of women in the local assembly, it is imperative to apply sound principles of hermeneutics. John R. W. Stott remarks about the need for sound principles of interpretation, "The danger of declaring any passage of Scripture to have only local (not universal), and only transient (as opposed to timeless), validity is that it opens the door to a wholesale rejection of apostolic teaching, since virtually the whole of the New Testament was addressed to specific situations. Whenever we can show that an instruction related to a particular context, shall we then limit it to that context and declare it irrelevant to all others? For example, the command to 'be subject to all rulers and authorities,' was addressed to Cretans whose rebellious spirit was proverbial; does it therefore not apply to non-Cretans? We might also argue that what Paul wrote about homosexual practice, simplicity of lifestyle, the uniqueness of Christ, world evangelization and many other topics was fine for his day. But times have changed, we belong to different cultures, and (some would add) we know more about those things that he did. So what he wrote had no authority over us."[xix] One of the problems as seeing Paul's prohibitions as being merely cultural rather than universal and timeless in scope is that Paul is teaching theology referenced elsewhere. To this end Packer asserts,

"The man-woman relationship is intrinsically non-reversible… This is part of the reality of creation, a given fact that grace restores nature, not abolishes it."xx

The Clear Passages

Hitch-hiking off Stott's remarks, it must be remembered that 1 Timothy 2 and 1 Corinthians 11 are the two most foundational chapters in the New Testament governing the conduct of women in the local assembly. When interpreting these seminal texts, it is imperative to keep in mind the cardinal hermeneutical principle that we must interpret the obscure scripture by the clear scripture. Both 1 Timothy 2 and 1 Corinthians 11 are undisputable prescriptive passages containing issuing clear prohibitions delineating the woman's role in the church in every era.

Moreover, it must be kept in mind that sound hermeneutical principles inform us that descriptive texts are subordinate to prescriptive texts of scripture. An example of this is viewing the narrative reporting that Philip had seven daughters who prophesied (Acts 21:9), as subordinate to the prescriptive texts of 1 Timothy 2 and 1 Corinthians 11 which clearly define the woman's role in the local assembly.

The Dual Role of Women in the Local Assembly

Two complementary imperatives form the dual roles of the woman in Paul's house order. The first imperative defining the Christian woman's role is defined positively in 1 Timothy 2:11, "for the woman to learn in silence with all submission." This phrase assigns to the Christian woman both a passive and submissive role of learning in the local assembly. In the local assembly, they are instructed to quietly learn from the teaching elder (1 Tim. 5:17). The second set of imperatives is stated subsequently in verse 12, "And I do not permit a woman to teach, nor to usurp authority over a man, but to be in silence." In this verse the imperative of women not teaching in the local assembly is stated negatively. It compliments Paul's previous instruction that the "woman learn in silence, with all submission." Paul adds a second prohibition, "nor to usurp authority over the man" (v. 12). He reinforces both prohibitions by repeating, "but to be in silence." Both of these imperatives are given in the context of Paul's house order for the local assembly.

God's House Order for the Church

In an effort to undergird the headship of Adam and avoid the deceptive plight of Eve, Paul outlines a house order for worshipping community of saints in the New Testament era. The Bible unequivocally asserts that God is a God of order rather than confusion. Paul writes to the carnal Corinthians church whose public worship was in a state of disarray, "For you can all prophesy one by one, that all may learn and all may be encouraged. And the spirit of the prophets are subject to the prophets. For God is not the author of confusion but of peace, as in all the churches of the saints" (1 Corinthians 14:32–33).

Implied in Paul's instruction of the Lord being a God of "peace" rather than "confusion" is the need for a "house order," which Paul establishes in the Pastoral epistles and 1 Corinthians 11–14. The most explicit statement in the New Testament pursuant to this house order is stated as Paul's purpose for writing his young pastoral protégé Timothy, in 1 Timothy 3:14, "These things I write to you, though I hope to come to you shortly; but if I am delayed, I write so that you may know how you ought to conduct yourself in the house of God, which is the church of the living God, the pillar and ground of the truth."

Paul imparted timeless truths concerning the house order of the church that he would prefer to offer in person. However, in the face of Paul's uncertain itinerary, the next best option was to write a letter establishing this house order for public worship. As the Apostle of grace writing by the Spirit of God, he establishes some strict guidelines of conduct for when the saints assemble to worship. Paul specifically outlines the conduct during the worship service in 1 Timothy 2:1–15.

"I desire therefore, that the men pray everywhere, lifting up holy hands, without wrath or doubting; in like manner also, that the women adorn themselves in modest apparel, with propriety and moderation, not with braided hair, or gold or pearls or costly clothing. But which is proper for women professing godliness, with good works. Let a woman learn in silence with all submission. And I do not permit a woman to teach or to have authority over a man, but to be in silence. For Adam was first formed, then Eve. And Adam was not deceived, but the woman being deceived, fell into transgression. Nevertheless, she shall be saved in childbearing, if they continue in faith, love, and holiness, with self-control."

A Natural Interpretation

In this passage Paul issues no disclaimers or exceptions which would signal that his instruction is temporary (e.g., "for the present distress," see 1 Cor. 7:26). Again, sound hermeneutical principles inform us that Paul's instruction is normative and timeless rather than temporary. While this passage is one of the clearest didactic (instructional) passages in all of Paul's thirteen letters, many believers have taken exception to the contents of Paul's Holy Spirit inspired teaching (2 Tim. 3:16–17; 2 Pet. 1:20–22). Some have labeled Paul a bigot. Others have crafted creative interpretations to coincide with politically correct narratives. These interpretations are reminiscent of the sign at the entrance of a blacksmith shop, "Many twists and turns forged here!" The same could be said for contemporary interpretations of Paul's teaching concerning the role of women in the church. Ostensibly due to the invasion of secular feminist, many have hammered out a more politically correct interpretation of this passage. However, biblical integrity dictates that we seek "authorial" or "author's" intent when interpreting this passage while resisting the impulse of forging feministic values into the text. As a part of this house order, he discusses the content of public prayer, and the roles of both men and women during the worship service.

Perhaps anticipating the objections of some, he offers a rationale for why women are not to teach in the worship service. Contending for the timelessness of this house order, are Paul's introductory remarks in 1 Timothy 2:7. Paul introduces himself as "a preacher and an apostle-I am speaking the truth in Christ and not lying-a teacher of the Gentiles in faith and truth." By flashing his apostolic credentials, he lays the groundwork of timeless statutory teaching for the church in every generation.

Feminine Modesty in Every Respect

Writing under the inspiration of God's Spirit, Paul establishes a house order for women in the local church. A corresponding passage also offering divine directives for the role of women the church is 1 Corinthians 11:2–16. In a previous chapter the modesty of the Christian wife was addressed. This moral grace has become a lost art in our promiscuous American culture. While the world does not place a high premium on modesty, God does. The Lord values modesty in general and particularly during the worship service. The most noticeable external characteristic of the Christian woman is to be godliness rather than gaudy attire. The biblical mantra best capturing this primary trait of Sarahs as explained in Proverbs 31:30, "Charm is deceitful, beauty is vain, but a woman who fears the LORD shall be praised." Paul's instruction parallels that of Peter's in which the "hidden beauty of the heart," is "incorruptible," and priceless in God's sight (1 Pet. 3:4). The woman's quiet submission is viewed as an act of holy reverence which honors God as the assembly of the saints gathers to worship Him. The woman's humble submission first to the Lord, and secondly to her husband is critical as the angels are the heavenly spectators at every worship service (1 Cor. 11:10).

Submissive Wives and Worshippers

In this parallel text to 1 Timothy 2:8–15, it is clear that the Christian wife serves in a godly, subordinate role to her husband. This is evidenced by the phrase, "all submission." The Greek word, "panton," meaning, "every, all," denotes, "submission in everything." While many promptly explain away the word, "all, everything," Paul allows for no such ambiguity for excusing insubordination due to personal disagreements. The definitive "all" is intended to censure ungodly tendencies to superimpose carnal rationalizations on the text. Such thoroughgoing obedience is consistent with the biblical contexts in which submission in enjoined (Eph. 5:21–6:5; Rom. 13:1–7; Col. 3:17–25; 1 Pet. 3:1–6). The New Testament writers command:

> "Bondservants, *obey* in *all things* your masters according to the flesh." (Col. 3:22, italics mine)

> "Bondservants be *obedient* to those who are your masters according to the flesh, with fear and trembling, in sincerity of heart, *as to Christ.*" (Eph. 6:6, italics mine)

> "*Submit* yourself to *every* ordinance of man for the Lord's sake." (1 Pet. 2:13, italics mine)

> "Let a woman learn in *silence,* with *all submission.*" (1 Tim. 2:11, italics mine)

> "Children, *obey* your parents *in the Lord, for this is right."* (Eph. 6:1, italics mine)

> "*Render* therefore, to *all their due."* (Rom. 13:17, italics mine)

> "*Obey* those who rule over you and be *submissive* for they watch for your souls." (Heb. 13:17, italics mine)

> "Wives *submit* to your husbands, *as to the Lord."* (Eph. 5:22, italics mine)

"Wives *submit* to your own husbands, *as it is fitting in the Lord."* (Col. 3:18, italics mine)

"Wives likewise, be *submissive* to your own husbands, that *even if they do not obey the word,* they may without the word may be won by the conduct of their wives" (1 Pet. 3:1, italics mine).

"that they admonish the young women to love their husbands, to love their children, to be discreet, chaste homemakers, good, *obedient to their own husbands"* (Titus 2:4–5, italics mine).

Submission and Obedience the Ethic of the Kingdom of Christ

Just as a slave was instructed to submit to their masters in everything (Col. 3:22), Christ-followers to "submit to every ordinance of man" (1 Pet. 2:13–15), Christians were commanded to submit to their spiritual leaders (Heb. 13:17), and children were to obey their parents in all things (Eph. 6:1–3), so wives were to submit themselves to their husband in everything, in which they were not required to sin (Acts 5:29). As previously noted, many recoil at a teaching they might consider dictatorial or oppressive. One popular strained interpretation is that the wife submits to their husbands when they agree with their husband's opinion or conduct. Yet this is precisely what Paul does *not* command. Such a view would be absurd as it would issue a hall pass for a wife's insubordination in any area she disagreed with her husband.

Submission and Reverence

In the context of 1 Timothy 2 and other places where the role of the wife is defined, submission is not conditioned upon the sinlessness of the party being submitted to, but reverence for God. Reverence for God is best reflected in submitting to human authority (Col. 3:18–23; Eph. 5:22–24; 6:1–9). Again, this does not in any way imply inferiority to their husbands or men in general, but that she has been assigned a different role by God both in the marriage and the church. The pattern for such submission is Christ's submission to the Father. While not one whit inferior to the Father, Jesus voluntarily submitted Himself to the will of the Father. He testified to the Jews, "I always do those things that please Him" (John 8:29). Jesus submitted Himself to the Father's commandments and "learned obedience through the things which He suffered" (John 10:18; Heb. 5:8). Such submission did not militate against Jesus's equality with the Father as He was "One with the Father" (John 10:30).

One might object that Jesus by submitting to the Father, was submitting to a holy and sinless God. Wives unlike Jesus, are compelled to submit to a sinful husband. However, a wife's submission to her husband either in the home or in the worshipping community is not about her husband, but her Lord. Pleasing the Lord is the impetus for submitting to fallen authorities, such as masters, imperfect rulers judges, and police officers, disobedient husbands, and sinful parents (Col. 3:18–4:1). For just as trials are a test of our faith, so submission and obedience are a demonstration our reverence for Christ. Every Christ-follower is called by God to cultivate the fine art of submission. It is critical that Christ-follower recognize that submission is not about the person being submitted to, but about one's reverence for God. Both of these moral graces of trust and reverence are illustrated in the narrative of God's supreme test of Abraham's faith. After Abraham passed his most excruciating test of his faith, the Lord declared, "for now I know that you *fear God*, since you have not withheld your son, your only son from Me" (Gen. 22:12, italics mine).

Applications of Submission in the Community of Faith

The emphatic contrast in roles between men and women is signified by Paul's usage of the strong adversative, alla, translated, "but" in verse 10. By employing this adversative Paul is serving notice that women serve in a decidedly different role than men in the local church. This differing role encompasses the spiritual responsibilities of teaching and leadership. In this respect women are commanded by the apostle to neither teach nor occupy roles of leadership. Paul leverages his apostolic authority by unequivocally commanding, "And I do not permit a woman to teach or to have authority over a man, but to be in silence" (1 Tim. 2:13). The Greek infinitive, "to teach," "didaskein," occurs first in the Greek sentence structure. When a word occurs first in a sentence this means that it is "emphatic," meaning the most prominent idea being conveyed by the author. This means that imperative prohibition disallowing women to teach in the local assembly is Paul's primary emphasis. What Paul is saying about the subject of teaching is that Greek, "gunaiki" (woman, wife), are "ouk" (not) to teach. The complimentary prohibition is captured in the phrase, "oude authentein andros" ("nor to usurp authority over a man") is a blanket prohibition of a woman exercising authority over an "andros," "man, husband." The word, "oude" nullifies any possibility of a woman either teaching or exercising authority over a man. By employing the word, "authenteo," Paul is employing a generic term that simply means "to exercise authority." The negation of the word reinforces the prohibition of women exercising authority in the local assembly.

Practically, this prohibition makes eminent sense in 1 Timothy when one considers that Paul's leadership qualifications are addressed to men rather than women. Paul instructs in 1 Timothy 3:2, "A bishop is to be blameless, the husband of one wife..." While delineating the qualifications of deacons, he instructs, "likewise, their wives must be reverent," and "the husbands of one wife" (1 Tim. 3:11–12). This same stipulation is repeated by Paul in Titus 1:6 when Paul establishes the house order for elders. Paul again writes, "if a man is blameless, the husband of one wife." It is arresting to consider that Paul never says, "the wife of one husband."

Summarizing Paul's House Order

First Timothy 2:11–12 represent the clearest statement on the role of women in the worshipping assembly. The natural force of the grammar is that women are neither permitted to teach nor exercise authority. To reinforce the non-negotiability of this role, Paul employs the strong adversative, "alla" which contrasts the role of men as leaders in the worship assembly with that of the women.

The Natural Force of the Text

While some have performed radical surgery on this prohibition, Paul's terse imperative lacks the resiliency to be reshaped into an unnatural and amorphous command. Contextually, Paul emphatically prohibits women from teaching in the worshipping assembly of the saints, or holding positions of authority in which they lead men (see 1 Tim. 3:1–13). The imperative, "Do not permit" speaks of a clear prohibition of teaching and occupying positions of leadership in the worshipping community. This underscored by two strong Greek negations, namely, "ouk," and "oude." These negative Greek particles translated, "no, not," negate the verbs they modify, namely, "teaching," and "exercising authority."

Teaching, Pastoral Authority, and God's House Order

Teaching in the worship service where men and women are present is an obvious form of "exercising authority." This command is couched in the "house order" in which Paul delineates to Timothy in 2 Timothy 4:1–3, "I charge you therefore, before God and the Lord Jesus Christ, who will judge the living and the dead at His appearing and His kingdom: Preach the word! Be ready in season and out of season. Convince, rebuke, exhort, with all longsuffering and teaching."

Paul's solemn charge to preach the Word in his second letter to Timothy is heavily freighted with the language of pastoral authority. Implicit within the imperatives, "convince, rebuke, exhort, and teach," is the strong exercise of authority through the declaration of God's Word. Secondly, Paul's dual prohibitions of women teaching and exercising authority is a precursor to Paul's citing of the qualifications of a local church leader in the next chapter. Therefore, the phrase, "nor to exercise authority over man," is not merely perfunctory or obsolete, but is foundational to Paul's house order (1 Tim. 3:14–15). Paul serves unequivocal notice that teaching and leadership in the New Testament church is the domain of godly men (1 Tim. 3:1–13; Tit. 1:5–8). As previously stated, in such passages the qualified elders and deacons are "andra" (men, husband). One crowning mark of the elder is that he is a "one woman man," as opposed to a "one man woman."

The Rationale behind the Women's Role

Paul's command is not local, but global, not provincial, but pandemic. This is evident as Paul continues to offer a theological rationale for commandments that may seem draconian to a culture overrun by rampant feminism. After issuing joint imperatives concerning the woman's role in the church, Paul cites the order of creation and Eve's deception as the dual rationale for these imperatives. Paul explains in verses 13–14, "For Adam was first formed, then Eve. And Adam was not deceived, but the woman being deceived was in the transgression."

Paul's final explanation in verse 14, "but the woman being deceived was in the transgression," could indicate that one reason women are barred from teaching or leading in the church is due to the curse. Both Eve's deception, and attempted heist of Adam's headship, netted Eve a talionic punishment similar to "an eye for an eye tooth for a tooth, hand for a hand, foot for a foot, burn for a burn" (Ex. 21:24; Lev. 14:20; Deut. 19:21). Judgments on sin are frequently retributive (talionic) in this way. One example of this is Genesis 9:6 injunction of capital punishment for premeditated murderers. The rationale is given that if one premeditatively takes the life of another, they have slain God in effigy and automatically forfeit their right to life.

God's Order of Creation and Marriage

There are at least two additional contextual problems with imposing a local rather than a universal application on this text. In addition to Paul's emphasis on sacred and unchangeable theology when he reasons, "For Adam was first formed then Eve. And Adam was not deceived, but the woman being deceived, fell into transgression" (1 Tim. 2:13–14). While Paul was not absolving Adam of moral responsibility for the fall (Rom. 5:17–19), his purpose was to cite theological reasons for women not teaching or exercising authority. One is related to the order of creation, while the other is related to Eve's proclivity towards deception.

The Woman a Helpmate

Adam being created before Eve, represented God's choice as a leader in the field and in the home. Eve was created later, not to be the leader, but the "helpmate, suitable for him" (Gen. 1:28). Helpmate, or "helper," denotes "a completer, assistant." The word translated "helpmate" (ezer) is a noble word often used of God's assistance of His people. The concept is illustrated in Hebrews 13:6, "God is my Helper I will not fear what can man can do to me?" While God bestowed abundant honor on Eve as Adam's helpmate, He did not bequeath to her equal authority with Adam. For while Eve was inherently equal to her husband, as having been created in the image of God (Gen. 1:26–27), she was nonetheless subordinate to him in authority. Corroborating evidence for Adam's authority over Eve is his naming of his wife. Genesis 3:20 reads, "And Adam called his wife's name Eve, because she was mother of all the living." While this book has already addressed the topic of Eve and her daughters' proclivity toward deception, suffice it to say this is seen as a practical and theological rationale for women not leading in the church.

Why More Easily Deceived?

One reason why Eve and her daughters are more easily deceived is that by nature they struggle to separate truth and emotions. While men are scripted to compartmentalize emotions and reason, causing one author to quip, "men are like waffles, women are like spaghetti." Similarly, Christian marriage expert, Emerson Eggerichs asserted that men are hardwired by God with a segregated personality (waffles), women conversely sport an integrated personality (spaghetti). Men, as evidence by warriors in combat, police swat teams during a raid, or firefighters rushing into burning buildings, are able to shove their emotions into a lock box while risking life and limb. This same innate capacity empowers them to compartmentalize their emotions when forced to make a rationale decision. This makes godly men prime candidates to be spiritual leaders in the church of Jesus Christ.

However, God did not hardwire women with the same capacities. I recently heard of a female rescue worker who confessed that women are unable to process their emotions the same way men are when confronted with a life-threatening situation. This is because a woman's personality is like a tether that is seamlessly woven together so that each part impacts the whole. Therefore, in the arena of a woman's soul, an inner warfare often ensues when presented with the truthfulness of God's Word. Often in the war theater of the mind, their emotions inordinately conquer the truthfulness of God's Word. In this respect they sacrifice God's truth on the altar of their feelings. Even God-fearing women, occasionally fight the inner demons of fallen emotions and idolatry of the mind. In this vein, a woman's emotions become the *default* voice of God that drowns out the *true* voice of God as heard in His Word. This author has witnessed this struggle in conversing and counseling Christian women for nearly four decades. It has been my observation that when confronted with biblical truth, women are much more apt than men to dismiss God's commands on the basis of personal sentiments, peer pressure, political correctness, or group-think mentalities.

The Male Teaching and Leadership Gene

Just as God has innately programed women with intrinsic strengths born of nature and nurture, so He has equipped men with an analytics tools to advance objective arguments relatively free of personal sentiment or bias. This is not to say that men never struggle with bias, as prejudice is deeply embedded in the DNA of every person. Yet the male capacity for compartmentalization, makes them better leaders and teachers. Men make better teachers as they possess a better facility for objective thinking. Often when men disagree with each other they preface such dissenting opinions with, "I respectfully disagree." Conversely, women tend toward sentimentally lacking the true north compass of God's Word. Women when confronted with a minor disagreement will often opt for emotional subjectivity over biblical objectivity. The feminine propensity of permitting the tale of their emotions to wag the dog of truth, often leads to poor decision making and destructive conflict. Such is illustrated in Eve's deception leading to eating of the forbidden fruit. Her deception and attempted domination of Adam, made "naked and afraid," the new normal replacing the pristine status of "naked and not ashamed," in her relationship with God and Adam (Gen. 2:24–3:1–7).

Women in the Church

In this environment even Christian women who follow in Eve's train, may sow seeds of discord with whom they disagree to the point of character assassination. While invoking the spirit of Jezebel rather than Sarah, they will speak disparagingly of those with whom they even have an honest disagreement. I have witnessed this trend often in both believing and non-believing women. In the church, the net result is often a deeply divided local assembly in which Satan gains a firm foothold. Again, Paul states the matter clearly, "Adam was not deceived, but the woman being deceived was in the transgression."

In brief, men are less susceptible to deception than women. Eve was seduced by the serpent's beauty, "wisdom," and diabolic charm. In so doing, she casually brushed aside the truth Word of God, given to her by her husband Adam. The results were pandemic. She was deceived by him. She ate of the forbidden fruit. To cite the tired cliché, the rest is history.

The Woman's Role from 1 Corinthians 11

Corresponding to Paul's instruction in 1 Timothy 2:8–15 is 1 Corinthians 11:2–12. Here Paul admonishes,

> Now I praise you, brethren, that you
> remember me in all things and keep the tradi-
> tions just as I delivered them to you, But I want

you to know that at the head of every man is Christ, the head of woman is man, and the head of Christ is God. Every man praying or prophesying with his head covered, dishonors his head. But every woman who prays or prophesies with her head uncovered dishonors her head, for that is one and the same as if her head was shaved. For if a woman is not covered, let her also be shorn. But if it is shameful for a woman to be shorn or shaved, let her be covered. For a man indeed ought not to cover his head, since she is the image and glory of God; but woman is the glory of man. For man is not from woman, but woman from man. Nor was man created for the woman, but woman for the man. For this reason, the woman ought to have a symbol of authority on her head because of the angels. Nevertheless, neither is man independent of the woman, nor woman independent of the man, in the Lord. For as woman came from the man, even so man also comes through woman, but all things are from God.

After applauding the saints for following the traditions of the early church, Paul establishes a pecking order for divine worship. The phrase, "traditions as I delivered them to you," is code for sacred teachings of the faith. This is similar to Jude's words, "that you should earnestly contend for the faith that was once delivered to the saints" (Jude 3). By prefacing his remarks this way, Paul is serving notice that the instruction he is about to issue is solemnly timeless. This order involved both authority and submission. Moreover, the wearing of a head covering for the woman is a symbol of this subordinate role. Paul one again is teaching timeless theology when he asserts in 1 Cor. 11:7–10, "For a man indeed ought not to have a cover over his head, since he is the image and glory of God; but woman is the glory of man. For man is not from woman, but woman from man. For man is not from woman, but woman from man. Nor was man created for the woman, but woman for the man. For this reason, the woman ought to have a symbol of authority on their head, because of the angels." Stott correctly identifies the woman's complimentary role in the local church. He rhapsodizes,

> "We note that verse 11 and 12 contain two complimentary instructions to or about women. Positively, a *woman should learn in quietness and full submission* (11). Negatively, she is not *to teach or to have authority over a man* (12). Further, the antithesis is double. One the one hand, she is to learn in quietness and not teach. On the other hand, she is to be submissive and not exercise authority over a man. Or to express the double antithesis more sharply, a women's behavior in public worship is to be characterized by quietness and/or silence, not teaching, and by submission, not authority."[xxi]

A Role for Women in the Worship Service

A role that is given to women is that of prophecy, a gift distinct from teaching. A woman is permitted to exercise the gift of prophecy with her head covered, demonstrating her submission to her husband. The word prophecy means, "to speak before." It denotes the woman speaking a prophetic word given by God. In this sense they are not teaching, but simply and clearly giving a word of revelation to the local assembly. It speaks of prophecy in this sense is not viewed as an inordinate display of authority, but of foretelling the revelation of God. Both men and women were endowed by God with the gift of prophesy, and both were permitted to exercise it in the local assembly. However, a woman prophesying was conditioned on an outward demonstration of submission to her husband.

Resistance to A Woman's Role

Some protest this view contending it contradicts Peter's teaching of Christian wives being "heirs together of the grace of life" (1 Pet. 3:7). Still others say that Paul's instruction is reserved solely for the church of Corinth. This view is fraught with a plethora of practical problems germane only to their historical setting. These objections may all be swept aside in light of the timeless house order Paul issues for the Church of Jesus Christ universal. Therefore, the dual commands for women to refrain from teaching and demonstrate submission to their husbands are to be taken as normative. Well remembering Paul's charge to Timothy in 2 Timothy 3:16–17, "All Scripture is given by the inspiration of God; and is profitable for doctrine, for reproof, for correction, for instruction in righteousness, that the man of God may be complete, thoroughly equipped for every good work."

The Theme of Submission in the Church of Jesus Christ

The theme of submission of the wife in the local assembly and home is observed in Ephesians 5:22–24; Col. 3:18; and 1 Peter 3:1–6, and Colossians 3:18. Colossians 3:18, succinctly stating, "Wives submit to your own husbands, as it is fitting in the Lord." Within the parameters of the Christian woman's submission Paul grants freedom pursuant to the symbol of that authority. He issues the disclaimer regarding head coverings, "But if anyone seems to be contentious, we have no such custom, nor do the churches of God" (1 Cor. 11:16). Paul seems to be teaching that while a head covering may be optional, a symbol of the man's authority should be present during the worship service. Some have suggested that this symbol of authority can be a wedding ring. For in this text, Paul speaks of customs, or forms, may be transferable.

The Angels Observance

Paul's rationale for the woman's role in the worship service is threefold: 1) the order of creation; 2) Eve's deception; and 3) the angels' observance of public worship. Supplying granularity to the third rationale, Peter writes of the issues of salvation, "things which angels desire to look into" (1 Pet. 1:12). Since man was made "a little lower than the angels" (Psalm 8:5), the holy observance of the angelic hosts cannot be casually dismissed.

Paul draws a parallel between the impetus for creating man and women. Men were created for the glory of God (1 Cor. 10:31), women conversely were created for the glory of man. This is divinely decreed pecking order in God's chain of grace. The reality that Eve was created for Adam's benefit is clearly documented in the creation account of Genesis 2. The reason for the creation of Eve is also given. God says, "I will make him a helpmate suitable for him" (Gen. 2:18). The prosaic fact that Eve was created from Adam's rib speaks to Adam's authority over Eve. For just as the Lord's creation of Adam demonstrated His authority over him, so Eve being taken from Adam's rib, underscores Adam's authority over Eve. This authority is sealed in Adam naming Eve. For in the ancient Hebrew nomenclature, naming something or someone, was a show of authority. Paul underscores this chain of authority by asserting, "the woman is the glory of the man." This does not infer inequality in worth, but role and authority. To this end Lowery posits,

> "A woman's (a wife's) glory and image was derived from (1 Cor. 11:8) and complementary to (v. 9) that of the man (her husband). Man, then, was God's authoritative representative who found in woman a divinely made ally in fulfilling this role (Gen. 2:18–24). In this sense as a wife is the glory of man, her husband. If a married woman abandoned this complementary role, she also abandoned her glory, and for Paul the uncovered woman's head gave a symbolic expression of that spirit."[xxii]

As Strict as the Bible and No Stricter

Years ago, while pastoring I employed several slogans to express the mission of each church. One of those slogans was, "As strict as the Bible but no stricter." That mantra fits the role of women in the church. For while Paul did not permit women to teach or lead in the local assembly, godly women have splendid options for teaching in other contexts. Paul's dual prohibition concerning women teaching during the worship service and holding and being elders or deacons in the church, does not prohibit women from teaching in Christian High Schools, Bible colleges, seminaries or teaching in Sunday school.

What God Intends

Friedrich Nietzsche once opined, "If men won't be men, women will." I am convinced that one reason women gravitate towards teaching and leadership positions in the church is that men are all too eager to default on their responsibilities to teach and lead except in a carnal way (James 3:1). This cultural phenomenon does not square with God's design for men, but is rooted in Eve's fallen "desire" to dominate her husband. If men display the passivity of Adam, women will exercise the dominance of Eve. Such a pattern in many churches signals a departure from God's original design for men. A transformation of thinking is in order among Christian men as well as Christian women. If God has designed men to teach exclusively in the local worship services, surely, He wants them at the front edge of spiritual leadership and biblical instruction in the home and society.

The Beauty of a Godly Wife

Few things are more beautiful than a godly mother and wife. It must be emphasized that while women serve as the helpmates for the man, they are not in any way inferior to them. Therefore, women also have a critical role assigned to them in the church of Jesus Christ, namely, the role of a godly mother. Her salvation comes through childbearing. By this Paul likely means, "retention of dignity." For Paul concludes his instruction on the comportment of women in the church in 2:15, "Nevertheless, she shall be saved in childbearing, if they continue in faith and love, and holiness, with self-control." This statement hearkens back to the book of Genesis. Eve's "salvation" came through being the matriarch of a descendant who would deal a fatal blow to the head of the serpent (Gen. 3:15). The daughters of Eve likewise will find redemption in the role of godly motherhood. Similarly, the daughters of Eve will be restored to the rightful role for which God created them. The God who issued the cultural mandate to the first couple to, "Be fruitful and multiply, fill the earth and subdue it" (Gen. 1:26–28), restores godly Christian mothers to that very noble purpose. In this respect Paradise Lost become Paradise Regained. Concerning this Duane Litfin remarks, "A woman will find her greatest satisfaction and meaning in life, not in seeking the male role, but in fulfilling God's design for her as wife and mother with all 'faith, love, and holiness, with propriety,'"[xxiii]

The Legacy of a Godly Mother

In the New Testament church wives and mothers played a very strategic role in the rearing of children. Paul admonished his ministry compatriot, Titus, to charge the godly older women to teach the younger women, "to love their husbands, to love their children, to be discreet, chaste, homemakers" (Titus 2:4–5). Paul serves notice that Timothy was a favored recipient of godly mothering. Timothy's maternal pedagogy came from not only his mother Lois, but also his grandmother Eunice (2 Tim. 1:5). These godly women tutored young Timothy who "from childhood knew the Holy Scriptures, which are able to make you wise to salvation" (2 Tim. 3:14–15).

Paul's conditional clause speaks to the virtue of motherhood while mirroring the profile of the virtuous woman of Proverbs 31. He informs that Christian mothers will be honored, if they continue "in faith, love, holiness, and self-control" (v. 15). Such honor was accorded Hannah who prayed that God would give her a son (1 Sam. 1; 2:30–31). Godly mothers like Sarah and Hannah are women of faith and prayer. "They look for a city that has foundations whose builder and maker is God" (Heb. 11:10). Like Eunice and Lois, they leave a godly legacy of knowing the sacred writings while teaching them to their children and grandchildren. Like Ruth, Mary, Hannah, Abigail, Priscilla, Esther, and Martha, and so many other godly women past and present, they love God, their families, and their neighbor. Like Mary the express devoted love for Jesus and their neighbor. They are holy, like Anna, Lydia, Mary, Elizabeth, and Deborah. Like Sarah and Abigail, they exercise self-control while interfacing with disobedient and intemperate husbands.

These women, and scores like them, along with their maternal grandmother Eve, retain their dignity through the bearing and godly rearing of children. Paul instructed, "Nevertheless, she will be saved in childbearing if they continue in faith, love, and holiness, with self-control" (1 Tim. 2:15). This statement once again hearkens back to early Genesis. For though the pain accompanying childbearing was a curse, the gift of being able to bear children was not (Gen. 3:15–16; 1:26–28). Just as Eve's bearing of children, was a precursor to the redemption of mankind, so her daughters are also saved by the bearing and rearing of children.

Summary

A major premise of this book is, "few things are more beautiful to God than a woman who fears Him." Solomon's description of a godly woman coincides with Paul's description of what constitutes a beautiful woman in 1 Timothy 3:15. Paul's instruction regarding the house order of the church of Jesus Christ is timeless in its orientation, not cultural confined to the first century church. Such teaching is rooted in God's origin and design of men and women, and Eve's deception by the serpent. Christian women possess a subordinate role in the local church as they do to their husbands. While they are not to teach in the worship assembly or hold positions of authority in the local church, God has orchestrated a beautiful role for them, namely the godly rearing of children.

Questions for Review

1) This chapter begins with the true story of the author's colleague being seduced by a false prophetess. This prophetess convinced this pastor to leave his wife for her, and abandon the clear teachings of God's Word. Have you ever known such a false prophetess?

2) Jesus said that Jezebel taught "the deep things of Satan." It is important that Christ-followers understand what apostate teachings are lest they fall into the error of the church of Thyatira. What are some "doctrines of demons" suggested by the author in this chapter.

3) Jesus sternly rebuked some in the church of Thyatira for embracing a first century Jezebel who taught His servants to commit sexual immorality and eat meat offered to idols. Reflecting on this, do you believe that Jesus might be concerned with twenty-first century Jezebels?

4) When confronted with a Jezebel, it is important that believers "test the spirits" (1 John 4:1), and "earnestly contend for the faith once delivered to the saints" (Jude 3). How are these complimentary objectives best accomplished?

5) Paul issues a strong imperative in 1 Timothy 2:13 prohibiting women from teaching in the local assembly and exercising authority over a man. What support does the Paul give for women not teaching or leading in the church?

6) One reason Paul cites for women not teaching men in the local worship assembly is Eve's deception. Why in general are women more prone to doctrinal deceit than men? Peter describes women as the "weaker vessels" in 1 Peter 3:7. Is it possible that this weakness might pertain to the greater vulnerability women have to false teachers and teachings? Explain.

7) A reason that Paul gives for a wife's head covering and quiet submission is the angels' observance. On a scale of

1–7, how often do you reflect on the reality that the angels observe the worship habits of local assemblies?

1   2   3   4   5   6   7

8) As Paul establishes a "house order" for the local church (see 1 Tim. 3:14–15), he issues a strong prohibition forbidding women from teaching or leading in the local assembly. What biblical reasons does Paul give as a rationale for women not teaching or leading?

9) Paul explains that Adam being created first, and Eve's deception were two reasons why women should not teach or lead in the local church. What are the practical implications of Adam being created first imply?

10) Adam was not deceived, yet Eve sin was born of her deception. How does Eve's deception disqualify women from teaching or leading in the local church?

God has a very special role for Christian women. There are few things more pleasing to the heart of God than a godly mother. What is this role? As you examine the characteristics of a godly mother, what moral graces do you feel are strengths? What virtues are you working to refine?

HOPE FOR JEZEBELS

"Who wants to live forever? Who wants to live forever?"
—Queen

"Come see a Man who told me all things that
I ever did. Could this be the Christ?"
—John 4:29

Donna Rice is a name associated with one of the most notorious political scandals in American history. Her notoriety is due not to multiple indiscretions but to the powerful man to whom she was attached. Her now infamous relationship with frontrunning democrat Presidential candidate Gary Hart rocked America in 1987. While Hart was a leading candidate for the Democrat nomination, a photograph surfaced with Rice sitting on the then Colorado Senator's lap on the yacht *Monkey Business*. The tryst she had with the erstwhile Presidential candidate, was dramatized in the 2018 movie, *Frontrunner*.

The trauma for Rice was just beginning after Hart announced he was suspending his campaign in the aftermath of the scandal. She reflected, "The film ends where the trauma in my life began, after my name was released to the press by the Hart campaign. The ensuing frenzy was driven by the mainstream media, who for the first time in the 24/7 news era, went feral and viral." Rice further explains, "By the grace of God, I found healing and restoration and eventually came full circle. For the past twenty-five years, I have fought to prevent the sexual exploitation of children in the digital world through my organization, *Enough is Enough*."[xxiv] Shortly after this scandal rocked the nation, Rice went into hiding and made a hasty retreat to her Christian roots. The Lord used the most devastating event of her life to bring her back to Him. Now God has enlisted her to battle a modern global injustice. Donna Rice has truly found "healing and restoration."

Jezebel's Redemption

In business, the conventional wisdom is if you want a job done get a busy man. Jesus, seemed to sport a different mantra, namely, if you have an important mission to execute, recruit a *broken* woman who has been abandoned by the world. There was a woman who was a classic Jezebel. Though not a queen, she was an idolatress who was confused about God. She had embraced false ideas concerning the messiah and worship. Furthermore, the townspeople held her in such disdain that she was compelled to maintain strict social distancing. Until one day she experienced a close encounter of a powerful kind. The holy ground for this encounter was a historic well named after the Jewish patriarch Jacob. Jacob and his family had drank at this well. At this particular moment, what was most significant about this serendipitous rendezvous, was not the wells history, but the fact that Jesus was sitting on it. For it was not politically correct in the first century, for a Jewish rabbi to be speaking with an immoral Samaritan woman. Even more perplexing was that this rabbi had the effrontery to request water from her. Stunned, she inquired what prompted this social faux paus. For this woman had three strikes against being welcomed into the kingdom of Christ. First, she was a Samaritan. The Samaritans were half-breeds, half-Jews and half Gentiles. They were a people despised by the Jews, whose chutzpah compelled them to view Samaritans through the lens of Jewish supremacy. Secondly, she was a woman in a male dominated culture. In this respect she was considered chattel, a hairs breath above slave status. Thirdly, she was a woman with a checkered past with men. Her immoral past and failed marital history served to socially ostracize her from both the Jewish and Samaritan communities. She had been married and divorced five times and her sexual relationship with her current companion, only served to magnify her loneliness. Yet none of this discouraged the iconoclastic Jesus from clearing the decks of His messianic schedule to book a life changing appointment with her. For Messiah Jesus was an unrepentant butcher of sacred cows. For this unconventional rabbi constantly preached that the kingdom of heaven was upside down.

For this reason, John writes that it was absolutely imperative that Jesus take a necessary detour through Samaria to visit this despised woman (John 4:4). The word for must, "dei" denotes an absolute necessity. It was mandatory, not optional, that the Son of God should travel through Samaria to rescue this forlorn woman from a life of deprivation. Jesus had a soft spot for sinners. He specialized in reversals of fortune and restoration projects. Therefore, this woman would be the first witness to a miraculous sign of His omniscience. Jesus knew everything about this woman, but loved her anyway. Though well acquainted with her past, He was fixated on her future. A future that included using her as an instrument of His grace and glory. The Son of God wanted to transform this Jezebel from the inside out.

Bone weary from miles of travel, Jesus casually takes a seat on the mouth of the well before initiating conversation with this woman. "How is it that you being a Jew, ask a drink from me, a Samaritan woman?" (John 4:9). Her surprise was not unfounded given that "the Jews have no dealings with the Samaritans" (v. 9). The longstanding animosity between the Jews and Samaritans was well known. Needless to say, this woman was more than a little surprised by Jesus's casual initiating of a conversation with her.

Jesus Trafficked in Spiritual Realities

Jesus ignored her concern. Instead, He spoke of a purer, more organic brand of water, that would eternally quench the thirst of all who drank of it, including this despised woman. He answered her, "If you knew the gift of God, and who it is who says to you, 'Give Me a drink,' you would have asked Him and He would have given you living water" (John 4:9).

The woman responded, "Sir, You have nothing to draw with, and the well is deep. Where do You get the living water? Are you greater than our Father Jacob, who gave us the well, and drank from it himself as well as his sons and livestock?" (4:12). "Whoever drinks of this water will thirst again, but whoever drinks of the water that I shall give him will never thirst, But the water that I shall give him will become in him a fountain of water springing up into everlasting life" (John 4:13–14).

Jesus was no medical quack hawking an overpriced miracle tonic with the market value of tap water. His staggering claim was actually true! Jesus spoke of water that supernaturally transcended the chemical compound of hydrogen and oxygen. This woman was drawing water which could never satisfy her thirsty soul. Jesus offered her without cost a spiritual water that would eternally quench her thirst. One sip of the spiritual water of the new birth would flood her soul with eternal life and transform her into a child of God (John 1:12–13; 3:15–18; Rev. 22:17). All she needed to do was believe.

An Exposure of Sin that Pointed Her to Him

This living water was acquired by faith in Jesus. Two chapters later another encounter with the Jews, Jesus declared, "I am the bread of life, He who comes to Me shall never hunger, and he who believes on Me shall never thirst" (John 6:35). This ancient Jezebel was intrigued by the prospect of not coming to draw water ever again. Yet Jesus had to disabuse her of the faulty notion that she could find satisfaction apart from Him. Therefore, He gave her a sign of His messiahship by demonstrating Himself to be omniscient (see John 20:30). He summarized her life story in one sentence. She asked her to "call her husband" (John 4:16). The woman responded, "I have no husband" (4:17).

Technically, she answered correctly. "You have well said, 'I have no husband,' for you have had five husbands, and the one whom you now have is not your husband; in that you spoke truly" (4:18). The woman discovered that Jesus was no ordinary rabbi. Her initial perception that He was a prophet hardened into a conviction that He was indeed the Messiah of God. The conspicuous woman believed on Christ and was forever changed!

Jesus transformed this repentant Jezebel from the inside out. He transformed her. She was forever changed. What is more, she became a strategic ambassador for the kingdom of heaven. She went to the men with whom she had cohabited and perhaps others and spread the good news about this amazing man who knew everything about her.

The Samaritan woman was instrumental in bringing the gospel to Samaria. She paved the way for Philip, an evangelist in the early church, build on the work that this redeemed daughter of accomplished in Samaria. She became the premier evangelist sharing the good news of Jesus's transforming power. Like Esther, she was God's woman in God's place at God's time! She excitedly invited, "Come see a man who told me all things that I ever did. Could this be the Christ? Then they went out of the city and came to Him." (John 4:28). The response of the men was, "Then they went out of the city and came to Him" (John 4:30). The glorious result of the ministry of this foreign woman whom Jesus loved is recorded in John 4:39–41,

> "And many of the Samaritans of that city believed in Him because of the word of the woman who testified, 'He told me all that I ever did.' So when the Samaritans had come to Him, they urged Him to stay with them; and He stayed there two days. And many more believed because of His word."

Jesus Loves the B-Team

Jesus loves the B-team. Just as Jesus chose Mary Magdalene, a woman out of whom He exorcised seven demons to first witness His resurrection from the grave, so He chose this obscure, immoral, Samaritan woman to be His daughter and ambassador of His love. Jesus loves prostitutes like Rehab and Gomer, adulteresses like Bathsheba, and the woman taken in adultery, idolatresses like Ruth, and billions of other daughters of Eve who have been blindsided by sin. This obscure woman was uniquely chosen to till the soil of

273

revival in Samaria (Acts 8). God delights in opening doors of hope for the Jezebels of our world. He specializes in transforming the ugly ducklings of sin into the beautiful swans of His grace. Jesus took this humble vessel and shaped her into a beautiful instrument of His grace and glory!

A Message to Jezebels

Jesus loves you more than you could ever imagine. Like the Samaritan woman, He knows everything about you yet loves you infinitely. Regardless of what you have done or not done in your life, Jesus loves Jezebels in the same way He loves everyone. He descended the stairway of heaven to die for you. He invites you, to drink of the living water He provides that will quench your thirst for eternal life. Jesus has come that He might redeem your past, present, and future. He has "come that you might have life and have it more abundantly" (John 10:10). Jesus will massage your weary soul with His incomprehensible peace, flood it with joy, and infuse it with eternal purpose. He invites you to know Him. He loves you more than anyone else, including yourself.

This is why He wants to give you a free gift of eternal life. It is free in the sense that it is without cost. You can't work for it, it is a gift. The Apostle Paul wrote, "For by grace are you saved through faith, and that not of yourselves, it is the gift of God, not of works lest any man should boast."

John writes, "And let Him who thirsts come. Whoever desires, let him take the water of life freely" (Rev. 22:17).

Jesus once said to a man, "For God so loved the world, [including Jezebels), that He gave His only begotten Son that whoever believes in Him shall not perish but have eternal life" (John 3:16).

Jezebel's Salvation

I began this chapter talking about Donna Rice who like the Samaritan woman Jesus encountered on a decisive day next to a lonely well. Like this misguided woman, Jesus demonstrated inexhaustible quantities of grace. This redeemed woman of God best describes her Savior's indiscriminate love for profligate daughters. In her book, *Kid's Online,* she writes,

> "I am often asked by the media and others why I got involved with the issue of pornography on the Internet. It's a long story but here goes. After many years of living away from my spiritual roots, a journey that began with a series of little left turns, I found myself in 1987 in the middle of a scandal, caught in the crossfire of press, politics, and public opinion. In despair I saw my life fall apart around me. Feeling helpless, hopeless, and at the end of my own resources, I realized that it had taken my falling on my rear end in front of the whole world for God to get my attention. He got it, and I recommitted myself to him and to my faith. Trusting the Lord, I prayed, 'I know that in time you can heal the pain in my life and even use what appears to be a disaster for good.'"

Yes He can! This daughter of Eve was transformed into a beautiful Sarah. Whether Eve, a despised Samaritan woman, or a disgraced model trapped in the cross-hairs of a political scandal, God's grace is greater than all of our sins!

Questions for Reflection

1) In the aftermath of the scandal that ended Gary Hart's candidacy for the US Presidency, Donna Rice was viewed with contempt. Yet Jesus did not view this precious daughter, but lavished upon her abundant grace. What hope does her story offer to modern Jezebels?

2) The author opined that God's mode of operation is, "If you want a job done, get a broken woman who has been

rejected by the world." Where have you seen this either personally our in your sphere of living.

3) Reflect on some of the prominent women in the Bible. Who are some, who like the Samaritan woman who were rejected or ignored by society, but embraced by Jesus? How did Jesus show compassion to them?

4) What evidence have you seen in your own life that Jesus loves the B-Team?

5) Rehab was a prostitute. Mary Magdalene was a woman out of whom Jesus cast seven demons. Tamar seduced her father-in-law to have a son. Bathsheba had an affair with a king. Tamar, Ruth, Rehab, and Bathsheba, were all women of questionable morals, yet are listed in the genealogy of Jesus. I light of these past expressions of grace, quantify the faith you have that God wants to show like mercy to contemporary Jezebels. Do you have...

Much faith   Some faith   Little Faith

Circle one.

6) It is never too late to place your faith in Jesus Christ as Savior and therefore, drink of that living water. As long as you have breath, Jesus offer of living water is still available to you. The following is a model prayer to help you seal your new relationship with the Son of God.

7) "God, I know that I am a sinner in need of a Savior. I now recognize that you sent Your Son Jesus Christ to be my Savior. Jesus died that I might have life. He came to redeem my past, present, and future. I believe in Him as My Savior. Jesus forgive me of my sins, come into my life and save me. Thank you Jesus, I look forward to serving you the rest of my life. Amen."

ENDNOTES

i   John F. Walvoord, *The Revelation of Jesus Christ,* (Moody Press, Chicago, 1966, p. 74).

ii   Dinesh D'souza, *Hillary's America,* (Regnery Publishing, 2016, pp. 217–218).

iii   *Woman and the New Race*, Chapter 5, "The Wickedness of Creating Large Families." (1920).

iv   Bruce Wilkinson, *Personal Holiness In Times Of Temptation*, (Harvest House Publishers, p. 177).

v   Ibid, p. 174–175.

vi   Ronald B. Allen, *Celebrating the Word,* (Multnomah Press, Portland, OR, pp. 40–41).

vii   Dinesh D'Souza, *When Nations Die,* (docudrama, 2017).

viii   Ibid.

ix   Curtis Bowers, *The Agenda,* docudrama.

x   Nancy Leigh Demoss, *Lies Women Believe: And the Truth That Sets Them Free,* (Moody Publishers, Chicago, 2001, p. 129).

xi   D. Edmond Hiebert, *First Peter: An Expositional Commentary,* (Moody Press, Chicago, 1984, p. 172).

xii   Roger M. Raymer, *The Bible Knowledge Commentary:1 Peter,* (edited by John F. Walvoord, Roy B. Zuck, Victor Books, 1994, pp. 848–849).

xiii   Ibid. (p. 849).

xiv   Charles Swindoll, *Hope Again*, (Word Publishing 1996, p. 103).

xv   Janette Henning and Melissa Camp, *Melissa: If One Life,* (iDisciple Publishing, Alpharetta, GA, p. 18).

xvi   The movie *Ragamuffin,* 2013.

xvii   Zane Hodges, *The Epistles of John: Walking in the Light of God's Love,* 1999, Grace Evangelical Society, p. 175).

xviii   John F. Walvoord, (*The Bible Knowledge Commentary: Revelation,* Victor Books, 1994, p. 937).

xix   John R.W. Stott, *Guard the Truth: The Message of 1 Timothy & Titus,* (Intervarsity Press, Downers Grove, Ill, 1996, P. 78).

xx   J.I. Packer, *Women, Authority, and the* Bible, (Intervarsity Press, [USA], 1986, p. 299).

John R.W. Stott, pp. 78-79, *Guard the Trust: The Message of 1 Timothy & Titus,* (Intervarsity Press, Downers Grove, Ill. 1996, pp. 78–79).

xxi   Ibid.

xxii   David K. Lowery, *The Bible Knowledge Commentary New Testament,* (John F. Walvoord & Roy B. & Zuck, Roy, Victor Books, 1994, p. 529).

xxiii   Duane Litfin, (John F. Walvoord & Roy B. Zuck, *The Bible Knowledge Commentary,* Victor Books, 1994, P. 736).

xxiv   Aaron E. Tomlinson, *The Associated Press.* Rice, Donna. *Kid's Online.* (Fleming H. Revell: Grand Rapids, 1998, P. 7).

BIBLIOGRAPHY

Ronald B. Allen, *Celebrating the Word*, (Multnomah Press, Portland, OR).

Bruce, F.F. *The New International Commentary: The Epistles to the Colossians, to Philemon, and to the Ephesians*, (Wm. B. Eerdmans Publishing House, Grand Rapids, MI).

Demoss, Nancy Leigh, *Lies Women Believe: And the Truth That Sets Them Free*, (Moody Publishers, Chicago, 2001).

D'souza, Dinesh. *Hillary's America*, (Regnery Publishing, 2016).

Dershowitz, Alan. *Guilt by Association: The Challenge of Proving Innocence in the Age of #Me Too*, (Hot Books, 2019).

Dillow, Joseph & Linda, Pintus, Duane & Lorraine. *Intimacy Ignited*, (Nav Press, 2004).

Eggerichs, Emerson. *Love & Respect*, (Word Publishing Group, 2004).

Feldhahn, Shaunti. *For Women Only*, (Multnomah Press, 2004).

Gottman, John M & Nan Silver. *The Seven Principles of Making Marriage Work.* (Harmony Books: New York, 2015).

Henning, Janette, and Melissa Camp, *Melissa: If One Life*, (iDisciple Publishing, Alpharetta, GA).

Hiebert, D. Edmond. *First Peter: An Expositional Commentary*, (Moody Press, Chicago, 1984).

Hodges Zane, *The Epistles of John: Walking in the Light of God's Love*, 1999, Grace Evangelical Society).

Litfin, Duane, *The Pastoral Epistles*, (John F. Walvoord & Roy B. Zuck, *The Bible Knowledge Commentary*, Victor Books, 1994).

Lowery, David K. *The Bible Knowledge Commentary New Testament*, (John F. Walvoord & Roy B. & Zuck, Roy, Victor Books, 1994).

Packer, J.I. *Women, Authority, and the* Bible, (Intervarsity Press, [USA], 1986).

Ratushinskaya, Irina. *Grey is the Color of Hope,* (New York: Vintage International, 1989).

Raymer, Roger M. *The Bible Knowledge Commentary:1 Peter,* (edited by John F. Walvoord, Roy B. Zuck, Victor Books, 1994).

Rice, Donna. *Kid's Online.* (Fleming H. Revell: Grand Rapids, 1998).

Ryrie, Charles Caldwell. *The Role of Women in the Church.* (Moody Press, 1981).

Skousen, Cleon. *The Naked Communist,* (Izzard Ink Publishing, 2014).

Stott, John R.W. (*Guard the Trust: The Message of 1 Timothy & Titus,* (Intervarsity Press, Downers Grove, Ill. 1996).

Thomas, Clarence. *My Grandfather's Son,* (Harpers Perennial, 2008).

Swindoll, Charles, *Hope Again,* (Word Publishing 1996).

Walvoord, John F. *The Revelation of Jesus Christ,* (Moody Press, Chicago).

Wilkinson, Bruce. *Personal Holiness In Times Of Temptation,* (Harvest House Publishers).

ABOUT THE AUTHOR

Daniel Klender is a United States Navy chaplain current serving at Marine Corps Air Station Miramar, in Miramar, California. For over three decades, he has been a pastor and Bible teacher in both the private and military sectors. For fourteen years, he pastored churches in the Southwest and the Pacific Northwest. Since receiving a call to minister to Sailors, Marines, and their families, Chaplain Klender has ministered throughout America as well as in Iraq, Asia, Europe, and the Indian Ocean Territories. Chaplain Klender received his doctor of ministry degree from Phoenix Seminary in Scottsdale, Arizona; a master of theology and master of exegetical theology in biblical studies from Western Seminary in Portland, Oregon, and a bachelor of religious education degree from William Tyndale College, formerly in Farmington Hills, Michigan. He is the author of *The Uzziah Syndrome: 40 Keys to Finishing Your Life and Ministry Well,* and *Living With the End in View: Escaping the Tyranny of the Here and Now.* He has two grown daughters.